EXPERIENCING CREATIVITY

´EXPERIENCING CREATIVITY,

On the Social Psychology of Art

ROBERT N. WILSON

Transaction Books
New Brunswick (U.S.A.) and Oxford (U.K.)

Library of Congress Catalog Number: 85-16554
ISBN: 0-88738-045-X (cloth)
Printed in the United States of America

Library of Congress Cataloging in Publication Data
Wilson, Robert N. (Robert Neal), 1924-
    Experiencing creativity.

    Bibliography: p.
    Includes index.
    1. Art—Psychological aspects. 2. Arts and
society. I. Title.
NX165.W48   1986   700′.1′9   85-16554
ISBN 0-88738-045-X

Contents

Acknowledgments

Grateful acknowledgment is extended to the editors of the following publications, in which these articles first appeared, and which hold the respective copyrights: *The Journal of Aesthetics and Art Criticism,* "Literary Experience and Personality" (September, 1956) and "The Poet and the Projective Test" (March, 1958). *Psychiatry,* "Poetic Creativity: Process and Personality" (May 1954). Prentice-Hall, Inc., "The Poet in American Society" (in *The Arts in Society,* ed. Robert N. Wilson, 1964). *Harvard Magazine,* "Conrad Aiken: An Appreciation" (July/August, 1980). Harcourt, Brace and Jovanovich, "High Culture and Popular Culture in a Business Society" (in *The Business of America,* ed. Ivar Berg, 1968). General Learning Press, "The Sociology and Psychology of Art" (1973). *Social Forces,* "The Courage to Be Leisured" (December, 1981).

Introduction

Neither the creative process nor the art object, singly or together, has been often in the forefront of sociological attention. That these matters have been of consuming interest to me during the past thirty-five years is probably the result of two accidents of temperament and environment: the first is my having had a rather old-fashioned liberal arts education that included some months reading English at Trinity Hall, Cambridge; the second is the fortunate befriending of my academic mentor, Henry A. Murray, who first encouraged me to scrutinize creative activity and as a student of society and personality to take the arts seriously. As a beginning graduate student at Harvard I wrote a term paper (later published as "Literature, Society, and Personality") exploring certain connections between literature and the social sciences. Murray proved receptive to this line of thought, called me in to talk it over, and eventually hired me as a research assistant in his ongoing series of investigations of fantasy and creativity. My first assignment, one which was to be decisive in shaping my scholarly career, was to administer a projective test called TAT II (described in chapter 3) to a sample of creative writers. Although the results of this inquiry were inconclusive, I found myself caught up in the mystery of creativity, determined to keep exploring how innovative people did their work. As described in chapter 4, I concluded that the creative process and the creative personality are so closely intertwined that neither can be understood apart from the other. In addition, and reflected in several of the articles assembled here, I soon realized that any comprehensive approach to the social psychology of art needed to consider the content or characteristics of the art work itself and the responsive posture of the audience/appreciator. That is, a perspective ample enough to encompass the diverse events called up by the phrase, "experiencing creativity," must first necessarily try to grasp the complex interplay among creator, product, and recipient that makes up the whole artistic transaction.

American sociologists, like Americans in the culture at large, have long tended to regard the arts as a luxury. Art as fringe or ornament, as a marginal social territory, may occasionally inspire pleasure, or even awe, but can scarcely merit sustained professional attention. A representative textbook writer of mid-century is forthright and emphatic:

> The arts, in sum, are the least important and the most variable of the elements that enter into the social structure. They are the designs embossed upon the textile of social life. The designs must please to be effective; but no

1

matter how pleasing, they will in no way affect the utility and durability of the fabric itself.[1]

Whether it be the pervasiveness of the Protestant Ethic, the primacy of the economic sphere in an industrial society, a lingering frontier Philistinism, whatever, social scientists generally have consigned art to the trivial and essentially irrelevant. I argue in chapter 8 that art in its playfulness and gratuitous character belongs to the realm of leisure. As a most unleisurely people, we relegate art to the residual category where it joins other leisurely phenomena in being what is left over after the serious work of life has been duly attended to.

Surely other reasons for the sociologist's neglect of artistic creativity may be readily adduced. Innovation is clearly grounded in a series of intrapsychic events—something original arises within the individual—and hence may be consigned to the clinical psychologist. And indeed the psychologist, whose province is the interior world, has made the most plentiful and valuable contributions of any of the social scientists to understanding creativity. Again, creative activity is elusive; it resists both conceptual closure and quantitative assessment, and this obdurate open-endedness makes many researchers uncomfortable. Finally, sociology as a youthful discipline has been concerned with distinguishing itself and emancipating itself from the humanities from whence it sprang. Making and appreciating art, thinking about its origins and effects, has been the task of the philosopher, the literary critic, the art historian. The sociologist has been in the main content to leave it to them.

If art and artist have not been seen as potent social influences, as significant forces in shaping the way we live, how have social scientists regarded their other traditional role: that of reflectors or indicators of the nature of the world around them? Here again, with few exceptions, art has been taken lightly if at all. Sophisticated content analysis has had its notable practitioners—for instance, Leo Lowenthal and James Barnett in literature, Paul Honigsheim in music, Vytautas Kavolis and John Manfredi[2] in painting and sculpture—but sociologists have concentrated their attention generally on a variety of other social indicators: census reports, economic indices, questionnaire tabulations, and first-hand observations of social interaction. The relative neglect of art-as-reflection is probably rooted in the same cluster of factors as the neglect of creativity itself, but the quality I noted above as elusiveness may be especially underlined. We find it exceedingly difficult to discover how to "read" what art indicates, because the indication is so commonly subtle and deflected. Emily Dickinson gave poetic point to this aspect of art's truth-value:

> Tell all the Truth but tell it slant—
> Success in Circuit lies

Too bright for our infirm Delight
The Truth's superb surprise

As Lightning to the Children eased
With explanation kind
The Truth must dazzle gradually
Or every man be blind—[3]

The humanist's voice claims, with persuasive rhetoric if not with wholly convincing evidence, that art is the most reliable of all testimony about the character of our lived experience. The philosopher and literary critic William Barrett is exemplary. Barrett quotes Sartre quoting Hegel to the effect that "history is what takes place behind our backs." We aren't able to see what is really going on until after the fact. But the artist is. Thus Barrett recasts Aristotle's dictum that "poetry is more philosophical than history" to say that "Poetry—or as we should prefer to say here, art—presents us a deeper truth about human life than all the researches of the behavioral sciences."[4] And further:

> Art is thus quite literally, repeat literally, an expression of the collective soul of its time. The forms of imagination that any epoch produces are an ultimate datum on what that epoch is.[5]

Whether we look upon art as La Piere's "embroidery" or Barrett's "ultimate datum," or as a vehicle of some measured significance falling between these extremes, we surely need to focus all available scholarly resources on the analysis of the creative act. Faced with the complexity and vagaries of creativity, we may be tempted to pronounce it all a mystery and abandon the effort to understand. Indeed, both Freud and Jung, among others, often came perilously close to this position. Alternatively, we may render creativity in some sense more manageable and comfortable by essaying a species of analytic reductionism, attributing all or most of the causal weight for original behavior to a single explanatory level. In contemporary social scientific attempts to cope with creativity in art and other fields, such reductive emphases have tended to assume one of three forms.

By far the most conventional and intuitively appropriate explanatory level is that of psychodynamics. The testimony of creative individuals, arguably the bedrock of exploration into the process(es), tends understandably to focus on experienced events inside the skull. It is obvious that nearly all of the inquiries collected in this volume, too, are centered in the interior world of the creator. That is where I started: quizzing poets about making poems. An exemplary excursion in this vein, perhaps the most sophisticated and comprehensive in recent scholarship, is Albert Rothenberg's *The Emerging Goddess*.[6] Drawing on both psychoanalytic theory and his own empirical research, Rothenberg presents a convincing analysis of creative thinking.

He is especially concerned with the creative individual's conscious control; the artistic daydream is construed as the obverse of our uncontrolled night dreams. He shows with a wealth of illustrations how innovative behavior pivots on the ability to fuse symbolic and physical opposites, what he terms *Janusian* and *homospatial* thinking and imaging. Rothenberg deliberately eschews the social context and cultural tradition of creativity as at least temporarily beyond his purview.

A few writers have investigated the social structure in which creative work occurs. Much attention has been devoted to artistic circles or coteries, the clustering of artists in social space and time. Presumably the interaction of group members has some discernible effect on the birth of an art product from any one of them. Instances abound in literature (Bloomsbury, the Fugitives, Paris in the 1920s) and painting (the Impressionists, the abstract expressionists of the New York School), but the threads of mutual influence are difficult to disentangle, and to specify with respect to any single work of art. Other elements of social structure that have been identified as influential in shaping creativity are, for example, the family background of creators and the institutional settings of artistic communication, such as the publishing industry. The most radical exponent of the position that creativity stems as much from social interaction as from individual impulse is Howard Becker.[7] In *Art Worlds* he argues persuasively that art is basically a collective production, a collaborative effort, whether it be in the overtly group context of drama or symphony or the seemingly isolated labors of the literary artist. Further, he establishes the social structural nature of the aesthetic response, the way in which the very definition of art and the assessment of its quality rest on a socially shaped consensus.

Finally, there are the several advocates of an extreme cultural determinism of creativity. Here the late A. L. Kroeber is perhaps the most uncompromising: he contends that genius, the individual talent for creating, is presumably evenly distributed in human populations; yet works judged to be of significant aesthetic import occur in pronounced peaks and valleys throughout history and across societies. In *Configurations of Culture Growth*,[8] Kroeber traces the appearance of creative outbursts, or *florescences*, to the immanent potentials for expression inhering in the stylistic configurations of various art forms. The possibility of making original work, that is, is severely bounded by the timing and amplitude of the formal tradition.

I think we may safely assume that art is multidetermined, and that an adequate explanation of creativity will draw upon the conceptual and evidential resources of psychology, sociology, and anthropology. Neither pschodynamics nor social interaction nor cultural patterning, taken alone, can account for the inception and reception of art. At present, however, while our knowledge of creativity is so partial and fragile, the optimal combination of these three analytical modes remains rather more an agenda than an accomplishment.

Notes

1. Richard T. La Piere, *Sociology* (New York: McGraw-Hill, 1946)
2. Leo Lowenthal, *Literature and the Image of Man* (Boston: Beacon Press, 1957); J.H. Barnett and R. Gruen, "Recent American Divorce Novels, 1938-1945," *Social Forces* 26 (March 1948): 332-37; K. Peter Etzkorn, ed., *Music and Society: The Later Writings of Paul Honigsheim* (New York: Wiley, 1973); Vytautas Kavolis, *Artistic Expression: A Sociological Analysis* (Ithaca, N.Y.: Cornell University Press, 1968); John Manfredi, *The Social Limits of Art* (Amherst: The University of Massachusetts Press, 1982).
3. From Emily Dickinson, The *Complete Poems of Emily Dickinson*, ed. Thomas H. Johnson (Boston: Little Brown, 1960), pp. 506-7.
4. William Barrett, *Time of Need* (New York: Harper & Row, 1972), p. 10
5. Ibid.
6. Albert Rothenberg, *The Emerging Goddess* (Chicago: The University of Chicago Press, 1979).
7. Howard S. Becker, *Art Worlds* (Berkeley: University of California Press, 1982).
8. A.L. Kroeber, *Configurations of Culture Growth* (Berkeley: University of California Press, 1944).

1
Literary Experience and Personality

This paper grew out of the charged atmosphere of the Harvard Psychological Clinic Annex during the two years (1949-1951) I spent in happy and
exciting inquiry there. I was at the time a graduate student in sociology and
had been taken on by Harry Murray as a research assistant. In the early
summer of 1949, Murray hir'ed me to replace Henry W. Riecken on a project
because Hank had decided to devote the summer to research for his
dissertation. At the end of some months of psychological testing of writers, I
joined the Clinic Annex staff in its wide-ranging and very ambitious
investigation of fantasy. Building on his classic *Explorations in Personality*
of the 1930s, Murray wanted to see how the life of the imagination in its
many guises might contribute to the understanding of personality. Hence
our research group was inspired by Harry to embark on a multipronged
research into the connections between experienced and created fantasy, and
the total profile of the individual's psychodynamic functioning. To this end,
we scrutinized twenty Harvard College undergraduates, volunteers drawn
from large psychology classes, finding out all we could about their fantasy
lives. Evidence included self-reports of day and night dreams, responses to a
variety of projective tests, autobiographical accounts, and lengthy interviews on diverse subjects. Because I was especially interested in the relation
of literature to personality, Murray encouraged me to inquire whether there
was any significant association between the fantasies an individual had
read and the shape of his or her psychological make-up.

The individuals Murray had assembled in a restored old house on Mount
Auburn Street were as varied as his own protean scholarly appetites would
suggest. But we came together as a working group with a quite remarkable
zest and a shared commitment to the exploration of fantasy. We not only
united in research, but formed a sort of extended family; the milieu was
rather more that of a large, eccentric household than of a university office. I
have seldom known a stage setting or a cast of characters since that time
that was a match for the Clinic. Murray, Christiana Morgan, and Marjorie
Ingalls presided jointly over the house, which was comfortably furnished
and adorned with many paintings; Van Goghs tended to dominate, perhaps
because they were so rich in Jungian archetypical symbolism, to say
nothing of the fascination exercised on a gaggle of psychologists by the
painter's own tortured psyche. Christiana and her cook supplied extraordinarily fine luncheons, really occasions for long, informal seminars punc-
tuated by wine and dialogue that were both free flowing. Verbal fireworks
were regularly ignited by celebrated luncheon guests, talkers with panache
of the likes of P.A. Sorokin, J.L. Moreno, and I.A. Richards. The core staff
members who ate, drank, and dreamed of academic glory together included

Gardner Lindzey, Hank Riecken, Goodhue Livingston, Mortimer Slaiman, and Bob Harlow. Without this background, these immensely talented and witty colleagues, the innovative guidance and goading of a genius like Harry, I should probably never have mustered the audacity to try the investigation reported here.

Although Harry Murray is rightly regarded as one of the innovators in psychological research of our time and as one of the most original theorists of personality, his most lasting influence may well be as teacher and stimulator. He had an astounding gift for leading others into new perceptions and innovative inquiries. I have never known anyone so thoroughly sophisticated who could assume such a deliberately naive posture; if the creative person is in some important respects childlike, bold and unafraid to ask fresh questions, then Harry perfectly fit the description. It was said of Albert Einstein that he was remarkable for the number of things he didn't understand. That is, he questioned the received wisdom. Just so, Harry could approach psychological issues as if someone had raised them out of the blue that very morning. So the world was born again and scrubbed clean each day.

Despite advances in our thinking about readers and texts during recent decades, especially those advances accomplished by reader response theory and the searching openness conveyed by the term *hermeneutics,* the nature of the aesthetic experience remains relatively unexplored. We are still inadequately informed about the receptive counterpart of creativity. If the creative act is really incomplete until the appreciator has forged the last link in the chain, we need to pay further close attention to that link.

The reading of literature is a type of experience to which social scientists have paid very little attention. Reading consists of the presentation of a symbolic stimulus and the response to this stimulus. The exposure to aesthetic symbols must be distinguished from other varieties of symbolic apprehension such as, for example, the exposure to the symbols of scientific discourse. One might in fact posit an idiosyncratic symbolic pattern for the exposure to each of Morris's[1] sixteen major types of discourse, as well as for the nonlinguistic discourse of gestures. Our primary task, however, is to define the nature of literary experience in terms of the theory of action and of personality psychology, and to separate it clearly from one other type of discourse which is presumed to lie, in some sense, at the opposite pole from aesthetic discourse: namely, the logico-scientific.

Aesthetic experience is characterized as being first of the *cathectic* type, as defined by Parsons and Shils;[2] it involves an immediacy of action which is to be separated from either the cognitive or evaluative mode. This is not to say that art is not rife with cognitive and evaluative elements, but merely to affirm the primacy of cathectic interests. The place of the term *value* in this discussion may be clarified if we point to a distinction between *valuing* and *evaluating* as action modes. Certainly aesthetic products are *valued* intensely in the form of immediate gratification; *evaluation,* however, implies the invoking of standards and the differential integration of object choices or ways of behaving. Evaluation, one might say, is the function of the aesthetician or critic; valuing, the function of the minimally alert reader in contact with a literary vehicle. The reading of literature, we would propose, is indeed action, a way of behaving. It is the living through, in symbolic terms, of the experiences of the author and his characters, forms, and language. It may help at this point to bring in the distinction between discursive and presentational symbolism proposed by Susanne Langer. Discursive symbolism is the type-case of science and logical exposition; it involves abstraction from experience for certain purposes, principally the cuing of reader response toward relevant aspects of life—relevant to extrinsic purposes such as definition, prediction, and control. Presentational symbolism, on the other hand, is the type-case of the arts; here a rounded image of experience is given to the perceiver in global form, not a verifiable statement but an intuitively congruous portrait—congruous with the experience as it actually occurred to the symbol creator. We may say that both forms of symbolism abstract, but that they do so for different purposes: the scientific cognitive symbol abstracts in order to point to some relevant aspect of experience, the aesthetic cathectic symbol abstracts in order to present a formula (T.S. Eliot's "objective correlative") for the recreation of the author's experiential mass in the mind of the reader. The participation in presentational symbolism must be distinguished from the instrumental apprehension of discursive symbolism.

By defining aesthetic experience as participation on the perceiver's part, we realize that reading literary works involves a closeness to the symbols. This closeness is of a special type, the type of appreciative immediacy. The aesthetic symbol always implies an intrinsic teleology in that the stimulus is valued in and for itself. What Morris has termed the *iconic* property of symbols is relevant here: their "meaning" is that of being valued for their own sakes. At their purest level, as in some painting and some nonprogramme music, their only reference is to themselves. In literature the iconic emphasis is most marked in poetry, but even in novels, plays, and so on, the iconic element is vital. To what do aesthetic symbols refer besides "themselves"? They refer to experience as ordered by a writer. This experience can only be adequately perceived if the reader is willing to give himself over to the experiential "set" of the author. The giving over requires at least a minimal sacrifice of self-identity, because the reader's autonomy, if fully maintained, would block out the author's vision. Successful appreciation is possible only where rigid autonomy is sacrificed to the flexible taking of the other's role.

And so, if we expose ourselves at all to literary experience, we bring into play those ill-defined mechanisms of empathy and identification. We might say that this mode of appreciative action is marked by at least a temporary and partial identification process. As students of personality, our interest is in the most important identifications a person has made. Since identification is always involved in literary experience, that experience is a fertile area for catching certain crucial types of identification in a reading individual. What we should look for is a pattern of ways of identifying, of recurrent objects of identification, which are characteristic of the personality under observation.

We can readily discern the relation of literary life history to the concept of projection. Several varieties of projection may occur as phases of the aesthetic identification processes. A set of aesthetic symbols is a type of projective test for the very reason that art allows for varieties of individual interpretation.[3] MacLeish tells us that "a poem should be equal to, not true," and what it is equal to for the appreciator is his or her own apperception of the creator's experience and intentions. For art can only be apperceived; inherent in it are many types of ambiguity and this is its main difference from strict cognitive discourse.

Parsons[4] has noted that expressive symbolism is one of the least well-developed facets of the theory of action. This special case of expressive symbolism, the aesthetic, may be germane to investigations of culture patterns, social interaction, and the individual dynamics of perceptual organization, as well as to the construction of personality portraits.

The Congruence of Reading Experience and Personality Configuration

Reading maketh a full man...
—Bacon

Although most people would agree that reading may generally be efficacious in directing an individual's development, few attempts have been made to define its influence more precisely. Pollock describes three phases of the literary process—the creative effort itself, the art object as object, and the response of the reader—and notes that the third phase has seldom been investigated: "Indeed, it is not a great exaggeration to say that as a scholarly interest it is almost entirely neglected except as part of the analysis of literary influences on particular writers."[5] The authors of *What Reading Does to People* agree: "We have yet to find any comprehensive study of the effects of students' reading."[6]

Reading experience, as a portion of the individual's history, is closely bound up with the total personality. Absorption of ideas, attitudes, facts, from the printed page is an activity which, in a sophisticated, highly literate culture, corresponds to overt responsive action. We live in a world of symbols; to a great extent our behavior is geared toward words and concepts.

The intense exposure to symbols which typifies alert readers, can therefore be as effective in molding their personalities as are certain of the more objective, basic experiential events such as crises of interpersonal relations. This is not to confuse books with life, but to insist that reading materials make up an important order of life phenomena.

The involvement with reading, especialy in its aesthetic forms, may be allied in two ways with the personality configuration obtaining at a given time, and is usually part of an interactional chain embracing both of these ways. First reading may be an effective agent of psychological growth or change, in a situation such that literary experience moves the individual to act in a specific way or to order ideas in a definite manner.[7] The sphere of reading-as-agent is obviously, like all life events, amenable to overt and covert analysis since the individual may be quite conscious of the weight of a written passage or may take in all varieties of impressions and ideas without an explicit realization of the process. The corollary of this view is that literary forms may be experiences in the framework of psychological predispositions; such predispositions might have either a literary or non-literary efficient cause, or some combination. Not only is the choice of particular areas of books, or concentration on peculiar ideas, in its way a projection of the personality, but the very decision to read or not to read a specific volume or style of work is probably a consideration which hinges upon the personality extant.[8]

Thus, we may posit a congruence of reading experience and preference and the contemporary personality configuration. A congruence is in fact assumed in most social psychological studies of themes in mass media. As a rule, the notion that reading creative material (or more generally, seeing or hearing it as well) is an *effective* agent in development is far less emphasized than the companion thesis that this form of experience exhibits themes which fit a preexisting personality pattern, upon which the individual can, as it were, congenially, "feed."[9]

The query, "Does A read books about athletic heroes because he admires such figures, or does A admire proficient athletes because of having read a great deal about them?" may be one of the falsely dichotomous chicken-egg variety; yet assuming the interactional maxim of social science, it may be valuable to shift emphasis and perspective toward the less fully examined pole, and examine the possible influence of reading experience as agent. That changes of attitude on a mature level of perception are possible is the key assumption of propaganda techniques, for instance, despite the caution that effective propaganda is maximally congruent with the preexisting dispositions to believe.

The present research is aimed at a modest appraisal of the degree of congruence between reading experience and personality. In order to test the degree of "fit" we propose to:

1. Obtain a pencil-and-paper choice of favored books and fictional characters.
2. Scale the respondents on a rough measure of familiarity with literary works—the person who has read only slightly would presumably exhibit less "congruence" in our sense, since he has experienced less material and (probably) done so less intensely.
3. Obtain a written account of the individual's reading history and a subjective estimation of what force this history has exerted.
4. Conduct an interview in which the individual's reading experience, current lifestyle and attitudes, and overt personal characteristics are explored.
5. Derive from steps 1 to 4 a succinct personality statement.
6. Compare this personality statement with a total personality portrait derived from projective tests, life histories, interviews, inventories, and so forth—the ultimate (in our context) clinical diagnosis.
7. Compare a rank order of readers rated on the scope and depth of their literary experience with rank orders of the same readers on the following variables:
   a. introversion-extroversion;
   b. adequacy of precollege school adjustment;
   c. degree of peer-group integration;
   d. originaity of stories told on the Thematic Apperception Test [TAT];
   e. certain needs and presses as exemplified in TAT stories and other projective protocols.

The scope and relevance of personality statements derived in this manner are widely variant from individual to individual, but the current status of the procedure would seem to be at least that of a highly relevant auxiliary tool. In certain instances, an individual's remarks about literary-aesthetic topics may provide a flash of insight which the clinician could not gain by means of any of the more standard techniques. This is especially true of affective statements about imaginary characters, most often when these characters appear to stand as ego-ideal figures. In one sense, the subjects' written appraisals of reading experience and the unstructured interview comments may be viewed as projective documents.

Perhaps the most importat task is to investigate the manner in which two classes of phenomena interrelate in reading experience and personality dynamics: (1) ego-ideal and ego-alien figures, and (2) themes of a psycho-sociological nature: personality establishments, lifestyles, values and goals.

Then again, we may survey the possible significance of reading as a gross category of experience, a way of behaving, which influences other actions in a global fashion. An example would be acute emphasis on books as compensation for inadequate satisfaction in other areas of life, regardless of the *specific* content of the literary fare. A few pointed instances of these relationships follow.

Studies of Ego-Ideal and Ego-Alien Figures

Cracker.[10] Cracker spent a good share of his early years immersed in fable and fact about classical atiquity. He read avidly in Greek mythology and in historial reconstructions of the classical period, developing an abiding interest in the Greek way and an admiration for the heroes of myths. Above all, two aspects of this era stood out for him: the ideal of mind-body harmony as embodied in athletic Greek youth, and the ideal of the voyaging hero exemplified by Odysseus.

As a college sophomore, Cracker has become a brilliant track star, outstanding in sprint events. A champion runner, he practices faithfully, consciously training his body to respond to strict competitive demands; the laurels of the race are his with great frequency, and he experiences the adulation of large audiences. Yet this classical athletic pursuit (and it is quite possible that the ideal will come appropriately full circle in Olympic competition) is meshed with a superior academic record and rational career planning. The notion that athletic excellence must be complemented by mental acuity is always with him. It is not difficult to observe a striking correspondence between the early literary experience and the later fulfillment of a classic ideal.

For the past three summers, Cracker has been a merchant seaman, sailing to several countries and gaining repute from his officers as a worthy sailor. The voyages of mythological figures, especially Odysseus, are roughly recapitulated in Cracker's quest. He has sailed "...beyond the sunset and the baths of all the Western stars..." has known adventure, exotic scenes, fleeting sexual encounters. He hopes to continue such maritime wanderings for many more years, and may in fact attempt to stake out a career in international trade.

One finds Cracker's personality far more understandable if some knowledge of his reading history is available. The mental-physical harmony of the Greek youth, the voyaging orientation of the mythical hero, are here seen in modern dress: they are never far from Cracker's vision. In addition, attributes of the ideal classical individual, such as rationality and a measured control of affect, are upheld by Cracker. His is the examined life of the philosophers.

Toast. Toast comes from a cultivated home in which he was exposed to a variety of literary influences. Because his scope of reading experience is so great, it is difficult to isolate specific figures of unusual psychological import. Nevertheless, among the many fictional characters admired by him, the prototype is Levin, the young serious man, musing on large philosophical problems. Not only Levin's personal manner, but also his whole style of life as etched in *Anna Karenina,* are important to Toast.

If we look at the individual involved, we find that he is serious, scholarly, and not to be dissuaded from wrestling with knotty problems. Despite his success in academic activities, and his position of leadership in his group, he does not rest on past achievements. He continues to probe for certainties, to explore the possibilities for a richer, more intelligent life. With a continued record of high achievement, he nevertheless expresses self-doubt, especially on the less controlled level of projective fantasy. There is thus a fairly clear-cut congruence between the figure admired by Toast and his own personality: high seriousness, leadership, gifts of character and intelligence, fundamental doubts about the world and one's place in it, and a refusal to grow complacent about one's problems.

Beep. At early adolescence, Beep chose Sherlock Holmes for a fictional hero; he pursued this ideal with gusto, to the point of buying and wearing a Holmesian deerstalker cap. In college, he still mentions the master sleuth as an admired prototype.

Beep himself is an introverted, anxiety-ridden youth, superb in his academic specialty but socially inept and burdened with portents of a diffuse insecurity. He sees the world as a hard and bitter arena, in which the very strong subdue the very weak, to the tune of a bleak unmelodious disenchantment. He is grossly unhappy, fearful, and unable to form strong interpersonal ties, yet he makes a minimal adjustment via the path of intellective dominance, sensing that his superior mastery of science will assure him of an acceptable and perhaps distinguished social role despite his personality inadequacies. His admiration for Holmes, the omniscient detective, who masters his environment through mental prowess, is not fortuitous. Who could constitute a firmer ideal than the cool, logical Holmes, who never permitted emotional nuances to interfere with the intellectual task at hand? One sees that rational dominance of people and things is closely allied to Beep's security needs, highlighting his strongly logical bent and covering up interpersonal maladaptation.

On the other hand, his ego-alien choices are most revealing: his scorn is directed at the classic instance of an irresolute intellect. He finds himself unable to sympathize with Hamlet, referring to the Dane's "disgusting lack of decision." Thus we find him repelled by indecisive thought processes, unable to countenance an unstructured play of the mind. Hamlet is to him weak, and he despises the weak because of his own frailty. Further, his rigid intellectual ideal will not admit of the penetration of the irrational into considerations of human conduct. Himself prey to night thoughts, he disavows the somber recesses of the mind, gasping for the bright dry plains of logical argument. He rejects Hamlet's obscure imaginings in favor of Holmes's demonstrations of the heretofore not-so-obvious.

Bruise. Bruise is a moderately successful, athletic undergraduate. Handsome, controlled, he impresses one as being quite smooth and interpersonally unruffled. But the first glimpse is complicated by his own tales of unhappiness in youth, by the fund of aggression in his projected fantasy. We learn that his mother has been overweening, demanding, has martyred herself deliberately at the altar of Bruise's sensibilities. He has come to detest her while paying her overt homage. He has set up a dichotomy of the "good woman," and the "bad woman," and the bad woman is a bitch who makes the lives of men close to her unbearable.

The ego-alien figure upon whom he fastens is Hedda Gabler, the bitch heroine of Ibsen's play who fitfully destroys her artist husband. Hedda is a focus for Bruise's hate; he noted that it was "too bad she couldn't have died a lingering death." His ambivalence toward women comes out in many contexts—while speaking of Ibsen's Nora or Hemingway's Lady Brett for instance—but the primary theme of malice toward the cruel, demanding, inconstant female dominates his discussion of literary heroines. There is thus a striking interplay between the significant literary figures and the actual complex of this individual's attitudes toward women.

Studies of Themes

Grope. Grope is a representative of what has been termed the Icarus Complex, a syndrome marked by overwhelming ambition, the need for group adulation, low ego-strength, and rapid descent from high-level performance or expectations upon the withdrawal of external motivational support. He had been a great success in early school days, but found the competitive and anomic quality of life at a major university anathema. Lack of persistent encouragement or startling success caused him to lose interest and stop trying; his achievement drive became crippled, and the consequent atrophy of directed effort resulted in failure and dismissal from college.

An exploration of his literary experience revealed that he had an unusual taste for exotic escape literature; that science fiction, for example, allowed him to dreamily leave the field, to let unsupported and fantastic ambitions preempt reality. The escape from academic striving and the escape from the real world in fiction coincided. Moreover, the *content* of his escapist fare implied a focusing on certain peculiar and highly relevant themes. For instance, the heroes transported to other planets of future ages seemed always to dominate their environment. In strange settings, they assumed leadership prerogatives. Questioning elicited the fact that Grope had been engrossed, at an early age, in the tale of the Swiss Family Robinson. The notion of island retreat, of leadership in a small society, of a free field for the exercise of burning ambition: these themes interlaced to indicate Grope's desire for untrammeled dominance and the wholesale allegiance of imagined admirers. He said he daydreamed of dominance, of vast control exerted through thought waves and electrical batteries.

Grope's reading history, then, meshed with his personality structure; it afforded rich evidence of the pervasive nature of the ascension-adulation theme. The exotic tenor of his current literary tastes illuminated the escapist fantasies engendered by his present dismal situation. It is pertinent to note that his "realistic" appraisal of his future prospects following academic failure emphasized the (never fulfilled) aim of flight training, the *zeitgeist* type-case of glamorous ascension.

Thaw. Thaw has lived in an aura of warm nurturance, the darling of mother and sister since the mother's separation, many years ago, from the father. He has built for himself an ideal of service and pastoral communion in a western county; marked by firm religious-moral tenets, he looks forward to integration within a group rather than to high personal striving.

Thaw exhibits a neat correspondence between a reading theme and a life goal. At the age of thirteen, he was confined to bed for several weeks. While there, he read a biography of the doctors Mayo, and the account so impressed him that he vowed to follow the career of medicine. As a college junior, this goal is still paramount. Despite the obvious causal force of his nurturant family and semirural environment, and the example of his older sister (a social worker), it is not too much to assign a measure of significance to the medical biography. At any rate, this experience in reading and his later career choice are decidedly aligned.

Nob. The great aim of Nob's life is to be securely fixed in upper-class status, to have the wealth and leisure for many activities. He desires to associate with persons whom he believes to be of an appropriate social rank, of "his own kind." Nob is not currently quite secure in the upper class; his family has lost money, but he does his best to keep close to elite friends and indulge in proper activities. He believes firmly in a hierarchical social order and the dominion of persons boasting assured talent and position.

Of his reading, Nob selects the novels of John Marquand as best illustrating a favored style of life. He cathects the manner of Marquand characters and delights in the portrayal of upper-class foibles. He wants the satire to be gently humorous, to lightly taunt the privileged while steadfastly upholding the essential rightness of their views. Nob expresses the belief that only those who know the type of life intimately—as he does—can fully appreciate Marquand's talent. With his mother or with favored friends, he can laugh at the subtleties of fictional treatment, indulge in a shared class viewpoint. A further congruence of literary themes and personal attitude occurs in Nob's enjoyment of *A Forsyte Saga,* and his admiration for old Jolyon Forsyte who represented, to him, the epitome of responsible, dignified capitalism. One should, Nob feels, conduct a career of financial aggrandizement with grace, style, and unobtrusive striving. Thus depictions of upper-class lifestyle and ideals in literary form reinforce his own striving and class consciousness.

Studies of Reading as Gross Category of Experience

Neater. Neater has long hoped for unusual intellectual achievement and a philosophical structure of his world. Unfortunately, he is not unusually gifted in an intellectual vein; he is actually rather slow and ill-equipped technically. His early life was characterized by a strict, overnurturant mother, a patriarchal father and superior older siblings. He never felt wholly part of the family, and never seemed able to measure up to his father's example.

When Neater was at boarding school as an ill-adjusted adolescent, he discovered that other family members each had an ideological "line," well supported by dialectical ammunition. He then began to search for intellectual scaffolding, to collect arguments, so that he might hold up his end in family controversy. Neater read widely, if slowly, at this point, wading through deep tomes in pursuit of certainty and sophistication. His teachers warned him against going over his head in reading fare, but he typically plowed along, searching for *the* answer in *a* book. Today he reads widely but has a mediocre academic record; he has great difficulty in retaining what he has read.

Here we have several facets of Neater's personality emphasized by his literary history; his desire for compensatory knowledge, his quasi defiance of more powerful or talented figures, his determined striving in combination with a paucity of underlying ability, and his compulsive hope that books will give him definite answers if he can only encompass them carefully.

Choice. Choice is a brilliant student who easily outstrips most of his competitiors. He is tightly controlled in his pursuit of status and achievement, extremely rational and self-assured. He is steady and balanced, unlikely to deviate from the mean of manageable life activities. Avoiding extremes, he runs a smart race down the center lane of rationality.

Choice's literary background emphasizes the themes of control and omniscience; he likes to be "on the inside," sharing the author's superior perspective, and savoring a measure of conscious control. He notes that he is unable to empathize with fictional characters. He preserves his rational autonomy to the extent of not giving in to the demands of aesthetic participation. Choice avows a shrewd noncommitment to heroes, lifestyles, or imaginative ideals; he will not be lured to excessive cathexes under any conditions. Always in the forefront we find his cerebral filter winnowing imaginative experience. He applies the dictums of sensible moderation, as in his comment that the philosophy of the *Rubaiyat* is enticing, but probably not wholly worthwhile, or that the style of life of certain historical novels is exciting but physically uncomfortable. Represented in his reading experience and his reactions to books are the distinguishing characteristics of his personality: tight rational control, moderation, desire for power through knowledge, management of affect away from excesses of self-forgetfulness.

Heiner. As a boy, Heiner suffered a physical disability which shaped his personality and is a continuing factor in his psychic configuration. He had been a shy, introverted person before the onset of the disability, and when he became a partial cripple his withdrawal tendencies were accentuated. His poor peer-group relations became even worse as a result of enforced idleness. Today he is an excellent student but socially inept, expecting little warmth or encouragement from others and unable to give much himself.

For Heiner, reading served as an escape from unsatisfactory playgroup integration. He reveled in vicarious experience via the literary route, gaining both pleasure and a sense of distance and superiority from his peers: "I could sit in my armchair and have more thrilling experiences than any of my age mates playing so foolishly and ineffectually in the streets."

Stall. Stall is a gifted individual who may become a professional writer. Academic-literary pursuits were encouraged during his youth, especially since he strove to emulate an older brother who had a deep interest in reading. Throughout his life he has found literary experience personally valuable and socialy rewarding. The sharing of imaginative events and ideas has been a constant theme, first with his brother and later with friends of both sexes. Stall has employed reading as an index to the character of others, expecting them to admire the poetry which he had enjoyed, and judging them on literary discussions. He ostensibly broke with a girl because of her insensitivity to certain literary values. Of his interest in poetry he writes: "In the past, I made my closest friend partly on the basis of this interest, and one of my rationalizations for breaking up with the girl I thought I loved was that she didn't appreciate poetry."

Scope and Depth of Literary Experience Related to Certain Personality Variables

The subjects were ranked from 1 to 20 on the scope and depth of literary experience. Rankings were derived partially from scores on a pencil-and-paper test of literary familiarity, and partially from the researcher's considered judgment of the data contained in the written literary histories and the interview hour. This rank order was then compared with rankings on several dimensions of personality and life history material. Spearman Rank Correlation Coefficients were computed, and may be summarized:

1. Reading Rank and Extroversion: $r = -.28$
2. Reading Rank and Adequacy of precollege school adjustment: $r = +.36$
3. Reading Rank and Degree of peer-group integration: $r = +.30$
4. Reading Rank and Originality of projected fantasies on the Thematic Apperception Test: $r = +.38$

5. a. Reading Rank and need Cognizance: r = +.64 (significant at .01 level)
   Need Cognizance, based on projective protocols and autobiographi-
   cal-behavioral data, concerns the strength of the individual's desire
   for knowledge of all varieties.
   b. Reading Rank and need Construction: r = +.52 (significant at .05
   level)
   Need Construction deals with the strength of the desire to build
   ideas or objects, to execute projects and create new things.
   c. Reading Rank and need Passivity: r = −.26
   Need Passivity characterizes the individual's need to retire, rest,
   sleep and avoid action.
   d. Reading Rank and need Succorance: r = −.14
   Need Succorance refers to the individual's wish for comforting
   attention, helpful superordinates and benevolent supporting figures.
   e. Reading Rank and need Autonomy: r = +.001
   Need Autonomy refers to the individual's drive toward freedom from
   authoritative restriction, toward self-fulfillment and self-manage-
   ment.
   f. Reading Rank and press Lack of Human Support: r = −.16
   This press indicates the degree to which supportive figures are
   missing from the individual's environment.
   g. Reading Rank and Oral Complex: r = +.01
   The Oral Complex rating is derived essentially from orthodox
   Freudian indices of oral fixation, in imagery and action.

Of these correlations, 1 was expected as fitting in with the common-
sense idea that extroverted activity and quantities of reading should be in an
inverse relationship. In this sample, extroverted individuals were decidedly
less likely to rank high on literary experience. The correlations in 2 and 3
were unanticipated, for it was thought that wide reading experience at an
early age played a major role in compensating for poor integration within
the group. It may be more nearly correct to view literary adventures as a
further reaching out, on the part of already adjusted individuals, for
fantasied increments of warmth. Reading might be seen as an index to
potential capacity for the formation of solid social ties. The result of 4 lies in
the predicted direction, although we had expected it to be even more
positive, for fantasy production seems to require a base, an experiential
fund, which may be partially provided by a wealth of vicarious experiences
and identification. Similarly, 5a and b were anticipated, although the
magnitude of b was greater then expected. Quite obviously the person with
a thirst for knowledge should appear also as a wide reader. Similarly, the
desire to reach out toward the creation of new things, to build ideas, may be
seen as related to the kind of reaching out in a search for new experience
which is involved in reading. We did not expect the results of 5c and d, since
it was thought that the reader would be more passive than the nonreader,

and would exhibit a stronger desire for help and comfort. If one conceives of literary experience as activity, however, 5c becomes understandable: the individual who is generally active and energetic is also active toward the world of books. In a sense, 5d through 5f may indicate that a person who has had wide reading experience has thereby had a certain portion of his or her succorant need satisfied, while the nonreader is likely to have a stronger succorant need, partially as a result of the lack of imaginative literary sustenance. The results of 5e were extremely surprising, since it was thought that the reader would be a person who had used literary experience as a means of satisfying autonomous desires and exerting independence from authority figures, demonstrated, for example, by the part played by reading in the stereotype of the adolescent revolt. We were mildly surprised by 5f: generally, reading is seen as often compensatory for lack of support, and as providing a satisfaction which interpersonal relations in the real world have not afforded. We computed 5g in a semi-facetious vein, to test the trite phrases "voracious reader," "hungry for knowledge," "thirst for literary experience." No relation was found between orality and reading—a fact that is surely food for thought.

Notes

This chapter is a small portion of a major investigation of fantasy conducted at the Harvard Psychological Clinic under the direction of Professor Henry A. Murray. It was facilitated by the Laboratory of Social Relations, Harvard University.
  1. See Charles Morris, *Signs, Language and Behavior* (New York: Prentice-Hall, 1946).
  2. Talcott Parsons, et al., *Toward a General Theory of Action* (Cambridge, Mass.: Harvard University Press, 1951).
  3. The definition and investigation of *projection* as a psychological phenomenon is of course an accepted branch of contemporary personality psychology (Lawrence Abt and Leopold Bellak, *Projective Psychology* [New York: Knopf, 1950]). It is crucial to stress the emergent conviction, on the part of Murray and others, that projection embraces a larger area than Freud originally hypothesized. In particular, it involves positive elements, such as ego-ideal components, as well as the traditional displacement of hostility and other less attractive psychic characteristics.
  4. Talcott Parsons, *The Social System* (Glencoe, Ill.: Free Press, 1951), p. 205, chap. 9.
  5. Thomas C. Pollock, *The Nature of Literature* (Princeton, N.J.: Princeton University Press, 1949), p. 205
  6. Douglas Waples, Bernard Berelson, Franklyn R. Bradshaw. *What Reading Does to People* (Chicago: University of Chicago Press, 1940), p. 12.
  7. Examples might be W.I. Thomas's case of a girl whose reading brought about alienation and separation from her parents, or China's Mao Tse-Tung's great admiration for heroic novels at a youthful age, or the role of the classrooms of Eton in preparing British leaders by steeping them in accounts of leadership, from Caesar to Nelson.
  8. Previous researches at Harvard have also tapped these areas of behavior: "The

subject may be asked to give a history of the fairy stories, fables, myths, adventure books, novels, plays, operas, pictures, paintings, sculpture and music that have most impressed him since he was a child....This procedure is based on the principle that a subject is most impressed by and remembers best the stories and creative productions which represent aspects of his own fantasies. A given presentation may light up hitherto latent tendencies or it may merely serve as a conduit for existent fantasies....Thus, a psychologist who simply notes a subject's artistic preferences may sometimes guess correctly the unconscious processes that are active within the subject. From H.A. Murray, "Techniques for a Systematic Investigation of Fantasy," *Journal of Psychology* 3 (1936): 115-43.

9. Cf. Ruth Benedict's illustration of Japanese character congruence with the tale of the "Forty-Seven Ronin" (in *The Chrysanthemum and the Sword* [Boston: Houghton Mifflin, 1946]), or Donald V. McGranahan and Ivor Wayne's study of themes in German and American drama, "German and American Traits Reflected in Popular Drama" (*Human Relations* 1 [1947-48]: 429-55).

10. Each individual discussed bears an arbitrary code name.

2
The Poet and the Projective Test

Although I had read a fair amount of poetry and had even published one slim verse in the college literary magazine, I had never met a practicing poet face-to-face until the summer of 1949. In many ways that summer changed my whole life: I became absorbed in the art and the artists, beginning what is by now a thirty-five-year devotion to the psychology and sociology of literary activity. Harry Murray had presented me with an extraordinary opportunity to live among poets and to make a professional mark as undeniably the first, if not the best, sociological interpreter of the poet's role. But at the time of the inquiry described in this article, I was concerned only with trying out a new psychological instrument in the hope that certifiably creative individuals would dazzle the researchers with innovative outpourings. They did not, and thereby hangs the tale.

Failed research can often be as instructive as it is disheartening. On the surface, especially considering previous experience with the Thematic Apperception Test in psychological diagnosis, Murray and I were perhaps justified in expecting a spate of imaginative fertility when writers were shown our picture cards. But in retrospect we appear to have been naive in not recognizing several significant factors; the test instructions called for narrative, and modern poets are seldom narrators in any straightforward sense; our pictures were contrived, rather obvious goads to fantasy without much intrinsic aesthetic merit; our subjects, creative writers, were far less inclined to accept the dictates of the tester and the rationale of the test than had been college students or patients in therapy.

If the collection of TAT responses did not yield the anticipated portrait of "the creative personality," the venture had nevertheless a certain import. What I call the interstitial nature of the poet's time-sense is highly relevant to the frozen moment that marks much contemporary poetry: the conjunction of memory in simultaneity rather than narrative sequence. The poet's authenticity and independence are amplified by stubbornness in the testing situation and insistence on genuine stimuli as the coin of exchange for genuine responsiveness; and preference for the ambiguous, the complex, the asymmetrical, so apparent here, is confirmed by Albert Rothenberg, Frank Barron, and others. Not least, the poet's exquisite attentiveness to the word, which threads through all the test records, underlines the rooted precision of the artist as maker and namer. As Boris Pasternak has it in simple eloquence:

> For a moment she rediscovered the purpose of her life. She was here on earth to grasp the meaning of its wild enchantment and to call each thing by its right name.

23

One of the central questions in the psychology of art involves the manner in which the artist uses experience as the springboard for an elaboration of fantasy. We know that he or she is affected by a variety of stimuli, and that this stimulation is transformed into a coherent pattern, usually a very selective one. It is true that the artist imposes a pattern on the formlessness of existence, but equally true that the material comes from the real world which imposes a finite fund of sense impressions on the artist. In a previous account I have described the way a group of contemporary poets go about their creative tasks.[1] The present report will consider a rather audacious attempt to elicit fantasy from poets by means of an artificial stimulus.

The father of the Thematic Apperception Test, Henry A. Murray, has devised a version of the test which departs from the original set of pictures in the direction of looser structure, less realistic scenes, and the use of color. Through these elaborations of the standard TAT, it was believed that professionally creative people might be challenged to exert their imaginal gifts in the artificial milieu of a projective test. Essentially, the testing of poets had a twofold aim: to learn more about the personalities and creative patterns of poets, and to determine the utility of the test itself in provoking the imagination. The research was avowedly exploratory and tentative, but at the very least we expected to glean a rich and varied harvest of fantasy. If projective tests elicit fantasy from ordinary individuals in many walks of life, should they not draw forth a much more vivid and complex response from people who devote their lives to creative literary effort?

TAT II, as the new form of the test was termed, has not yet been published for general use. It consists of twenty pictures, administered one at a time in two sessions of ten pictures each, with about an hour allowed per session. Several of the pictures were colored by a professional painter; several feature exotic backgrounds of tropical foliage, animals, and so on; several are dominated by enlarged faces or figures arranged in a photomontage effect. The variety is perhaps greater than that found in the standard TAT. Subjects are given the same instructions that they are usually given in the TAT, namely to tell a story suggested to them by each picture, using the materials offered therein in the most dramatic and imaginative way they can.

The sample of poets who took the test is unique in certain ways. The twenty subjects constitute an elite sample, in that each member is a recognized figure in American poetry, the author of much published work and the recipient of critical esteem. At the time of the research, they lived in the eastern part of the United States. They earn their living in a variety of vocations, including editing, fiction or critical writing, teaching, business, and medicine. Characterized aesthetically, they might be associated primarily with the avant-garde, although their poems have now gained substantial recognition. The little magazines print their work often, but so do regular commercial publishers. Included in the group are several Pulitzer Prize winners, National Book Award winners, and holders of the Poetry Consultantship at the Library of Congress.

Thematic Analysis

Thematic analysis has been most often employed in a clinical setting as an aid to depth understanding of the individual personality. The TAT has in general proved its utility to the clinician, not as a complete and independent description of personality but as one portal among many opening on the essential individual dynamic.[2] In group contexts, however, where the goal is to establish common patternings of response rather than to probe any single test for its ultimate analytic clues, serious questions of reliability and validity arise. Here it becomes less possible to profit from random scraps of information and fortuitous insight, more necessary to isolate well-defined themes. Moreover, the winnowing of group uniformities requires that the responses be maximally comparable; the rare colorings of the individual person must be blurred over in a search for gross pigments of behavior. The present study, which was aimed at describing a group of writers, suffers from both lack of an adequate analytical framework and low comparability among test responses of group members.

Responses given by writers to TAT cards were not amenable to clear-cut evaluation under any extant method of scoring, nor was it possible to devise a scoring technique which would well represent the themes embedded in the material. The primary reason for this failure to derive full psychological potential from the response patterns seems to lie with the unique character of the responses. These reactions defeated the rationale of the test because the respondents refused (or were unable) to adhere to the test instructions: what emerged from the test in an overwhelming number of instances was not a set of plots, of narrative structures detailing individual behavior, but rather a variety of free associative responses. Such a welter of musings and fragmentary philosophies resisted straightforward thematic analysis and minimized the chance of discovering foci of dynamic comparability. The TAT rests on the assumption that respondents will tell stories of a conventional dramatic character, including a chronological narrative flow, a dominance of one or a few themes per story, and a limited set of actors. Traditional forms of short story, play, or novel provide the structural model for the test and its psychological evaluation. Poets, however, found the narrative mold uncongenial, and few of their responses conformed to conventional expectations of plot and action.

Nevertheless, the tests were scored as far as possible according to the categories of need, press, and state ordinarily employed by Murray.[3] The completed profile of group responses was then compared to a profile of twenty college undergraduates who had also been tested with TAT II. While, for the reasons outlined above, no great confidence can be placed in this phase of analysis, the few significant differences between the artist group and student group may be of interest.

Results were as follows:

The state of conflict was represented in poets' responses more frequently than in the students'. Interviews obtained during the research, which I have summarized at length elsewhere (see note 1), were marked by a persistent willingness of poets to recognize and accept tensions within themselves as reflections of the "invariant doublets" of experience. Poets stressed openness to varieties of experience, the capacity to face life honestly, as a desirable and in fact necessary characteristic of the artist's personality. The poet's acute sensitivity and permeability to impressions implies that he is unusually aware of polarities and conflicting themes, quick to perceive inconsistencies. Faithfulness to reality, wherever that reality may lead, is a schooled imperative for the professional perceiver or poet. The artistic code does not allow easy glossing over of ambiguities or pat resolutions to conflict.

It may also be hazarded that themes of unresolved conflict in projective responses reflect something of the poet's own ambiguous situation in contemporary American society. No matter how certain the artistic purpose, it is perhaps inevitable that tensions involved in filling a social role which is ill-rewarded and marginal to primary American vocational emphases should infiltrate the poet's fantasy.

The outcomes for the central figures (heroes) of the projected stories were significantly less successful in the poet group than in the student group. Moreover, the ratio of successful to unsuccessful resolutions was reversed; poets described five successes for every seven failures, while students postulated three successes for every two failures. This finding may be partially related to the previous one. A situation of sustained conflict, and a refusal to posit an easy solution, would obviously mesh with the presence of more fantasied failure. The scarcity of success stories, correspondingly, may be traced to the poets' reluctance to supply a trite plot twist, to wrap the response up neatly before proceeding to another card. Part of the poet's business is to raise the questions which remain unanswered—and, perhaps, unanswerable.

It is probably fair to say that dominant American values stress an optimistic view of life. But the poet, again, is almost by definition the holder of a rounded perception. The subjective reports indicate that the capacity for enduring, if not reaching out for, all varieties of experience is highly appropriate to the creative function. It must also be borne in mind that the writers in the sample were far more mature than the group of students and could probably be expected to voice more disillusion, the disenchantment of maturity. Above all, the poet is sensitive to the tragic mode in human affairs, knowing that tragedy is the stuff of art as surely as are the other chords of experience. An older poet mentioned colloquially during his response to one card:

> The girl has a vacant face...the sort of creature who perpetually passes by in life. I think possibly in that sense we could say that the sinister figure in the background didn't approve of Suzanne for that very reason, as if saying, "without tragic sense of life what have you got? In fact you ain't got nothing."

Two negative findings are of interest. Poets and students were not significantly different on either the need for achievement or the need for autonomy. We had believed that poets would exhibit less need for achievement, since in their own vocation, conventional success is not the normal pattern; the TAT, moreover, seems to allow greater opportunity for the expression of overt "success" in situations of external strife than for the accretion of quiet satisfaction through triumphs in more contemplative or spiritual contexts.

Even more strongly held was the impression that the poet would stress the need for autonomy, on the assumption that the desire for untrammeled freedom in work and thought would be an overriding consideration. Perhaps the poets in this study had long since worked through the struggle for independence of action, as a part of normal professional development in the artistic vocation.

The thematic analysis of the tests, then, must be assessed as a failure, since few important uniformities of psychological disposition were uncovered. Creative people appear to vary greatly in personality structure, despite their sharing a common core of vocational concern and artistic process. It seems highly unlikely that we can isolate a distinctive psychological make-up for poets or other varieties of creator that will be clearly different from the patterns of butcher, baker, or bureaucrat.[4]

Formal Analysis

The most important data derived from projective testing in this research cannot be expressed in terms of the usual scoring procedure. Far more impressive than any specific content of the protocols was the general way in which the artists handled the task imposed on them. Rapport was felt to be quite good throughout, so that some confidence can be placed in the responses as indicative of more than interpersonal factors, as a genuine reaction to the test itself.

An analysis of the form of the poets' responses revealed the following significant qualities. These characteristics are distinct from specific psychodynamic content:

1. Aesthetic criticism of the TAT pictures.
2. *Double commentary*—a response to the picture plus an analysis of that response by the subject.
3. Self-reference and private associations.
4. Artistic distance.
5. Linguistic virtuosity.
6. *Interstitial* or nonplot mode of reaction.

One of the more striking occurrences was the statement of aesthetic criticism of the TAT cards.[5] While not every poet expressed an opinion, most of them had a variety of comments about the style of the pictures. Nearly all of those who paid particular attention to design thought that it was aesthetically poor, even if interesting for other reasons. Obviously, the test was not constructed as an art object but as a stimulus for storytelling; yet it appeared that the absence of true aesthetic quality drastically interfered with the aim of eliciting a full response. Many times poets mentioned that they would prefer the challenge of a genuine work of art, a painting or piece of sculpture, to what they felt was the contrived quality of the test stimuli. Perhaps artists can only be met on their own grounds; that is, they may have to be presented with real art or undistorted nature if we expect them to make a deeply felt response. Poets seem to feel cheated when asked to open up frankly in response to an artificial stimulus. We propose that the tone of criticism indicated a far-reaching aesthetic quality in the poet's perceptions, so pervasive that even tasks are judged in terms of aesthetic criteria. The artist's vocational mood may be supposed to generalize into many other areas of life. If, as a poet stated, the writer is working twenty-four hours a day, then one must assume that whatever enters his ken is perceived in its aesthetic relevance.

Representative comments on the aesthetic qualities of the test might be illustrated:

> Oh, this makes me again hopelessly....stopped at the aesthetic gate.

> I am not going to comment on the artistic value of these pictures that I have been looking at. It is not high....What I should like to comment on is the triteness of the stories suggested.

> I don't know...to me it's very uninteresting, colorless, bad, poorly drawn...it evokes nothing from me.

> To me again, not very stimulating; your question and answer dictated by the picture itself. Your imagination is stopped as it were by the dictates of the picture.

A second interesting theme in the formal response was the *double commentary,* entailing the overt performance of the poet plus interjections *about* that performance. Most of the respondents were self-conscious, and as critical of their efforts as of the pictures presented. They observed their own progression through the test, and frequently asked for judgments from the tester about the relative proficiency with which they performed. It was a clear illustration of the theory of the "spectator self": the artist plays a double role in having to act as creator and critic at the same time.

A certain portion of this self-analysis may be seen as a defensive reaction. Artists are not among the most friendly onlookers of social scientific operations, and if part of their hostility is based on aesthetic abhorrence, another part undoubtedly lies in a fear that too much will be discovered or that their delicate mechanisms will be positivistically pilloried.[6]

Self-reference is further illustrated in the profusion of private associations; again and again poets were thrown off the narrative track by tangential anecdotes and impressions. Often these were of great interest in their similarity to free association. Poets associated to faces, situations, backgrounds—all the elements of the pictures. Aside from its relation to egoism, the maximizing of the stimulus' relevance to the respondent's personal history, this practice of private associations ties in with the important position of memory in the poetic craft. Immediate events jog the poet into a reawareness of pertinent elements in his lifelong impressionistic stock. When pictures forced recall, the remembered moods or incidents were often described with the greatest precision and richness. The critical role of memory in the poet's work is analyzed by Stephen Spender in his autobiography, *World Within World:*

> For memory is the root of creative genius. It enables the poet to connect the immediate moment of perception which is called "inspiration," with the past moments in which he has received like impressions. This relating of the immediate impression with past ones enables the poet, through the moment, to strike a kind of chord across time, made up of notes which are similar impressions felt at different times and connected with one another in a simile within which all are contemporaneous.[7]

Poets appeared to hold their fantasied characters at a distance, to examine them sympathetically but impartially, as if judging their significance for artistic usefulness. Artistic distance is related to a penchant for psychological analysis of characters: acuity in motivational analysis was one of the most striking features of the protocols. As one poet demanded of the professional writer:

> He should have empathy, intuition—the ability immediately to understand other people, even if he doesn't like them.

The poets brought the TAT figures to life, even if they were only adumbrating a mood picture, by endowing protagonists with psychological depth.

That the responses were marked by verbal fluency and, frequently, brilliance of expression, is not at all surprising. Even in the performance of this artificial task, the poet inevitably brings his linguistic capacity to bear. The concern with words and virtuosity in their use stands out. We often noted the process of searching for the exact expression, the precise metaphor; for instance, adjectives would be strung together as a poet came ever closer to just the word required. A poet might toy with descriptions of a central character, putting forth alternative expressions until one designation seemed to fit most appropriately. The hunger for exactitude was most pronounced, a very yearning toward "the word." The responses were rarely sloppy, even if they held to no concrete story line, for digressions were caught in the same sharp focus as central points. A concern with naming was brought out in the appellations of characters; part of the test instructions called for the designation by proper names of the major characters in the pictures, and rather than tagging figures with a common, meaningless name, the poets usually tried to conceive a designation which would be appropriate to the personality they had in mind, to psychological moods as well as physical characteristics. This virtuosity and love of precision made the testing an agreeable experience; as in listening to an expert conversationalist one is often enchanted with the by-play of a fine mind, so here the test sometimes had the pleasant, exciting flavor of a dramatic performance.[8]

But the tests were, after all, a relative failure. Why? They fell short partly because of aesthetic animosity toward the stimulus. This was not the primary difficulty, however; the crux of the failure lay instead in the refusal or inability of many poets to perform as requested, that is, to tell a story. The TAT is based on the assumption that some kind of narrated plot will be available for analysis; the plot is what enables investigators to make inferences about projected themes, and concomitantly, about the psychological characteristics of the storyteller. Test instructions emphasize that a story is desired, and an attempt is made during the course of administration to hold the respondent to a narrative, reminding him of what is required. Yet over half of the poets did not approach story form in their reaction to the pictures. Instead they tended to produce a wandering, musing mood portrait. This might involve deep character description, free association, an exploration of nuances in the pictorial stimulus, or simply a play on word combinations. The effect was that of a frozen cross section of time, caught for artistic analysis, but never pursued backward to origins or forward to conclusions. Rapport, as indicated, was excellent, and the feeling throughout was that a serious attempt was being made to follow instructions. Yet stories did not quite come off; instead, the narrative form was approached gingerly, then often discarded in favor of a more congenial method. We have designated the two major styles as *narrative* and *interstitial.* The interstitial form of response involves an absence of orderly story progression, a beginning, middle, and resolution; in a very real sense, as the term implies, it is a temporal "lying between," in which the time flow is arrested in favor of an intensive examination of the trapped instant.

We regard the high incidence of interstitial responses as the truly novel, and most important, result of projective testing with this sample. It is the one feature which could not very well have been predicted; in fact, our belief was that professionally imaginative people would construct longer, richer, better-formed narratives than any other group. The first, most obvious explanation lies in the nature of contemporary poetry. The ballad and epic forms, the lengthy tracing of a series of incidents, are decidedly not characteristic of modern verse. Poets repeatedly explained that they had no narrative gift, that they were unused to structuring their world view in lineal progression. There is a lack of professional artistic interest in "plotfulness." Modern poetry is generally shorter, more specific than traditional types, tending to pinpoint and explore a limited emotional or dramatic range. Further, the tendency to stress ambiguities—the multiple linguistic-emotive meanings—in events or relationships serves to divert attention from the prosecution of a clear-cut story line.

The poet has been described as an exceptionally aware person. This awareness is nowhere more clearly demonstrated than in a reluctance to hew to a plot structure. Aware of all the facets of the stimulus, and unable to connect them fully in the spontaneous, time-limited situation of the test, the poet gives a somewhat chaotic, sensitive, disorderly response, and "sees too much" in the wandering, tentative approach. This (for test purposes) overawareness substantiates a point made by Schneider[8]: the artist has a greater capacity for the identification of multiple implications.[9]

In a speculative vein, we might note that the interstitial mode involves a definite conception of time which is akin to both stream-of-consciousness novels and modern physics. Lineal causality and narrative description are abandoned; mutual interaction, temporal relativity, and constant change of state are emphasized. Edith Cobb brought my attention to a possible convergence of literary and scientific vanguards in which time is conceived, not as a rope marked by "knots" (hours, days) at intervals, but as a concentric coil in which the precedence of events is relative. (The image of the coil was first expressed to me by Anthony Rossiter of Jesus College, Cambridge, during a discussion of the differences in the time perspectives of Proust and Joyce.) Perhaps, as in the case of the aesthetic qualities of the pictures, we shall find it unwise to try to impose a conventional criterion of time when analyzing and testing creative personalities.

Two further steps are suggested by the projective data:

First, a replication of this research with the aim of verifying or disproving the correctness of the analysis. Replication is especially necessary with reference to what we have termed *formal characteristics,* since these were so peculiar to the present sample.

Second, the construction of a new model of projective test, designed especially for artists. The TAT employed was not of maximum utility. It tended to stand in the way of free-flowing response, to block the expression of intensely felt themes. The aesthetic blockage may in fact have been crucial in our failure to uncover more uniformities at the content level. Any such test should be designed with a view to its *aesthetic* effectiveness, so that it might stimulate artists the more by possessing in itself an aesthetic validity. All testing is artificial, but it seems essential here to minimize the falsity by providing the respondent with something to chew on which more nearly resembles a real bone.

Notes

I am indebted to the encouragement of Dr. Henry A. Murray in this project. The research was facilitated by the Laboratory of Social Relations, Harvard University.
1. Robert N. Wilson, "Poetic Creativity: Process and Personality," *Psychiatry* 27 (May 1954): 163-76.
2. The evidential basis of the TAT is well summarized in Gardner Lindzey, "Thematic Apperception Test: Interpretive Assumptions and Related Empirical Evidence," *Psychological Bulletin* (1952): 1-25.
3. Henry A. Murray, *Explorations in Personality* (New York: Oxford University Press; 1938), esp. chap. 3.
4. The failure to discern a large number of striking uniformities in the test records of creative workers has been experienced by another researcher: "It was my impression that the painters I studied were rather heterogeneous in personality structure....I must say, though, that so far as any unity of 'creativity' is concerned, I don't think it exists, or if it does, it isn't caught by TAT or Rorschach—or anything else that I know of." Dr. Anne Roe (personal communication).
5. In many instances, the test seemed to inhibit, rather than stimulate the expression of fantasy. In Barron's phrase, some of the cards acted as a "stimulus-constraint." Barron's investigations are exceedingly relevant to this discussion since they emphasize the preference of artists for complex, asymmetrical patterns, and it may well be that the TAT is ill-suited to the professional perceiver just because it presents the conventional ingredients of melodrama. Barron further highlights the pertinence of formal, stylistic elements of personality as compared with elements of unique content. Cf. Frank Barron and George S. Welsh, "Artistic Perception as a Possible Factor in Personality Style: Its Measurement by a Figure Preference Test," *The Journal of Psychology* 33 (1952): 199–203, and later papers by Barron.
6. Derogation of scientific "coldness" in contrast to lively poetic warmth has been a favorite theme of poets for several generations:

> *Science! true daughter of Old Time thou art!*
> *Who alterest all things with thy peering eyes.*

Why preyest thou thus upon the poet's heart,
Vulture, whose wings are dull realities?

—E. Allen Poe, "Sonnet to Science"

Thou shalt not answer questionnaires
Or quizzes Upon World Affairs,
*   Nor with compliance*
Take any test. Thou shalt not sit
With statisticians nor commit
*   A social science...*

—W.H. Auden, *Nones*

7. Stephen Spender, *World within World* (New York: Harcourt, Brace, 1951), p.53.
8. This element of pleasure brings to mind the rich vein of humor throughout the responses. It is important to note that the poet has a love of the comic, as well as the tragic, spirit. Part of the roundedness of the creative mind is an ability to sense the comic in situations—and in self-analysis. It would be unfortunate to present artists as dreary, monkish spirits. They are not.
9. Daniel E. Schneider, *The Psychoanalyst and the Artist* (New York: Farrar, Straus, 1950).

3
Poetic Creativity: Process and Personality

Although the attempt to uncover the design of the creative personality through psychological testing was a relative failure, as described in the previous selection, it did lead me to what I think is a rather more successful description of poets' intrapsychic and interpersonal lives. I had discovered during the testing enterprise that these were among the most interesting of men and women, and that various questions about how they did their work and conducted themselves in society were engrossing puzzles for a social scientific inquirer. Moreover, they proved companionable, easy to talk to, furiously engaged in their craft and hence engaging in conversation about it. Being young and naive, I easily cast myself in the role of neophyte, perhaps an apprentice writer with some hint of poetic sensibility. Abjuring the deflected approach of the projective test and the distanced impersonality of the questionnaire survey, I set out to ask what I hoped were direct and searching questions.

The research was compounded of paradox and pleasure. Paradox was at the center of the poet's existence in the mid-twentieth century: how *could* these people do what they did, throw their considerable talents and powerful energies into this vocation that promised neither fame nor riches, that had been fittingly titled by T.S. Eliot, one of the first among them, as "a mug's game"? Pleasure was inherent in the sheer joy of intercourse, in being welcomed, bantered, jolted by such entertaining individuals.

Interviewing poets about the activities entailed in writing a poem proved indeed to be "experiencing creativity," or as close to doing so as an observer could come. I went at this exciting task with a semistructured format: that is, I had contrived a list of topics that I believed would provoke reflection on aspects of composition, but by altering sequence and encouraging spontaneity still leave ample room for the conversation to make its own way. The poets' hospitality, not only in tolerating a lengthy interview but in affording a relaxed, informal setting for dialogue, contributed mightily to whatever merit this sketch of the writer at work may have.

In retrospect, the main features of the creative process and personality set forth here hold up quite well. My emphasis on craftsmanship and productivity, on poetry as hard and technically demanding work, is still valid; however, this analytical stress suffers, perhaps, from the historical climate of the research. The 1940s and 1950s may well have been marked as the apotheosis of the Protestant Ethic in American occupational life, the post–World War II rush for glory and gold, which had been somewhat stoppered by the Depression. So there is rather too much of solemnity and professionalism, even of rational calculation here. Today I should place greater weight on the writer's essential playfulness (as in fact I do in chapter

8 on leisure), on the poet's joy and delight as well as his or her manifest responsibilities.

At least two of the major elements in creativity that I tentatively identified have since been underlined and clarified by the studies of the psychiatrist Albert Rothenberg. Where I spoke rather vaguely of the writer's taste for ambiguity, Rothenberg demonstrates convincingly how the delicate balance of holding opposites in tension lies at the very heart of creativity. This he terms *Janusian thinking* after the Roman god of the hearth, who faced two ways. And while I argued for the poet's conscious mastery of his material, Rothenberg strengthens the case by his incisive contrast of creative work and dreaming: the innovative artist, he asserts, is the converse of the night dreamer. Creativity is the mirror-image of the dream, sharpening and revealing what the dream life confuses and hides.

Yet discovering how we create is very probably an endless if necessary quest. We seem to draw closer to understanding through successive approximations, but a complete grasp eludes us. In olden times in the field artillery, long before the computer emerged to tell us how to aim our guns, we tried to home in on our targets by bracketing, firing a round too long and then one too short, hoping that an in-between range splitting the difference would be effective. Exploring creativity may be construed as scholarly bracketing.

There have been many theories of creativity in the arts, and its relation to the artist's personality. No single construction satisfies all the vagaries of creative work. Perhaps one reason for the generally confused state of psychological formulations in this area lies with the problem itself. By definition, creativity is in a very deep sense resistant to analytical efforts: if the entire process could be neatly blocked out, it would no longer possess the novelty and freshness which is expected of original activity. Prediction and control, the prime goals of science, would in their fullest application contravene the quest for the new. Yet it may be possible to build a model of the process which seems to recur when people achieve some original product.

One must distinguish creative artistic effort from other forms of creativity. Although many similarities seem to exist between artistic and other kinds of creativity, especially the scientific, it would be dangerous to generalize too far. Even further from the central focus, but still akin, is the notion of living creatively.

The basic assumption about literary work on which this discussion hinges is that the process of writing and the personality engaged in it are parts of the same whole. Since there are many sorts of people who write poetry, the most obvious thing they hold in common is this artistic role. To say that only people exhibiting a special psychological dynamic are capable of creative writing is a form of crude reductionism; it leads to the nothing-but fallacy in which complicated patterns of talent and effort are dismissed with a nod toward Oedipus. Moreover, it seems wiser to start with some-thing on which a good deal of evidence is available—the process of writing—than with the vague impressions of partisan observers, who regard all writers as gods or psychopaths.

Thus in this chapter, I shall report a study of artistic creative effort in which the problem was couched in terms of a special kind of verbal innovation—namely, the writing of a poem. The study was confined to practicing professional writers, and the method used was to ask for their introspective analysis. Despite obvious drawbacks—particularly the fact that people may be very mistaken about themselves, as modern psychology has demonstrated—this attack may be useful, for we cannot observe the writer at his work, nor induce experimental controls into our study. Thus the primary data consist of poets' testimony, elicited through semi-struc-tured interviews, on the characteristics of their craft. I shall present these data within a conceptual framework which is drawn in part from the main body of opinion, among both creative writers and psychoanalytic theorists, on the writer and his craft.[1]

The Process of Creative Writing

Dividing the process of writing into discrete segments is of course a violation of reality. Like all processes, creativity is an ebb and flow, only artificially divisible into sections. Yet the breakdown of writing into chron-ological foci may help us to grip what would otherwise be too slippery to analyze. Then, too, there is an obvious progression involved, from blank page to finished poem, although it seldom occurs in a straight line without much backtracking and crisscrossing. A rough paradigm of the stages of poetic creativity would include at least the following elements: the selective perception of the environment; the acquisition of technique; the envision-ing of combinations and distillations; elucidation of the vision; and the end of the poem and its meaning to the poet. I shall discuss each of these elements in some detail.

Selective Perception of the Environment

From the moment of birth the person is exposed to a multitude of stimuli. These may be mainly physical at the start, but are soon overlaid with emotional experiences in great variety. Accompanying the emotional learn-ing involved in the cathexis of the mother and other significant figures is a learning of bodily motions and of the relations among objects. The child in due course discovers himself, realizes his individuality and identity, and perceives relations between this self and external entities. All of experience accumulates to form a store of impressions, images, and ideas—the self upon which later excursions in life, artistic and otherwise are founded. The particular combinations of stimuli are idiosyncratic; but at the same time individuals in a given society partake of a common fund to greater or lesser extent. From the first fact stems the inherent individuality of the human being, and the capacity for creating something utterly personal; from the second, the insurance that what is created will have sufficient social relevance to be minimally communicable. The total fund of experience is the "well" of J.L. Lowes,[2] the source of material for creative effort. At this point it is unnecessary to distinguish subportions of this experience; certainly it is a store whose stock includes sensory impressions and a variety of mental content, both conscious and unconscious. Psychoanalytic knowledge would certify that it is always more extensive than the person can consciously realize at any point in time. The acquisition of experience is variable in both extensity and intensity. It is probably true that the artist registers more experience than the noncreative person, but it is certain, and more important, that the experience is registered with greater intensity. The qualitative difference in intake between creator and noncreator may be subsumed under the overworked concept of sensitivity. It is a criterion of the artist that he is more aware than others, more permeable to the impressions of outer and inner stimuli.[3] We must note, however, that the highly aware person is not guaranteed creative gifts, that sensitivity is a precondition but not an assurance of creativity. An extremely sensitive person may never learn how to use art forms or have the energy necessary to disciplined expressive action. Further, the sensitivity which facilitates rich experiencing must, in the case of the artist, sooner or later be allied to a discriminating function, so that experience is weighted according to some value scale. This scale is implicit, but must be present if we are to distinguish the artist from an amorphous sponge soaking up everything in sight regardless of worth.

Four major sources of stimuli may be posited as essential to the formation of the creator's experiential fund: the gross natural environment, interpersonal relations, symbol systems, and the self.

The gross natural environment includes the world of nature and human artifacts that do not constitute a recognized symbol system. Much of the imagery on which the word-artist depends has roots in nature—process and object—and in inanimate things.[4]

As to interpersonal relations, the artist grows and lives in an atmosphere of human interaction. From the immediate mentors in the family comes the capacity for love and identification. Emotional responses are learned, and the techniques of empathy are nurtured. Interpersonal relations are the focus for our learning to take the attitude of the other, and to be fully ourselves. This order of experience is critical to future expressive activity, and especially to creative work; it implies that the artist can learn to judge motivations accurately, and transmit art to others in such a form that they can recognize its validity in human terms.

One symbol system—language—underlies all actions of the type termed verbal creativity. Language is the mold for the bulk of our experience, and the form into which impressions of all kinds must be translated for communication. Fortunately much of the translation takes place almost immediately on the reception of stimuli, so that what is later recalled is already in symbolic linguistic form.[5] The word-artist is usually a person infatuated with language, ultrasensitive to its shadings and differential impacts, and to precision in its use.

Theodore Spencer gives poetic point to the verbal artist's concern with language:

A Reason for Writing

No word that is not flesh, he said,
Can hold my wavering ear; but when
That golden physical flesh is clear,
I dance in a glory like your glory
With force to stir the dead.

No word that is not thought, he said,
Can hook my slippery mind; but when
That silver accurate thought I find,
I dance in a glory like your glory
With force to stir the dead.

Words both flesh and thought, he said,
Hold and hook my heart; and when
The gold, the silver, shudder apart,
Still in a glory like your glory
I'll dance to stir the dead.[6]

Language becomes for us all the mirror of the world; most of us use it with a fairly low level of alertness, but it is the peculiar virtue of the literary artist to employ words with a maximum awareness of their special qualities. Some have suggested that the cultural pressure of linguistic convention forces upon the child an acceptance of stereotyped ways of seeing and thinking, and that adherence to a conformist view of things is therefore built in by the inexorable demands of a common language. According to this view, the creative person would be one who in fact rejects the conventions of word usage in favor of a more perceptive concentration upon exact meanings, one who can retain the capacity for seeing as the child supposedly sees, in complete freshness and wonder.[7] There is considerable support for this notion in the emphasis placed by artists upon the maintenance of curiosity, of the gift of wonder. It would seem that the truth of this conception is valid but partial—that the artist must indeed preserve the facility to see anew each day and to be unfettered by the deadening force of trite expressive mechanisms, but that he must also hold to a minimal acceptance of linguistic convention if communication is to occur. Moreover, although we may inveigh against the restraints of ordinary usage, it is obvious that the child must receive the cultural imperatives of a philosophy-in-language[8] before being able to go on to refine, reject, and revivify that philosophy. Unless an initial acceptance is posited, then the artist would be without the weapons for social life itself, to say nothing of creative effort. Thus, it is necessary to both accept and discriminate in linguistic intake. A civilized being must be nurtured in some culture, accept some predetermined ways of seeing; otherwise, we would expect feral children to be the world's greatest literary artists. Creativity does not occur in a vacuum.

In the realm of symbol systems, it is important to mention that particular subsystems may be among the most potent stimuli for the artist. The environment which is perceived and sensitively amassed as the basis of creativity includes the heritage of past creators. The primitive is a rarity even in painting, and is in verbal creativity almost unknown. The tradition of the art form to be pursued is as much an essential element of the experiential well as the images of natural objects themselves. There are few literary artists of today who would be subject to Dr. Johnson's criticism of the playwright who had written more than he had read. The individual must work within a culture even if he or she is bent on eventually transcending certain portions of that culture. Not only is there an internalization of a specific art form, such as poetry, there is also an accumulation of philosophical, historical, religious, and even scientific knowledge, which in many cases exceeds that of the professional scholar.

The self is a part of the environment of the developing person. Perception of the self by the self forms a significant component of experience. It is a truism that the creative artist uses the self—that is, employs individual experience, seen as object, in the expressive effort. The picture of the self which the person infers and constructs in introspective maneuvers is the artist's prime source of material and knowledge. It is the basic insurance that motivational insights will be accurate, and is the first testing ground for the validity of conceptions. This is so despite the fact that the person may introspect in error as gauged by certain objective standards; what is seen within is true for the individual and is the creator's last resort. The meaning of great art work for large numbers of people and through many generations, attests that the single creator's self-examination is not infinitely distorted. If it were, there would be no communication by means of art and no standards of esthetic value and relevance. As science in the last analysis rests upon the consensus of informed observers, so verbal art survives through an implicit agreement in the hearts and minds of men and women, that what the artist has said is true—at least for them. The poet explores the self, and thus the self that is tapped must be a richer, fuller whole than in others if the work is to be maximally pertinent.

The Acquisition of Technique

The most splendid experiential mass leads to no art product unless it is transmuted by a mode of expression into recognizable form. Eliot somewhere remarks that the sign of distinction in a young poet is not the content of his work, which is likely to be trite, but the way in which it is set forth, its technical quality. Unless the artist acquires a skill in manipulating the forms of the craft, the most sensitive insights are likely to be lost on others. Perhaps the major flaw of thousands of "mute inglorious Milton[s]" is their lack of technical mastery, their ignorance of the rules of their art. The number of really important creative acts, in art or science, which have been performed by fundamentally untutored persons is very small. Just as the physicist must be immersed in the problems of science for long hours before the creative insight occurs, so the artist must be grounded in the problems of his craft, especially in its formal aspects. This is necessary to the exciting creative effort itself, because at the time of discovery the more mundane dimensions of procedure must be already second nature to the creator; otherwise insight will be clouded over by technical difficulties, perhaps even smothered. The imperative to acquire technique is obviously bound up with the experience of symbol systems. Probably the main way in which formal mastery accrues is a combination of discriminating exposure to past models—the artistic heritage—and a constant exercise of skills based in part upon those models. As the old saw goes, the way to learn how to write is to write. Unquestionably, a large segment of the technical rules can be taught and learned in a rational manner. This segment insures some formal felicity. The question of form itself, however, is not so simple; the highest skill is in fact not divorceable from content. It is a part of the art product, an organic component, which is involved in the very essence of the created thing. Thus, a particular type of versification can be rationally acquired, while the "ear" of Ezra Pound, his uncanny juxtaposition of sounds, is more than a transferable skill.

The Envisioning of Combinations and Distillations

If one point in the creative process can be singled out as of prepotent significance, it is the moment of vision, when an original formulation occurs to the artist.[9] Without this realization of possibilities of expression, the experiential fund and the technical mastery have no theme upon which to play. The realization may be called insight, inspiration, intuitive flash: it is the feeling of immediate knowledge of connections, of the sight of truth or coherence or pure symmetry. The content of experience becomes meaningful in a selected manner, and with such impact that it cries for expression. This occasion cannot be planned or rationally ordered; it seems to happen to the person without conscious effort, at once a surprise and a fulfillment. The happening is related again and again, by scientists as well as artists, and always with a tone of mystery.[10] It is in the best sense a discovery; because the discovering has been going on for some time in the unconscious, it sometimes appears as a rediscovery of a vision once known and then forgotten. This is probably the basis for Wordsworth's feeling that new insight is a recollection of the divine wisdom of the child.

Perhaps most frequently, the moment of insight embraces a combination of elements of experience. If the segments have previously appeared, they have been unrelated and disparate, but now they suddenly attain an intimate emotional-logical relatedness. Metaphor is a typical example, if the metaphor be of wide and deep implication.

Yet the intuition need not be in the form of connections; it may be a distillation, the intense grasp of essential properties of an object or action. In this guise, it approximates a Platonic recognition of first qualities at the core. For this moment, an image or event stands naked before the creative perceiver, revealed in its intensity of being and is-ness.

The great envisioning may take various forms: it may strike as a purely mental flash in a moment of relaxation or dissociation; it may be the end-point of a deep consideration; it may be physically cued by sensory stimuli. The vision of "Kubla Khan" might be an example of the first variety, a long philosophical poem an example of the second, and the chain of associations spurred by Proust's cake and tea an example of the third. The envisioning may be taken as the starting point of the poem proper. How do authors themselves think verses begin?

The poets interviewed affirm that each poem is a unique transaction. Not all poems, even if in the same genre by the same author, begin in an identical manner. In a way, each special mood or subject matter imposes its own requirements, the kind of process most congruent with it. At any rate, the starting point is the least fully known of all creative stages. There is substantial agreement that a stimulus of some sort is involved, and apparently this stimulus can be structured in three different modes: (1) it can arise from outside in the form of a striking occurrence or physical object; (2) it can be a combination of outside image and an inner recall, a linking of concrete event with stored memory; or (3) it can be an almost wholly conscious self-stimulation, in which one sets up the goal, intellectually, of writing a poem.

Virtually all poets describe a combination of (1) and (2), abjuring the third category as a less significant and less successful variety of process. A start can be made in the third way by an experienced craftsman, but to the practiced eye it will be an exercise, an imitation poem which lacks integrity. The chief grounding for (1) and (2) is expressed as a *generalized state of awareness,* a heightened consciousness which acts as a prepared ground for stimuli from without and within. For example, comments from the poets interviewed were as follows:[11]

Keep oneself in readiness for a poem to occur.

Let us be as conscious as possible.

The starting place is a "prepared-for experience."

What happens to stir this awareness, to bring about the actual crystallization of experience in poetic form? Poets testify that the stimulus can be almost anything—a smell, sight, or sound, an unanticipated idea, word, or image, but they emphasize, too, the thesis that this specific jog is not entirely isolated from other experience. It may represent an agglutination of stimuli, a chance symbolizing of recurrent ideas and emotions. Expecially important is the point that this special occurrence ties in with past experience, so that memory enters the picture as a crucial variable. The stimulus, to be poetically transformed, must be connected back to a fund of impressions and valuations. The well, or store of impressions, provides a perspective from which the immediate experience can be viewed:

> Cues come from the memory; a smell or sight, à la Proust, may release stored impressions.
>
> Childhood impressions are often recalled from when one's photographic plate was more clear and sensitive. Childhood experience is strong; it is my freshest file.

The word *inspiration* has a way of complicating this initial segment of the process. Some poets vow that inspiration is everything; others maintain that what is called inspiration is really an explicable concatenation of factors made up roughly of prepared ground, stimulus, and linkage with the impressionistic fund. Regardless of their degree of adherence to such a concept as inspiration, with its bedrock of mysticism, poets describe the experience itself in similar terms. It consists of a more or less sudden shock by which one immediately and intuitively is thrust into a poetic theme, or better, into a reverie from which such a theme may emerge. There is constant reiteration of the feeling that something "comes," "pings," "bursts," "twists":

> A tune came.
>
> I seldom search for anything, but let it come to me.
>
> Short poems spring quickly into consciousness, often after awakening in the morning.
>
> There is a burst, a visitation. In one stark experience the poem comes as a whole.
>
> A poem is a spasm, a shock, twisting open the unconscious.

> There is an initial strong feeling about a subject; this immediate conception starts one off.

> Inspiration is invaluable...some initial attraction, which may never recur.

Two cases may be cited as striking examples of the inspired beginning, demonstrating the total impact of poetic genesis. Richard Eberhart states that he has a poor memory and must jot down his thoughts as they arise. He looks upon the beginning of a poem as a gift. At times the words pour out. "The Groundhog,"[12] perhaps his best-known poem, was written in half an hour. One group of his poems was written in the middle of the night. He got out of bed, jotted down lines on three-by-five slips of paper; the result was twenty six-line poems in one hour, their form being dictated by the size of the paper at hand. Gene Derwood stresses that the poem is a total experience, involving her entire mental-physical being. She feels the poem starts as a shock, speeding up all her activities, "like a kick in the solar plexus." She experiences great physical excitation for several days, and at the poem's completion may suffer a severe heart spasm.

It should be emphasized that this facet of the process is no guarantee of artistic production. Although the immense jump has been made, the art work itself has not yet begun. The vision must be shaped and clothed, formed into an artistic whole. The vast thrill of the conception waits upon a mature execution. The unconscious has done its most important duty. Although the great energies of the id will be called on again and again throughout the process, they have here performed their most notable function. The focus which is here termed *envisioning* is the high point of unconscious forces, and the least amenable to ego mastery.

Elucidation of the Vision

The vision must be concretized if it is to be enduring and communicable. There is a conscious application of energy to the task of making the combination or distillation meaningful. The task involves an explication of the insightful moment in such a way that its character becomes significant, both to the creator and to the potential audience. Here the technical facility acts as a reagent upon the visionary mass, giving it a discernible structure. In Schneider's terms, creative "thrust" from the unconscious is broken to the bit of creative "mastery," in which the reality-oriented ego is of first importance.[13] The artist must endure the inevitable disharmony between conception and execution, and attempt to recapture as much of the insight as possible. The personal relevance of the period of intuition must be transformed into a broader relevance in this era of elucidation, the words made socially significant while retaining their distinctive idiosyncratic overtones.[14] This is the key point of Rank's "will to form": the will exerts itself toward the attainment of a suitable structure for the imaginative insight, and insists upon imposing the order of artistic criteria on the loosely given vision.[15]

But elucidation of a predetermined insight is not the sole occurrence at this stage. The maker of an art product does not suddenly stop and merely impose form on a given set of images or ideas. The creative process is fluid; it persists in giving rise to novelty at each stage of the creator's development. And so, when the artistic creation is in the shaping stage, it may be quickly illumined by a further insight of the nature described above. Discoveries take place at every point; the poem shapes itself by suggesting its own further progress. The word used to convey a specific idea keys off a chain of other ideas which may be immediately applicable to the course of the work at hand. Thus through associative serendipity, surprising facets of development may be in store for the creator.[16]

At this stage of elucidation, the artist comes to terms with reality in the psychological sense. This is not to say that the vision is compromised, but that in making it socially meaningful it is necessary to demonstrate an element of control, a discrimination between pure fantasy and the demands of the concrete world "out there." Poets return to a psychoanalytic state of grace which distinguishes them from the psychotic who lives in illusion and the neurotic who is incapable of self-mastery. They prove that the psychic azimuth is directed not to a world of dissociated illusion but to the real world, even though it is a unique perception of the world, enhanced and informed by the power of the dream.[17]

Elucidation embraces the conscious effort to shape lines of verse on paper in such a way that they transmit the poet's full intent. Poets report that this process of working through their material is a combination of conscious and unconscious strivings, but that rational mastery is relatively more important here than in the previous stage of envisioning or inspiration.

The first draft of a poem may consume a few hours or several days. It must be recognized that, in all but a few cases, the poem does not arise full-blown in direct consequence of the stimulating experience. Rather, it is keyed to the experience, and to the vital word or phrase which first symbolized that experience, but goes on to develop in its own way.[18] One might say that most poems are like complicated chemical reactions, in which the outcome is uncertain but each occurrence sets off another, related occurrence. The working through falls conveniently into two phases: the first draft formulation (which may in some cases be the finished poem) and the subsequent revision and polishing. It has been pointed out that the first draft is in part a voyage of discovery, in which the poem grows by associations to, and refinements of, the original key symbol and each successive extension. There is a suggestion that the poem has a certain autonomy, that it fulfills itself according to subtle patterns of growth:

> The process of writing a poem is like climbing a mountain...steep, although there are easy spots. The unanticipated insight is most important; one comes upon it in the ascent up the mountain.

Every image should evoke another image.

During a long "murmuring period" the lines work themselves out and I repeat them audibly, voicing my progress.

The poem develops as a musical structure. There is an eagerness to fulfill the phrase. Each thing suggests another; one doesn't know in advance what he's going to do. The poem is an environment. The poem may be compared to the dance. There is the same repetition of learned steps, and a consistency of overtones.

There is a feeling of confidence that the poem will shape itself to an end. After its genesis in a particular emotional experience, the poem moves away from the concrete, is "transvalued" so that it gains a general dimension.

Many poets consider revision to be the crucial portion of the creative process. The emphasis is on technique, craft, and patient work. One is here one's own critic, and may be exceedingly harsh, demanding a score (or more) of rewritings. In Marianne Moore's aphorism, "rewriting is rewarding." This phase of the effort is highly sophisticated, drawing heavily on the poet's artistic experience and linguistic virtuosity. Yet there is a hint in the poets' comments that revision is more than a conscious working over of material; the strain of exactitude may in fact stir the unconscious springs of expression to new oscillations and taut precisions:

Writing a poem is mostly revision; new insights may come during the revision, the poem may change entirely. In revision, one gets closer to, not further from, the unconscious.

If value cannot be transferred, of what value is it? Craftsmanship is indispensable and actually inseparable from value to be conveyed.

Revision is the most important part of writing. The real work lies in judging and reforming initial lines. There is a sense of competition, of striving toward an impersonal standard, like par in golf.

Revision entails, often, an entirely fresh rewriting, since each word must fit the whole structure of the poem.

The End of the Poem and Its Meaning to the Poet

The final stage to be abstracted from the creative process is barely distinguishable from the fourth. It is the reappraisal of what has gone before, the last intimate probing which completes the art product. Here the patina is added to a rough-hewn creation through censorship, revision, and close attention to details of technical perfection. This stage is not always vital; the poem, in certain cases, may arise full-blown from the initial visionary elucidation, as in the instance, again, of "Kubla Khan." But often such a last step may find the brick that fulfills the artist's mosaic, a particular word or phrase long-sought but for a considerable time unattainable. Thus A.E.

Housman describes a poem of which several stanzas came to him in the first elucidation, while the last stanza was more akin to literary carpentry and required several efforts.

Here the spectator self,[19] the other observer internalized, functions to enhance the communicability of the art product. Self-criticism opens up the poem for an aesthetic reappraisal, and leads to changes which may increase clarity, adding point and force to the creation. One might conceive of an artistic superego energized by the pride of craft, so that no aspect emerges in the final version which is less perfect than possible. Of course artists may vary greatly in their self-demandingness, from the person who spews forth a great volume of work relatively unchecked by critical conscience to the true perfectionist whose constant rewording brings him only to what he regards as a heightened approximation to desirable form.

What do writers feel they gain from their poems, and how do they regard the finished effort? The question of reward is an intriguing one, since it is clear that modern poets, with very few exceptions, can anticipate neither riches nor fame. The answer can only be, "Because I like to do it," or "Because I have to do it." The notion of function pleasure, or rewards accruing from the work process itself, is at the heart of creative endeavor.

> The poet's reward is derived from the poem itself.
>
> The personal, not grandiose, pleasure of hooking an idea, of getting it trapped in words, is perhaps more elating than actually finishing the poem.
>
> Why do dancers dance?

Self-assertion is often given as a reason for writing, the hope that one will master the medium and gain appropriate recognition, and the more distant hope that one will achieve a measure of immortality:

> Ego-assertion is part of writing poetry; one wants to capture one perfect thing, to survive after the bubble breaks.

Finally, some poets state that poetry is for them a release from psychic tensions:

> Poetry is a release for the psyche.
>
> It fills the need to "get it out." It afforded a release of grief after my wife's death; even sad poetry gives its own pleasurable feeling.

What are the feelings which accompany the completion of a creative task? The most frequently mentioned state is one of pleasure, elation, even exultation:

> There is a feeling of catharsis and exhilaration.
>
> There is elation at the completion of form.
>
> It is a satisfaction to have stated it, to have gotten it, a joy that "they can't take that away from me."
>
> There is a good feeling after the poem is out, a desire to read it aloud, to show it to people.
>
> The normal feeling should be one of exhilaration, tempered with anxiety.

The other major theme concerns the necessity of leaving the work behind, in order to get on with new efforts:

> There is a first flush on completion; one should then forget about it forever.
>
> A poem is never finished. It is abandoned in despair.

Thus considerable agreement appears among writers about the process they undergo in the creation of art products. It is psychologically appropriate to believe that the creative personality is related in a meaningful way to this process.

The Personality of the Artist

In psychoanalytic theory, Freud, Rank, and Jung all pay close attention to the problem of formulating the artist's personality. They tend to view the poet as a person who utilizes particular psychic conflicts to nourish the achievement of a socially relevant product. Although they recognize the possibility, in fact the probability, that the poet is a highly unusual person whose emotional patterns diverge from the "normal," they emphasize just as strongly that talent and real contributions set the poet off from the unproductive neurotic or psychotic. These earlier theorists, who were themselves educated in the humanities, refused to dismiss the artist's *work* as an essential factor in the estimation of his or her personality. So far was Freud from writing off the poet as unbalanced that he gave full credit to artists as people ahead of their time, who knew of, and used, the unconscious before it was ever scientifically described.

Certain recent writers in the analytic vein, of whom Bergler is the most conspicuous example, have forsaken this large, generous view of the poet in favor of theories which posit a single psychological pattern. They typically study a few sick people, who happen also to be writers, and then generalize from this study that all writers evince some stock conflict, some basic neurotic design. It seems wiser to focus our attention on the positive equipment of the poet, which facilitates the creative process, rather than on those inadequacies which the poet shares with all people to some extent. Anyone can exhibit an oral neurosis or a destructive rage; few can create, from their own hearts and minds, poems which speak to human beings, present and future.

The imperatives of the creative process center around two kinds of strength in the personality. The process is complicated and, fully considered in life terms, very long. So the person must have vitality sufficient to carry out a lengthy job of accretion and formation. Although a play function certainly exists, artists bear testimony to the fact that art is work. Artists need more than the energy required for routine living, enough more so that they can project a part of themselves out into the created object. In addition to this sheer vitality and exuberance, a kind of integrative strength is required. One might term this balance, capacity for adjustment, or ego-strength. At any rate, artists are people who use themselves mercilessly, who rake and strain at their inner dynamic, deliberately provoking elements of conflict and terror within. They may not prod the unconscious, as certain of the romantic poets did, with alcohol or laudanum, but they prod it. (Incidentally, references to "it," "the thing," and "my neurosis" are legion among poets, and fit well with the literal translation of the title of Freud's book, *Das Ich und das Es* (The I and the It).[20] Karl Shapiro writes that, "the poet is different from the non-poet in that he makes greater demands on his Unknown than anyone else, and that he brings to light certain riches which are accorded a universal value."[21]

The element of integrative strength leads into the next important component, which is a capacity for perceiving associations among things or ideas, linking them at times and at other times holding them balanced in conflict. A largeness, a generosity toward impressions, enables the creator to accept irreconcilable modes, resolving them if possible, but encompassing them if necessary under the rubric of self. That is, the artist may recognize multiple meanings and enjoy them in their variety. As the poet associates the dissimilar, he or she may dissociate the similar, peeling off layers of meaning or "types of ambiguity," as William Empson has termed them.[22] The poet can perceive in more than one way, especially in other ways that the conventional ones. This too requires a kind of strength and breadth of perspective, for the tension between widely various ideas must be maintained without compromise, without arbitrarily narrowing one's vision in the interests of psychic ease.

As the foundation for creative activity, poets need a certain type of sensitivity; they are permeable to impressions. This is a schooled sensitivity, one in which keen and discriminating observation is more vital than mere gross impressionability.

If these impressions are to become meaningful to others, then they must be *formed* artistically. A desire to capture the essential character of a person, situation, or mood is typically a poetic desire. Here is the chief significance of the traditional concern with words on the poet's part. W.H. Auden writes:

> A poet is, before anything else, a person who is passionately in love with language. Whether this love is a sign of his poetic gift or the gift itself—for falling in love is given not chosen—I don't know, but it is certainly the sign by which one recognizes whether a young man is potentially a poet or not.[23]

Infatuated with words, the poet wills communication, and if the aim of explicating the obvious or subtle is not there, then works of art will not be forthcoming, and the person is not performing the full poetic role. It is well to remember that in the explication phase, the poet need not necessarily be writing for a public or even for one other person: most usually, he is not, but in making something clear to the social self within—the spectator self—it will thereby be made meaningful to *some* others. (If the work contained no clues for *any* other observer, then it would be schizophrenic art, whose value is diagnostic, not esthetic.)

A summing up of the imperatives for the creative personality shows certain characteristics essential to the functioning poet. Whatever the particular personality dynamic may be, it cannot be understood fully without reference to the following technical boundaries: *strength* (both vitality and ego-strength or integrative strength); *a capacity for association and integration* (of ideas and images—a generosity toward impressions and ability to encompass tensions); *sensitivity* (discriminant permeability); *a desire for form and explication* (linguistic facility or infatuation with words); and *intelligence*. Regarding the last of these characteristics, it is obvious that the role requires a rather large portion of what is ordinarily called intelligence. But above a certain level of competence, the concept of raw I.Q. means very little. A poetic intellect is not the same as a scientific intellect, although they share a common baseline of "better than average" mental functioning. I have been speaking here of particular parts of intelligence as seen in their significance for the artist; they happen to be the special forms which artistic intelligence takes.

The responses of poets to the question of what constitutes the personality necessary for artistic creativity tend to support the foregoing assumptions, although in modified form. The poet as person, affirm the artists, is interesting but superfluous. The best of the man is in his work, and the work is the key question in artistic activity. Nevertheless, there is a series of requisites which must be fulfilled in the poetically creative personality as ideal type. Any one poet may show certain features and fail almost completely to manifest certain others, but each must approach a core complex of capacities which underlies the vagaries of indvidual personality makeups. The characteristics of poets are indeed various. Experience with practicing artists impels us to cast aside nearly every initial generalization which might be made concerning overt personality traits, such as: poets are very introverted, fairly extroverted; very effeminate, very masculine; simple livers, lovers of luxury; aggressively irritable, benevolently kind. Yet when called upon to designate characteristics which they felt were crucial to poetic endeavor, or at least exceedingly germane, the poets evidenced remarkable agreement.

Both the wide variety of facets mentioned and their striking interconnection suggested that *a complex of capacities* was the appropriate conceptualization. There was no single dynamic mechanism suitable to serve as the aegis of the characteristics without a forcing and warping which would violate the facts. At the same time, the variety was not infinite, and it was soon apparent that more than random listing was involved. It seemed best, then, to emphasize that the personality make-up judged most desirable tended to approximate a pattern; this pattern had form without being extremely close knit or exhaustive.

Four outstanding capacities may be staked out for consideration, and on these the congruence of subjective responses is high. These are the capacities for *experience,* for *ordering experience,* for *exploring and using one's own personality,* and for the *use of language.* A fifth, extremely knotty area is essential to this report, but on this area there are crucial disagreements; this is the question of whether the work of the poet requires *a harmoniously organized personality or an imbalance of personality.*

The Capacity for Experience

The stress here is upon sensitivity, intensity, awareness, and enthusiasm. A poet must have great curiosity about people and natural objects, an attachment to the world so intense that the satiation point for experience is above most other people's. Included, too, is the capacity for absorbing shock, for flexibility of mind:

> A poet must have enthusiasm for life, for what you encounter in the world.
>
> There must be sensibility: a more highly nervous organization of personality.
>
> He should possess the capacity for living at a higher pitch: spontaneous combustion, effervescence. Also, he should have empathy, intuition—the ability immediately to understand other people, even if he doesn't like them.
>
> There should be a capacity for a general awareness of humanity, complete association with society: all humanity are his relatives.
>
> The acute awareness is partly physical. I recall how upset Robert Frost was by his having drunk a cup of tea pressed upon him by his hostess after he had first refused it.

He should have the feeling of being more alive, of being able to experience life at several segments and levels.

There must be an ability to live more than others, not to become bored or satiated.

He should have "imagination," a marvelous "forgetter," the ability to scrub his brain clean and come up fresh.

The Capacity for Ordering Experience

The poet desires to shape and objectify experience, but first and most vitally to somehow capture it. Paramount in this drive for order and experiential conquest is a kind of detachment which complements the deep attachment of the experience itself. It is as if one had to move away from, and precisely represent, the idea, image, or feeling which has occurred. There is the notion of strict honesty toward the materials of poetry. In ordering experience one must not distort it:

The poet must shape the materials offered: "objectism."

He should be dissociated from community life, "out of the swim," in order to gain perspective.

There must be a desire for a savage intensity of analysis.

Ideally, he should have docility, reflectiveness, tenacity of mind and act.

The Capacity for Exploring and Using One's Own Personality

Honesty toward the self, and a desire to probe the secrets of the self, are essential. Self-focusing is accompanied by a certain inwardness and egoism. Some egoism and neglect of others is implied by the necessity for self-regard. If many poets are too close to their work to live agreeably with others, it must be remembered that part of their work is self-exploration. An element of toughmindedness is involved, since a penetrating look at the self must be accepted without flinching:

One must have toughness of character.

The poet is ultimately concerned with his own personality. Unlike the "objective" scientist, he gnaws at his vitals. The poet is the spider with a web coming out of its belly.

A created work is nothing more than an extension of the man who does it.

Self-awareness is vital, a knowledge of one's own neurotic "drive." Consciousness is the highest morality.

The Capacity for the Use of Language

By definition the poet is a master of words. Facility in linguistic expression was mentioned more often than any other characteristic in the assessment of personality. Although this capacity would seem to lie on a different level from the three previous ones, being more of an ability than an enduring personality characteristic, it is really commensurate if properly understood. A special attachment to language, an intensity about words, is closely bound up with the capacity for ordering experience. Involvement with words is a concomitant of, and in part an expression of, the desire to entrap and mold experience. Of course nonpoets may have an equally intense love of the world and appreciation of rich experience; the mark of poets is that their experience is couched in verbal form, so that words are for them truly *the* medium of expression. To the writer, words are living things, and seldom merely instrumental, and the talent which masters them is thereby doing more than training or playing; it is exhibiting a deep personal need:

> Language is itself nonmaterial, but the poet's success depends on how well he makes it an object. Let the language lead the dance...put the self behind.

> The poet must have a sense of "the word," must be a word-lover.

> Language must fit the subject. One can die of linguistic virtuosity. Words cannot be dissociated from the poetic theme. Yeats: "How can you tell the dancer from the dance?"

> Love of words is important, but overfacility takes the tension, the carven quality, out of the poem.

The Harmoniously Organized Personality versus Imbalance

The exaltation of a state of harmony, and the idea that this harmony of the faculties underlies imaginative achievement, is a pronounced theme in many of the interviews. Most of its adherents seem to be embracing the classical-humanistic view of the whole person, to whom nothing is alien, whose efforts stem from a sense of balanced interest and well-being. The artist, they say, should be "more normal" than other people, more self-possessed and more keenly aware of his own stability:

> Imagination stems from harmony.

> The poet should be a person of wide interests and normal psychological make-up.

But another view is stressed more frequently: that art originates in tensions, that the fully integrated person feels no need to be an artist. Its advocates state that a measure of imbalance is at the root of creative effort. Inner conflict, in effect, is regarded as the seed from which poetic growth is possible. Although personality flaws are thus countenanced or even blessed as the *sine qua non* of art, it should be noticed that they are always bound up, for the poet, with the goal of productive artistry. That is, the poet speaks of them as a spur to something else, to be used for the work at hand. There is no glorifying of illness or imbalance for its own sake. The vocational emphasis is so strong as to suggest that the achievement is worth the price in suffering or interpersonal maladjustment:

> Is life itself to be sacrificed to discipline in work? If being a poet is determined by certain psychological instabilities, the question is whether these can be turned to fruitful effort and production.
>
> There should be an imbalance based on sexual dissatisfaction, so that the poet is "hopped-up" with sexual vitality.
>
> No poet can be emotionally mature, or approximate "the adult personality." No itch, no poetry. There must be a conflict, or else just quiet sitting. I've got my conscious pretty well under control, but Jesus, my unconscious!

Poets provoke their own unconscious by deliberately exposing themselves to the strains of exact expression, and by torturing symbols—the words—to fit reality as well as they are able. Of course they may in addition have neurotic tendencies which antedated the concern wth art, but these are not typical of artists. Lionel Trilling[24] observes that one cannot single out the artist for psychoanalytic explanation—that if the poet's power stems from neurosis, then so does the lawyer's and scientist's. The process of creative endeavor imposes a series of strains; the successful artist surpasses these strains and utilizes the pain they have engendered in order to produce an art product. All people are exposed to neurotic conflict. Poets intensify this conflict by delving into their own motives and representing irreconcilables to themselves. But the poet who actually writes, and writes well, has by that achievement gained a certain mastery over the self, and over the conflict-filled material of the symbolic fund. Again and again, acute students have stressed the poet's power of *control*: the unique ability to make of fantasy a socially valuable objective entity.

Coleridge, Rank, Schneider, Trilling, and many others bring out this crucial argument. Thus artists are regarded as triumphant over the forces of disintegration, precisely because they produce, and in producing create an esthetic whole which is the obverse of the neurotic's self-defeatism.[25]

The process of creativity is fraught with dangers to the creative personality. It requires of its practitioners a greater strength and sensitivity than most people possess. Aside from the imperatives of (1) vitality and integrative force, (2) capacity for association and dissociation, (3) sensitivity, and (4) desire for form and explication, the major theories have been concerned with the conscious-unconscious dialectic and the mechanisms for artistic control of unconscious material. The most general statement is that creative activity involves the whole person, that all facets of personality come into play, and that the integration of these facets in a constructive task is the problem of the artist, as it is the problem of every person. The artist, however, embodies an integrative working through in a traditionally valued vehicle: the work of art. What sets the artist apart from other people is not a peculiar personality structure inseparable from creativity as such, but the fact of being "in process" so much more fully, and emerging with a concrete result.

Notes

I am indebted to Dr. Henry A. Murray for encouraging this investigation. The research was facilitated by the Laboratory of Social Relations at Harvard University.

1. The sample of respondents included twenty-four American poets, all of whom have published extensively and command some measure of critical following. The poets were asked to describe the chronological sequence which occurs when they write a poem. Although it is apparent that each poem is in a very real sense unique, they were asked to try to generalize about what typically happens. The interviewer urged them to consider the relative importance of inspiration and conscious craftsmanship to their efforts, and to analyze their subjective responses to each phase of composition. This research is part of a larger effort to delineate the social role of the contemporary poet; the full investigation included projective testing and sociological questioning. Only the portion dealing with the *technical* role, the writing process itself, will be considered here.
2. J.L. Lowes, *The Road to Xanadu* (Boston: Houghton Mifflin, 1930).
3. This point has been brought emphatically to my attention by Conrad Aiken, who makes increasing awareness the key to his philosophy of artistic activity (personal communication).
4. James Laughlin entitles a book of his poems *Some Natural Things* (Norfolk, Conn.: New Directions, 1945) and has indicated in conversation that natural objects provide the main instigation for his creative efforts.
5. Karl Shapiro has emphasized that the predominance of the verbal is in him so acute that sense impressions must usually undergo an immediate transformation into words if they are to be fully meaningful (personal communication).
6. Reprinted in *Twentieth Century American Poetry*, ed. Conrad Aiken (New York: Random House, 1944), p. 307.
7. Ernest Schachtel, "On Memory and Childhood Amnesia," *Psychiatry* 10 (1947):1–26.
8. One of the great insights of the developing study of semantics is an appreciation of the extent to which language emobdies in its very structure the cultural way-of-seeing of its primary users. See especially B.L. Whorf, *Four Articles on Metalinguistics* (Washington, D.C.: Foreign Service Institute, Department of State, 1950); and D.D. Lee, "A Primitive System of Values," *Philosophy of Science* 7 (1940):355–78.
9. This moment is analogous to the sudden fruition of what the gestaltists term "insight." See W. Kohler, *Gestalt Psychology* (New York: Liveright, 1929): chap. 10. Gestalt theory is not maximally relevant to the problem of the artist because it is based on a special type of insight, that occurring in problem solution. Yet it could probably be made more relevant through proper extension.
10. Many examples are quoted by Hutchinson. See, for instance, E.D. Hutchinson, "The Nature of Insight," and other papers by the same author, in *A Study of Interpersonal Relations*, ed. Patrick Mullahy (New York: Hermitage, 1949).

11. The three statements that follow and all others appearing in boldface type are the interview comments of contemporary poets.
12. Reprinted in *Mid-Century American Poets*, ed. John Ciardi (New York: Twayne, 1950), p. 234.
13. Daniel Schneider, *The Psychoanalyst and the Artist* (New York: Farrar, Straus, 1950), chap. 5.
14. Otto Rank derives the essential creative act from a consideration of language in its social and individual characteristics. Discussing the historical parallels of Christianity and art, Rank says that "a power of new creation by speech is vouchsafed to every individual. It is only later that the poet comes to perform it for the rest and does so by harmonious fusion of the individual and collective forces, for though it is a language of his own, and therewith a world of his own, that he builds, it is yet such that it conveys something to others and helps them to build a world of their own." O. Rank, *Art and Artist* (New York: Knopf, 1932), p. 273.
15. In Richard Wilbur's words: "In general, I would say that limitation makes for power: the strength of the genie comes of his being confined in a bottle." In Ciardi, *Mid-Century American Poets*, p.7.
16. Robert Frost, in his essay on "The Figure a Poem Makes," expresses this "discovery" element: "It must be a revelation, or a series of revelations, as much for the poet as for the reader...A poem may be worked over once it is in being, but may not be worried into being. Its most precious quality will remain its having run itself and carried away the poet with it." In *Complete Poems of Robert Frost* (New York: H. Holt, 1949), p. viii.
17. The artist's conscious mastery is emphasized especially by Lionel Trilling in his important and extraordinarily perceptive paper, "Art and Neurosis." Lionel Trilling, *The Liberal Imagination* (New York: Viking, 1950), pp. 160–80.
18. "Paul Valery speaks of the 'une ligne donnée' of a poem. One line is given to the poet by God or by nature, the rest he has to discover for himself." Stephen Spender, "The Making of a Poem," in *The Creative Process*, ed. Brewster Ghiselin (Berkeley: University of California Press, 1952), p. 118.
19. "Spectator self" refers to Mead's concept of the reflexive character of the self. G.H. Mead, *Mind, Self, and Society* (Chicago: University of Chicago Press, 1934), part 3.
20. Freud, *The Ego and the Id* (London: Hogarth, 1935).
21. Karl Shapiro, "The Meaning of the Discarded Poem," in *Poets at Work* (New York: Harcourt, Brace & World, 1948), p. 86 Essays by Rudolf Arnheim, W.H. Auden, Karl Shapiro, and Donald A. Stauffer; introd. by Charles D. Abbott).
22. William Empson, *Seven Types of Ambiguity* (New York: Oxford, 1947).
23. W.H. Auden, "Squares and Oblongs," in *Poets at Work,* p. 171.
24. Lionel Trilling, *The Liberal Imagination*.
25.   Then as th' earth's inward narrow crooked lanes
            Do purge sea water's fretful salt away
                I thought, if I could draw my paines
            Through Rime's vexation, I should them allay.
            Griefe brought to numbers cannot be so fierce,
            For, he tames it, that fetters it in verse.

      (John Donne, "The Triple Foole," in The Poems of John Donne [New York: Heritage, 1970], p. 9.)

4
The Poet in American Society

As my inquiries into creative behavior continued, it seemed quite natural to widen the scope of attention, to move outward from the poet's interior world to his or her other perceptions and actions in society. As in the case of poetic composition, I chose to conduct a loosely patterned interview on topics ranging from self-conceptions to relations with fellow writers. The nature of the research was such that I enjoyed many opportunities not only to complete a scheduled talk about the poet's role, but also to be an informal participant-observer, a kind of houseguest-cum-sociologist of art. The chance to soak up the culture of modern poetry was at its most expansive in the instance of my long friendship with Conrad Aiken (recounted in chapter 5), but there were many other occasions to mingle fairly unobtrusively, to friend and be befriended.

The social researcher is of course often cautioned about the dangers of drawing close to his subjects, of losing objectivity, forsaking neutrality, in the extreme anthropological case of "going native" and joining those whom he is supposed to be observing. Here I make no apology for my subjectivity, indeed my advocacy of the poet's cause. Only by being myself an aspiring poet—if perhaps a poet manqué—could I begin to penetrate the special world of the artist. Rollo May contends that the researcher's neutrality is in fact a myth, that one can only comprehend deeply that about which one cares passionately. I wouldn't have dared agree with him in 1950, when I was studying poets. I do now.

Clearly, much has changed in the thirty-five years since I was first privileged to live among poets. My empathic groping toward a poetic subjectivity, so suspect in the positivistic, value-neutral climate of 1950, appears less odd today, rather better attuned to proponents of a phenomenological sociology or a reflexive sociology. Indeed, I have become a sociologist who writes a fair amount of poetry for publication, an indulgence that, although rare, is not quite beyond the pale.

Change is apparent in several other respects. For example, the gross underrepresentation of women in my sample of poets, which inspired only a glancing caveat then, now emerges as a serious distortion. Women poets in the present, at least in the United States, seem to be as numerous and as distinguished as their male counterparts; for example, women figure very prominently in the editing-publishing complex of literary journals, the "little magazines" that now, as then, are the very lifeblood of practicing poets. In all this we see embodied in the arts the enhanced participation of women in the American labor market. When I first analyzed poets I obviously had a male occupational model in mind, and the use of the masculine pronoun was not just for stylistic convenience. I confess not to

57

know whether more sustained attention to female poetic careers would substantially alter the sketch of the artist's role.

Altogether it would seem that the tight vocational model of mid-century, the controlled unemotional male striving for glittering prizes, has undergone significant modifications. The role strait jacket has been loosened, if not entirely cast aside, with an accompanying increase in variety and flexibility. I should guess that a more ample appreciation of femininity and a heightened stress on the virtues of autonomy and self-expression in recent decades have helped produce a more favorable climate for the artistic role.

The poet's role is a special case of unregulated and unplanned vocation. It is an exceptional, personally chosen position which has deep roots in the artistic tradition of Western society but is virtually excluded from the major patterns of contemporary occupational or recreational life. In David Riesman's terms[1] poets are acutely inner-directed, devoting their best energies to the elucidation of idiosyncratic visions of experience. Although the medium in which they work is thoroughly social, and the words with which they grasp reality are supposed to communicate intensively and extensively, their central activity is basically solitary. Of those who work alone in an American society dedicated to the abolition of solitude, the poet is perhaps most nearly comparable to the scientist. But the poet differs strikingly in that the scientist enjoys a fabric of external support and prestige, as well as a well-defined realm of objective data; the scientist is linked to research money, nuclear charisma, and circumscribed phenomena of interest. The number of scientists who actually work alone is also steadily diminishing. Poets, in their roles as verbal innovators, are adventurers in the minds and hearts of men. As such, they have no appreciable economic leverage, their names are unknown, and the potential field of attention is as wide as the universe. The fundamentally lonely nature of the task has been well described by Stephen Spender:

> Above all, the writing of a poem brings one face to face with his own personality with all its familiar and clumsy limitations. In every other phase of existence, one can exercise the orthodoxy of a conventional routine: one can be polite to one's friends, one can get through the day at the office, one can pose, one can draw attention to one's position in society, one is—in a word—dealing with men. In poetry, one is wrestling with a god.[2]

It is impossible to understand the poet's relation to the social milieu without taking into account the relation to the self and to the expressive medium—language—in which the self is absorbed. Unless this private world is recognized as the locus of the artistic role, we shall seriously misjudge the poet's intentions and importance. For the poet does not set out to tell the public a beautiful tale, nor is the impact to be gauged by the total readership of the tale that is told. Poets set out to capture for themselves the essence of experience. In this attempted elucidation of the ineffable, they work in and through the distinctively human medium of words. The obsession with language means that experience recaptured in privacy is in a fundamental sense more "real" to the poet than are everyday face-to-face encounters. Since we cannot look to overt, observable social interaction as the source of basic understanding about the role, we are thus, to some extent, disabled as sociological investigators. In effect, since the investigator can hardly watch poets at work or devise a controlled experiment to assess their propensities for various sorts of artistic behavior, the study of this distinctive social role is largely confined to an intensive probing of the subjective dimensions of the task, as they appear to the poets themselves. There are certain types of tangential information which offer some clues. These include literary criticism, psychological analyses of literary work, publishing and sales figures, and popular reactions to the artist as expressed in magazines and newspapers. Yet in the end we are compelled to look at the poet's personality, style of life, methods and goals, and above all the created product itself, through the poet's own lens. Only then is it justifiable, and indeed possible, to analyze the artist's role from a social psychological perspective. In John Ciardi's words, "Modern poets, in one sense, are the poets we know least about, and until time has made clear to us (and to them) their whole intent, until time has completed the circle whose arc they are now projecting, the poets themselves are likely to be their own best guides to themselves."[3]

The present research was initiated as an effort to explore the reactions of creative writers to a projective test. During the testing, we grew increasingly interested in the poets' behavior and writing habits and in their place in American society. It was decided, therefore, to enlarge the investigation, visiting the sample of writers a second time for a lengthy semistructured interview. The two visits, often occurring at summer homes far from public accommodations, afforded an exceptional opportunity for informal discussion and casual observation extending well beyond the limits of a normal interview.

This study is based primarily on a group of twenty-four poets who were the focus of intensive research, athough relevant data were secured from many other sources. The group interviewed and tested was thus small in numbers. It was, however, large in artistic excellence, so that it constituted an elite sample. The poets, all published writers of some stature, included several Pulitzer Prize winners and holders of the consultantship in poetry at the Library of Congress. They were, for the most part, residents of the northeastern United States, recipients of critical acclaim, and members of the more "advanced," experimental artistic sector often loosely termed *avant-garde*. There were no newspaper versifiers and no strictly regional writers, only one author of light verse, and only three women poets. It may be seen that the sample is sufficiently homogeneous to be internally comparable, but that it necessarily can afford only a partial picture of the very ill-defined entity, "the American poet." For an exploratory venture, it was felt that a limited range of cases studied in depth was preferable to a survey of any substantial number of people who might be designated as poets. Because of the limitations of the sample and the fact that writing is a highly individual operation, generalization is exceedingly hazardous. We shall nevertheless speak of "the poet" for convenience of exposition, without qualifying each statement in the several ways required for absolute precision.

A Psychological Note

The psychology of creativity cannot be developed in a brief treatment of the artist's social role. In another paper, the creative process in poets and the personality characteristics that seem to accompany the process were analyzed in some detail.[4] Yet the writing job itself has such important implications for the general behavior of the writer that we should mention a few prominent psychological concomitants of poetry making.

Creative writing is a process that involves the whole individual at his or her most alert level of activity. It demands great energy coupled with a capacity for probing and using the materials of one's own personality. The subjective immersion of the poet at work exposes him to psychic strain, as the deliberate use of the self tends to reveal and accentuate the deficiencies and conflicts, as well as the rich integrations, of that self. Creative involvement is critical to the social role in that much of the behavior often labeled eccentric or deviant in the artist's life, such as difficult family relationships, failure to keep social engagements, refusal to get caught up in community activities, should really be seen as a part of the writer's job rather than as evidence of perverse bohemianism or inherent marginality.

In addition to the vitality and flexibility required for intensive creative effort, poets cultivate a particular gift for experiencing the world fully. They can write only out of that experience, that combination of stored impression and current sensation which forms the creative fund. Poets are sensitive, then, but not in a mode of mere flabby impressionability; rather, they are selectively sensitive to their environment. Though it may be true that they actually experience a larger quantity of physical stimuli and ideas than do most people, it is perhaps more true that they experience with a heightened keenness and selectivity. For this is, after all, their job. The task is only begun by sharp perceiving, however; there remains the crucial element of ordering experience, of molding and trapping it in the web of language. The poet has a remarkably developed capacity for the use of language. One informant has emphasized that the predominance of the verbal is in him so acute that sense impressions must usually be immediately transformed into words if they are to be fully meaningful. W.H. Auden has remarked that the love of words is the distinguishing mark of the aspiring poet. Linguistic virtuosity, backed by a strong desire to make experience as meaningful as possible, is the poet's chief weapon in the creative endeavor.

Supplementing these required qualities of personality are technical skills of a high order. A knowledge of the forms and techniques of verse is essential. Technique alone is not enough, yet the most sensitive and gifted perceiver does not become a poet without mastering the formal properties of poetry. These skills should be emphasized, for the poet is sometimes wrongly seen as an untutored person engaged in a purely emotional response to the world. On the contrary, the technical equipment is quite as important and hard won as are the conceptual tools of any other professional. If poets are more than fine technicians, they are also more than primitive celebrants of sensuous joy. They are in the strict sense makers, craftsmen, artisans of language who transmute the flux of perception into a fulfilled order for their own (and others') pleasure.

The labor of writing is long. It moves through stages from first conception to finished poem, and each stage exacts from the poet a substantial measure of alert effort. If the artist then demands some privacy, some extra degree of disassociation from worldly concerns, this social solitude should be related as much to the intrinsic nature of the craft as to any conscious alienation from the social context. Poets' main connection with nature and human nature is through language, as they make experience meaningful to themselves and thereby provide the tongue and the knowledge for increasingly sensitive perception in society at large. The poet's primary function is not to lecture or serve on committees or lead political movements, but to write poems. The psychological satisfaction of art and intensity of self-definition in the poet's role will be prominent in the following discussion. Satisfaction and self-definition must be recurrent themes, for they are too easily lost in the rather clumsy and abstract framework of sociological consideration.

The Poet's Historical Role

It has been hypothesized by aesthetic and literary scholars that in some era of prehistory all people were artists, or perhaps better, that each member of society had skills which permitted him or her to assume the creative role at some time. The seemingly spontaneous elaboration of the primitive dance would lend credence to this view. Otto Rank[5] has maintained that the selection of an individual to voice the sentiments of the group occurred only in conjunction with certain religious forms. At any rate, the role of the artist in the West has typically been specialized and distinct, although in a few places and times it has been expected that educated people would occasionally indulge in art making apart from their full-time occupations. If the role has been specialized, it has also been traditionally arduous and unrewarded by the society in which it takes place. As Sir Arthur Quiller-Couch reminds us, "The inequity of it is accepted, proverbial, and goes back even to legend, to Homer—Seven wealthy towns contend for Homer dead/ Through which the living Homer begged his bread."[6]

The paucity of recognition enjoyed by most poets during their lifetimes may of course be related to the fact that the validation of artistic worth is a matter for posterity, that the poet as prophet may seem much more congenial and valuable to a later age than to his own. Yet it is true that the writer is an exceptional individual among nonwriters, and that a private excellence may be deprecated as a public excellence is exalted. Poets, after all, have seldom been able to offer anything of immediate public utility. At many times in the past, however, they have appeared to be more nearly woven into their society's major patterns of interest and behavior than they are today. Pindar wrote odes to military victory, and Elizabethan playwrights and musicians created for the monarch's pleasure; it is rather difficult to imagine T.S. Eliot celebrating the Battle of Okinawa or Tennessee Williams being commissioned to write a new drama for a presidential inauguration. (And yet the appearance of Robert Frost at the late President Kennedy's inauguration may prefigure a somewhat closer alliance of artistic and civic spheres.)

The poet has been an object of suspicion, to be sure. Plato excluded the "honeyed muse" from his ideal republic, and one of the first moves of modern dictatorships has been an attempt to force artistic conformity with the dogmas of the state. Perhaps only in the contemporary Western democracies has the poet been so sedulously disregarded. Critics have sometimes assumed that writers, as producers of a cultural luxury, were dependent on the favor of aristocratic patronage, so that the decline of aristocracy left them without a social anchor. Without the patronage of a ruling elite, they were exposed to the winds of the commercial marketplace. In the nineteenth and twentieth centuries it became a European fashion to speak of the artist versus society, as if there were some unalterable opposition between the creator and the social order. We are heirs to this romantic stereotype of the alienated writer. It is significant that the writer enunciated the enmity, and that there are very few instances of attack on the artistic role by government officials, businessmen, or whomever. It might be more appropriate for the contemporary poet to sue society for nonsupport than for alienation of affection. A classic statement of the poet's feeling of being hounded by an unsympathetic social environment is Baudelaire's:

> If a poet asked the state for permission to keep a few bourgeois in his stable everyone would be greatly astonished; but if a bourgeois asked for some roast poet, it would be considered perfectly natural.[7]

The case of the poet in America is especially interesting, because the very trends toward mechanization and bureaucratization of life which repelled European artists have here reached most acute form. It is generally accepted that the colonial and post-Revolutionary periods in the United States failed to produce artists of the first rank. We assume that citizens of that age were much too busy staking out a new republic and dominating the physical environment to devote much attention to the arts. Most of the productions of that and later periods were either too clumsy to merit critical consideration or too derivative of English models to stand as truly American literature. We note that then (de Tocqueville) as well as in the latter part of the nineteenth century (Henry Adams) there existed the primary antithesis between a pragmatic penchant for getting things done fast and efficiently and a much less common resolve to get things done beautifully if slowly.

Most critics point to the mid-nineteenth century as the golden years of artistic intensity in America. The Concord group and other figures in F. O. Matthiessen's American Renaissance stand for the plenitude of literary fruition. The names of Melville, Poe, Emily Dickinson, Walt Whitman, Emerson, Thoreau, are taken as climactic. Of the poets, it is Poe, Whitman, and Dickinson who are singled out for special praise as the progenitors of a native verse.

Matthew Josephson[8] develops the thesis that after this literary high noon, the serious writer became progressively alienated in spirit from the main facets of American life. Of course, Josephson can point to anonymity and marginal status of the artist even before the late 1800's, but it is in the booty stage of American capitalism, the post–Civil War expansion of railroads and industry, that he finds the locus of disenchantment. The mercantile emphasis, the stress on unaesthetic utility, the lack of public response, all contrived to produce in the artist a feeling of separation from society. Josephson assumes that this society rejected the artist; if the public indeed did so implicitly, it is certain that many writers proclaimed an explicit rejection of their country. The exiles went the length to physical rejection, as in the expatriation of Henry James, of Whistler, of Eliot and Pound in the early twentieth century. The stay-at-homes were in many cases unhappy with their lot. Recall Melville's "I feel I am an exile here." The individual who stayed in America seemed doomed to eccentricity: "The fatalistic, the silenced Melville, the outcast Whitman, the mysteriously secluded Emily Dickinson...." What reasons are adduced for this situation, which may err on the gloomy side but is nevertheless a largely correct summary of what writers felt their lot to be? Leveling and standardization of values and mechanization of life, which may be expressed sociologically as the dominance of a rational-legal, bureaucratic industrial system, are most often put forth as antecedents of artistic discontent:

The artist, then, appears most vulnerable. In a society increasingly collective and uniform in its interest, no place has been left for his lonely and personal labors. With such a world art in the older sense can no longer co-exist.

Under mechanism, the eternal drama for the artist becomes resistance to the milieu, as if the highest prerogative were the preservation of the individual type, the defense of the human self from dissolution in the horde.[9]

In this dilemma the poet represents one of the critical issues of contemporary Western civilization. Simmel stated the problem in general terms:

The deepest problems of modern life derive from the claim of the individual to preserve the autonomy and individuality of existence in the face of overwhelming social forces, of historical heritage, of external culture, and of the technique of life.[10]

To balance the picture of the artist as a social isolate of ignoble status, we may think of the Indian Summer of New England, of Chautauqua with its idolatry of "culture," of the general (and genteel) fashionableness of literary activity. Yet the critics affirm that those artists of sterner vein, who were to be recognized as giants by a later generation, were for the most part badly treated. So Dahlberg weeps for Melville buried in a poor grave:

Is it not fitting, so American, that the most astonishing genius that ever came out of the Western hemisphere, should be so uncleanly slabbed down in mean cheap dirt not among the pitiable poor but with the common drab bulk of rightly unremembered dead. Look upon his homely sparse tombstone and read the frugal inscription written thereon, "Occupation, Writer," and then utter aloud the pity for the artist, in America, alive or deceased, it matters not, that Hamlet so dolorously sighs forth before his father's apparition, "Alas! Poor Ghost."[11]

In 1913 we find Ezra Pound advancing a somewhat brighter view, although it is still weighted toward the dark strains of isolation and rejection. For Pound, although he stated in definite terms the obstacles to poetry in this country, had hope of a development toward better days: "I have declared my belief in the imminence of an American Risorgimento. I have no desire to flatter the country by pretending that we are at present enduring anything except the Dark Ages."[12] He sets up American vigor and "clumsy energy" against the flowering of the arts, noting that politics and business drain talented individuals away from the arts. Of the Americans he said:

One knows that they are the dominant people and that they are against all delicate things. They will never imagine beautiful plaisaunces. They will never "sit on a midden and dream stars," as the Irish peasant said to Joseph Campbell.[13]

The status of the American poet today is difficult to describe, for it is an ambiguous and various complex of attitudes and values. While certain observers profess to see a general raising of artist and intellectual in the public eye, stimulated by increased literacy and leisure, it is apparent that the poet's craft is far from the concerns of most members of American society. In one sense, the poet's position is bettered by the wide influence of poets and critics in academic circles and by a resultant increase in intelligent interest. Public readings of poetry have drawn large audiences, recordings by poets are stocked in libraries, and one poet a year has been formally recognized by the Library of Congress as Consultant in Poetry. Yet it would be false to suppose that the appellation "poet" evokes an unusually affirmative response from the mass of Americans, or that it implies any great respect. He is no culture hero but is probably more nearly disregarded than disvalued in any explicit sense. A *lack* of attribution of high status is not the same as the attribution of low status, for broadly speaking the poet is not scorned but neglected. The poet's role is simply not in the public ken, and this despite a healthy, important production of poetry in modern America. Many leading observers, in fact, emphasize that the writing of contemporary and recent native poets is of extremely fine quality, a true growth of poetic tradition matching other high points in aesthetic history.

Auden sums up the mixed, uncomfortable status of most poets today:

> Everyone in his heart of hearts agrees with Baudelaire: "To be a useful person has always seemed to me something particularly horrible," for, subjectively, to be useful means to be doing not what one wants to do but what someone else insists on one's doing. But at the same time everyone is ashamed to admit in public that he is useless. Thus if a poet gets into conversation with a stranger in a railway coach and the latter asks him: "What is your job?," he will think quickly and say: "A schoolteacher, a beekeeper, a bootlegger," because to tell the truth would cause an incredulous and embarrassing silence.[14]

Why should artists, specialists in symbolic creativity, hold a tenuous position in American society? They originate form and content which afford pleasure and more than pleasure, the rich insights and stark perceptions to make experience meaningful, yet they can seldom earn a living in this vocation, seldom count on any broadly based support in their chosen role; they must be as ready for depreciation as for appreciation, and this according to criteria seemingly remote from consideration of artistic excellence. If we analyze poets' work and life in the context of American values, it may be possible to see the frail roots of their insecure role in our cultural soil. It should be stressed, however, that American society only accentuates the traditionally precarious role of the artistic innovator. In nearly every place and time the truly creative individual has represented a threat to the norms people live by, since such an individual promises to shatter or transcend or at least drastically amend those norms. Creative individuals in art are the more dangerous because they challenge our ways of perceiving and our habits of expressing what we see. Unlike the political revolutionaries or social reformers, who would change the forms of social intercourse, artists would change our total response to the universe of man and nature. In this they are like scientists revising our perceptions of physical reality or the charismatic religious leader enhancing our moral perceptions.

The Poet and American Values

The texture of American culture is so rich and complicated that generalizations about specific themes of value and behavior are always hazardous. For every statement that this or that pattern is dominant or recessive, we can easily adduce contrary evidence. Although an analyst must arbitrarily break through the almost oppressive heterogeneity of social forms, it is well to begin by recognizing that pluralism is itself perhaps the most prominent theme. Pluralism of values is in fact a chief support of artists, in that it lets them work out a unique destiny of vocational fulfillment. Although it is true that cultural diversity complicates the effort to communicate, reducing the scope of any single shared tradition or contemporary frame of reference, diversity also provides poets with a range of alternative life styles, with economically rewarding pursuits other than poetry, and with several potential kinds of audience. Again, the habit of tolerance in religious and political matters tends to insure the tolerance of artistic heresy. If we let artists die of neglect it can scarcely be said that we hound them with demands for conformity to any particular doctrine of state or ideology. Underlying pluralism of tradition, however, there are a few generally recognized clusters of dominant themes against which the artist may be viewed.

The Protestant Ethic and the Spirit of Poetry

The Protestant Ethic as adduced, for example, by Max Weber, is in a very fundamental sense antipathetic to poetry. This is true despite the high rank of the greatest Puritan poet—Milton—and despite certain superficial congruities between the Calvinist ethical ideal and that of the artist-as-ascetic. While the concept of the "calling," of devotion to a disciplined activity, is very relevant to poetic dedication, the context of the poet's calling is singular. For such work by its very nature demands a breadth of enjoyment, an appetite for the pleasures of this world, which is foreign to the religiously derived work ethic. The Protestant Ethic, like the utilitarian doctrine, emphasizes the extrinsic goals of striving; salvation and profits are alike in their displacement from the work activity itself. Weber has shown how the goal of election into a celestial state of grace became subordinated, in the later development of Calvinist-inspired work ethics, to the idea that work is good for its own sake. Yet this Calvinist work is not the poet's work, since it is not to be enjoyed but grimly endured. Obviously an entrepreneur could not legitimately derive pleasure from a calling which had been imposed as dutiful striving.

The poet is too apparently a person who derives pleasure from his or her task, and that pleasure is a sensuous one. The immediacy of symbolic creation implies acceptance and deep enjoyment of affective nuances. Poets play with words and love them for their own sweet verbal sakes; they are stimulated by their own productions. The Protestant Ethic, rightly internalized, involves a positive distaste for pleasure, and especially for sensuous pleasure. We might recast Macaulay's famous remark about the Puritans and bear baiting by noting that American society rejects the poet not because of the pain (or ease) given to readers, but because of the pleasure obviously derived from writing. It is furthermore a peculiar feature of the artist's work that it rarely appears, to a casual observer, to be work at all. Actual writing is known to consume a rather small portion of the writer's day, even when in high gear. And there are periods, well described by E.D. Hutchinson as periods of renunciation in creative endeavor, when nothing happens to be going just right, no new idea has jelled, and the artist must stick it out. This sticking it out may take the form of loafing; although everyone agrees that a certain kind of loafing is crucial to any intellectually creative activity, it still seems to the public not quite right or wholly just. The public, as Bergler notes, envies writers while scorning them for their (seeming) ease. In a country where occupational life is characterized by intensity, especially "busy work" and routine, the person of no fixed outer demands is looked upon somewhat askance. This occurs despite the fact that there may be inner personal demands, in poet or scientist, more strict than anything the time clock or straw boss imposes.

Routine and Originality

In the rational-legal society of the West, occupations are very generally routinized. The complexity of huge bureaucratic-industrial organizations demands that the specific task assigned through division of labor be amenable to definite planning. The characteristic job should be ordered to standards of performance, technique, and interrelation with other closely allied functions. Not only is the job itself routinized, but the training that fits an individual for the position is specified and clearly established with an end in view of competent task fulfillment. All of this ordering and accountability means further that the vast majority of occupations are institutionalized; that is, the activities involved cluster into a set of definable expectations on the part of mutually interactive role players. Performance of certain roles is an accepted feature of the social system, and both role players and significant others know what is legitimately to be expected. The "public" or mass of social actors has, too, a disposition to regard as justified an activity for which formal social provision is made, which can be objectively "certified." None of these strictures applies to poetry as a profession. It is true that strict standards of competence are applied by literary critics, but even here the criteria are amorphous. Writing is a sedentary activity; the poet grows no calluses, goes to no offices, punches no time clock, gains no diploma, earns no certificate of competence. There is no current, universal measure of success or fitness; credentials are intangible, a passport without date, country, or occupation. Poetry is an undefined profession. It lacks both the institutional support and the popular appeal of science, with which alone it is comparable in terms of originality of contribution.

The Poetic Role and the "Revolt of the Masses"

Ortega y Gassett has made a profound analysis of the tremendous power of the "mass man." He posits the rise to dominance of the great bulk of average individuals, through the democratic franchise and the weakening of older hierarchical social organizations, as the primary fact of our times. Nowhere is the phenomenon more fully exemplified than in the United States. That this should result in a vast pressure toward conformity and mediocrity is not surprising. De Tocqueville made careful note of leveling tendencies in the United States over a century ago. Perhaps genius and talent are always suspect; one doubts that physicists or chemists are wholly understood or accepted in this country, despite the practical efficacy of their sciences. Mass dominance implies a standardization of values and a distrust of the unique. These tendencies are accentuated enormously by the media of mass communication, which insure that the value standard becomes a common denominator. The common denominator is not necessarily low for being common; it may be quite high, as exemplified in a very real intensifying of the interest in classical music, but it *is* weighted toward uniformity.

The poet is by definition the teller of a personal truth. He or she is unique and abides by an uncommon denominator. The poetic vision is necessarily too exacting for a generation schooled in the comforting prose of the *Reader's Digest* or the artificial excitement of quiz shows. As a minority of one, the poet falls under many of the strains imposed on other, more obtrusive minorities.

Pragmatism and Poetry

Americans do things and go places. Poets do things and go places too, only they do unusual things and go to uncharted places. This in itself may make them objects of suspicion, but they are guilty of a worse crime, and one that sets their role more incontrovertibly against the American temper: their efforts have no obvious utility. In this aspect the poet is more deviant than the gangster, whose role at least has an objective utility for himself in that it may make him rich before it makes him dead. The molder of aesthetic symbols may reform the language, transmute and communicate experience, delight the reader with originality of form, yet the popular pragmatist might ask, to what end are these things done? We accept the notion of pure research in the sciences because we have learned by experience that such efforts generally result in efficacious and profitable by-products. The poet does pure research in the human heart, but few Americans could be convinced that this work compares in importance with that of a specialist in coronary thrombosis.

The Artist and the Feminine Role

In American culture, women have most often been the carriers of the arts. They have not usually been of the first rank artistically or critically, but overall they have been the sustaining and encouraging audience. In a very real sense American males have delegated to their wives, and even more definitely to women of the "old maid schoolteacher" stereotype, the responsibility for what is popularly known as culture. A superficial explanation of this phenomenon might point to the frontier imperatives, which later became the business imperatives, of energetic effort, devotion to externals, and resolute "toughness" on the part of the male. As Erikson has so beautifully shown, one of the duties of the mother in this country has been to push the son firmly in the direction of untrammeled maleness and striving, meanwhile sedulously smothering his impulse to things sensual and immediate. This emphasis, of course, leaves the pursuit of poetry to women or to males whose socialization somehow did not "take."

Yet this is not the whole story. When Carol Kennicott, protagonist in Sinclair Lewis's *Main Street*, tried to bring the arts to Gopher Prairie (a typically womanish project), she was met not by a plain refusal but by positive male hostility. Why should American men avoid the artist's calling and tend to deprecate those who follow it?

We may suggest that, going deeper than the fact of the female as the functional art bearer in the American tradition, there are elements intrinsic to the roles of male and female which militate against men-as-artists. What has been called the American man's panic fear of homosexuality may be relevant to the ambiguous position of the male poet. As the Kluckhohns and others have stressed, it is comparatively easy for men to be scared out of being artists. A major basis for this fear may be that the themes of diffuseness and affectivity which characterize the feminine role, for example as outlined by Parsons, are also quite typical of the artist role. In this connection, Parsons has remarked upon the revealing use of the term *longhair* to describe artists and their works. We note that the term is ordinarily employed in a derogatory vein. May it not be a dramatic symbol of the hostility often directed against the artist who oversteps role bounda-ries? This correspondence of themes suggests that the fear and hostility the male poet often meets are contingent on his not "acting like a man" in role terms. The poet incorporates too much, refuses to be bound by conventions of role differentiation and exhibits an unmasculine concern with senses and sensitivity. He is not well socialized, for he breaks the mold by overincor-poration. Related to his greater *capacity* for experience is the possibility that his actual intake is too large for an easy distinction between masculine and feminine elements. Thus he takes in elements of both male and female roles, as do all men, but then refuses to be disabused of feminine affectivity and diffuse responsibilities at a later stage. Perhaps he never succeeds in unlearning the infant's play impulses or warmly sensuous responses to the world. A hypothesis might be, then, that the artist role and the feminine role are intimately related—often to the social detriment of the artist—not because artists are constitutionally "queer" but because our culture demands a role differentiation on the thematic, learned level, which the male artist is unable or unwilling to make. Unable to suppress his affective resonance and diffusely generalized response to life in favor of the more strict male occupational model, the poet finds himself too versatile in a specialized world. As "the apple tree, the singing and the gold" do not promote the world's work, so they do not provide a wholly acceptable costuming of social role for the male poet.

The Ideal of Self-Fulfillment

The American belief in an individual, self-determined destiny, which will express the essential talents of each person, is one of the strongest props for marginal roles. The idea that one's social role, far from being predeter-mined by accidents of birth or environment, represents the choice made by a relatively free agent, implies the right to choose odd life styles and seemingly incomprehensible goals. Thus, despite the very real pressures toward conformity, and especially toward a materially validated success, there is a range of tolerance for artists who are doing the kind of thing that appeals to them. The shocked disbelief that greets the announcement that one's son has turned to poetry or painting is not unmixed with a respectful envy, an admiration, however grudging, for the individual who hews to his own path. The spate of popular volumes which preach self-fulfillment and unique personal development bespeaks the resonance Americans have for such concepts, as well as the need for reinforcement of the ideal in a society which seems to force people into roles they might not choose again as free agents. It is true that the notion of an individual's "doing what he or she wants to do" is usually implicitly qualified by criteria of financial gain, but we must attach great importance to the fact that parents in this society feel guilty about pushing their children into uncongenial vocations. So a way is left open for the artist, who corresponds to an ideal type of self-fulfillment. There can be little doubt that of all men the poet is most concerned with the burgeoning of his own personality, sensitivity, and perceptivity. It is, after all, his only stock in trade, the only instrument he will ever have to perform miracles of words. The dramatic moment when Sherwood Anderson walked out of his paint factory, family life, and routine set of social roles to become a professional writer is perhaps a symbol for the right of self-expression. Today it is debatable whether an aspiring novelist would even have to walk out of the factory or out of a settled lifestyle; he might be encouraged in his native circumstances to the point where flight was meaningless.

Education and Leisure

Americans now have the highest general level of education and the most leisure time ever enjoyed by a society as a whole. The effect of this situation on the arts and the artist is not yet clear, but it will undoubtedly change the artist's role by transforming the nature of the audience. More people now have the humanistic acquaintance which is ncessary to make the arts individually meaningful, and they have free time to read, or visit museums, or listen to concerts. Respect for the professional artist may increase as more amateurs try to master the techniques of painting and writing. The tiny leisure class which has traditionally provided aristocratic patrons is being expanded in this country toward a kind of classless leisure, a potential source of broad support for artistic activities. It is certainly conceivable that creation and recreation may tend to merge if the mass media do not succeed in consuming all of everyone's spare hours. The great world of events piped into our livingrooms may come to be too much with us, so that the private world of one poet and one reader becomes an attractive sanctuary.

Innovation and Deviance: The Paradox of the Creative Role

Although we have seen that American values in their variety both harbor and reject the poet, it is obvious that the role diverges rather sharply from the vocational paths which people in this society are expected to follow. In part the divergence is negative, consisting of not embracing certain common goals such as economic gain or social position and not employing certain common means such as professional training or climbing the rungs of an organizational hierarchy. These negative elements are the core of the concept of the artist as deviant, but they do not lead us very far, because in these terms the poet is indistinguishable from the hobo or the psychotic. The really important questions arise when we ask what the artist puts in place of the behaviors he has rejected.

The poet as maker rejects the conventional perceptions of the world of men and nature. His implicit goal is to make the reader more aware of the complexity and ambiguity of existence, not by preaching but by vigorous example of fresh ways of seeing. The artist forces us to give up, at least momentarily, those routine, comfortable perceptual stereotypes on which we depend to keep the world under safe control. This is why full participation in aesthetic communication may be nearly as psychologically threatening for the appreciator as for the creator. The threat, like almost all challenges to an established behavioral system (for example, neurosis) has as much potential for growth and refreshment as for confusion or debilitation. Yet we naturally resist the challenge to follow the poet into novel modes of reacting to experience and novel words for expressing that reaction. It not only bestirs us, since art may in one sense be seen as the opposite of a state of rest, but it also confronts us with the imperative to grow, to enlarge our own perceptions enough to assimilate some part of the artist's perceptions.

Because the heightening of awareness is an endless occupation, halting only with death or complete unawareness, the poet cannot be said to have a "goal" in the usual sense. The essential goal is more of the same, that is, renewed involvement in the process of living and writing. It is true that the poet wants to achieve the perfect line, the absolute phrase; but this is an intangible end, really the prelude to the next perfect line,and it is so elusive that many writers would agree with the aphorism that, "a poem is never finished, it is abandoned in despair." If the artist's goal is difficult to define and tends to be a process rather than a static accomplishment, what may we say about poetic means? They are so extraordinary, when compared with the instrumental maneuvers of most individuals in society, that the question of "how poets do it," may put them further from the dominant patterns of behavior than the question of "why they do it." In large part, their means are simply to live as fully and sensitively as possible, to be a mobile perceptual antenna at the boundary of human consciousness. Because poets spend so much time doing and being these things, they may be and often are accused of being noncontributing members of society. When it comes to the job of writing itself, it is performed in a private world. Only when some reader happens to receive the gift and enter to a certain degree the universe of cognition and emotion which has been elaborated, does the poet come to have an obvious function.

As the creator of expressive symbols, the artist eventually has an effect. It is likely to be a slow and subtle one, like that of the religious leader, the philosopher, or the scientist, for it consists in changing people's basic views and reforming the tongue they use to express those views. We then face an interesting conceptual problem: the very innovators whose transcendence of common values has, in the long run, the most highly valued effect, are treated as marginal people in the contemporary social scheme. Many reasons may be adduced for this treatment, including the uncomfortable wrench the artist gives to conventional ways of seeing, and the time lag between what the artist does and what the potential publics may grow to accept. Fewer good reasons may be found, however, for the failure of social scientists to devote adequate attention to the exceptional person, the creative individual in whatever sphere. The theorists of social control and general societal maintenance have tended to accept their own cultural framework to the extent of dividing people into those who follow social prescriptions closely and those whose refusal to follow them results in deleterious (criminal or ill) behavior. They have neglected to consider the talented person who transcends social prescriptions in search of something better or fuller. Psychologists too, as Allport has recently maintained,[15] have been bound to a model of man as reactive organism, who could be seen as responding to external stimuli (therefore capable of accepting or rejecting sensations, including social norms) but not as initiating creative activity (therefore capable of devising new structures and refining old ones).

Since the creative individual is demonstrably important to society, we need a sophisticated theory of innovative behavior. Such a theory is required both for what might be termed *institutionalized innovation,* as in science, and for the singular creativity that occurs in noninstitutionalized spheres, as in art and religion. Some clues exist, in such diverse contexts as Max Weber's concept of charisma, psychoanalytic studies of the genesis of artistic behavior, and current investigations of personality characteristics of talented individuals. But a true social pyschology of creativity needs to be grounded in a series of detailed researches, embracing everything from childhood development to the style of life of the mature innovator. As Henry A. Murray has expressed it, the sociologist must turn from an exclusive preoccupation with assocational roles, which are characterized by observable patterns of social interaction toward some cognizance of monadic or individually creative roles. The problem of analyzing the role of the artist or scientist is not an exotic or peripheral one merely because their behaviors are complicated and they are a numerically tiny segment of the population. The poet and the physicist are not only highly significant in their society, but in their vocational paths they raise the major issues for the student of man: conformity and social control, the relation of the individual to various social groupings, the learning of cultural norms, the creation of percepts and values by which the social fabric is torn or mended or graven with bold new designs.

Aspects of the Poetic Vocation

Choice of the Career

The absence of the trappings of institutionalization means that in one sense there is no career for the aspiring individual to choose. That is, the job of poet is a unique system of literary and experiential patterns without many of the familiar guideposts we normally associate with an occupation: there are no training schools, no diplomas, no starting salary, no series of positions to which the able beginner might order his progress. This paucity of external criteria is quite fitting, since in other professions such criteria guide rational choice whereas in poetry the decision to follow the muse is seldom a matter for mature deliveration. It is, rather, a decision which generally occurs fairly early in life. Paradoxically, by the time one could accept or reject poetry as a way of life, he would have already to be a considerable poet. It might even be said that the role of poet overtakes the persistent and talented writer of poetry.

Literature as experience is the major force attracting recruits to the poetic role: they read, are astonished, and determine to create for themselves. Symbolic experience, the environment of the printed page, is often neglected in our quest for causal chains in human development, but it may be an important agent of growth, especially for personalities whose career fulfillment lies in literate sectors of the arts, professions, or government. One poet who made an early, explicit choice of the vocation recounted this event:

> I have never wanted to be anything else. At the age of nine, I read *Tom Brown's Schooldays*, which had an introduction containing two lines of verse:
>
> > *I'm the poet of White Horse vale, sir,*
> > *With liberal notions under my cap.*
>
> I asked my parents what a poet was, and when they told me I was fascinated. I went to school and saw several words listed on the board; I made a rhyme scheme, and this was my first poem. I always *knew* I would be a poet.

Even those who came to poetry somewhat later in life tend to stress the importance of literary stimuli:

> It was not deliberate, and was based on the pleasure principle. I read modern poems in high school, not dreaming that I could write one. Then one day I wrote one, loved the experience and wanted to repeat it.
>
> The exposure to literature is important; poetic activity must spring from somewhere. I wrote some poetry in college, but was not very involved with it. I wrote much prose, and becoming dissatisfied with it, turned to poetry.

The power of the poetic tradition is of course reinforced by the presence of some few mentors and colleagues, themselves sharers of the verbal heritage and partners in the creative enterprise. It is often an older colleague who will call one's work to the attention of editor or publisher. Ezra Pound's reputation in literary circles is actually based quite as much on his letters and encouraging overtures to young poets as on his own artistic contribution; many older writers feel that the nurture of young talent is a duty imposed on the established person, although it is to be sure a duty of enthusiasm rather than compulsion. Contemporary poets are vividly aware of influential exemplars:

> I had to quit athletics because of my health. After trying all the arts, I fixed on poetry. I met _____ at the university. He was a major influence on me, giving me good freshman literary criticism, not vague but in clear declarative sentences.

> I firmly settled on poetry while at Cambridge, largely under the influence of I.A. Richards and William Empson.

> What I need most is someone to fight like hell with. Women are to go to bed with, men are to fight with. My association with Ezra Pound helped inspire me to continue writing poetry. For years we waged a battle over the proper goal of the poet; I would say "bread" and Pound would say "caviar."

Finally, the inner drive toward poetic innovation appears to many artists as a given, a historical personal fact which must somehow be accommodated and woven into one's style of life:

> It was an accidental, not a conscious, decision. But I felt a lack when I was doing something else, as if I were not using myself.

> You're generally a poet because you have to be, not because you decide you want to be.

> In this art, in distinction from painting, one must begin early. There is the necessity of much practice, so that one achieves technical mastery before the finding of his individual voice. Poetry is always there. If it is with you, you will make a place for it.

Modern poets are under no illusion that the vocation they have embraced is likely to bring them any of the usual rewards of a profession. Twenty years ago the most famed contemporary, T.S. Eliot, put the matter bluntly:

> As things are, and as fundamentally they must always be, poetry is not a career but a mug's game. No honest poet can ever feel quite sure of the permanent value of what he has written; he may have wasted his time and messed up his life for nothing.[16]

Economic and Spiritual Support

Poets require at least two kinds of support from the environment: a living that makes existence economically feasible, and a variety of social response or reward that can bolster their own belief in the value of their writing. Economic maintenance cannot be based wholly on the sale of verse; among modern poets, perhaps T.S. Eliot and Ogden Nash could now survive on royalties, but even they were not in a position to do so until their careers were well advanced. Book sales bring in a few hundred dollars a year at best, so they will not support a writer despite a steady production. The average sale of a volume of poems is fewer than one thousand copies. Publication is, moreover, quite difficult, since the publisher must anticipate a loss and usually prints poetry only as a prestige item, an unprofitable but good book published as an aesthetic service. The magazine market for verse is not a great deal better. Serious poets are rarely published in mass-circulation magazines. *Harper's Magazine* and the *Atlantic* cannot afford to pay high prices; *The New Yorker* does pay well for serious work, but it stands almost alone. The "little magazines" often maintain high standards of quality, but they can pay little or nothing to their contributors.

In addition to sales of published work, there is a variety of more or less fortuitous chances for income or its equivalent in subsidized free time. These include prizes, gifts, appointments to summer art colonies, and occasional odd strokes of luck. Some few patrons still may help the artist with gifts of money or nonrepayable loans; colonies such as Yaddo or McDowell afford several months of quiet, secure living for a few painters, composers, and poets at work. Sheer windfalls sometimes occur: Conrad Aiken once began to throw an "advertisement" in the wastebasket when the figure of $750 caught his eye; it was a letter from a pharmaceutical house offering him this sum for a one-page poem to be written for the annual publication.

When all the possibilities are exhausted, it is obvious that most poets must earn a living through some other activity than writing poems. Thus the follower of a pervasive vocation, one which demands a more nearly total investment of the personality than most, has to fit this vocation into spare-time or part-time occasions. Poets feel the money-making job should be far enough removed from creative work that it does not drain their energy or capture their time to an intolerable extent. They try to avoid the kind of high-pressure involvement demanded by news magazines or films or many sorts of organizations. Yet they do hold a wide range of jobs in business, the professions, and the writing-editing-publishing complex, and these jobs do not appear to interfere greatly with serious artistic production. William Carlos Williams and Merrill Moore were physicians, Wallace Stevens was a business executive, and a great many poets hold academic posts. There is an idealistic conceit that artists should remove themselves to pastoral pursuits or manual labor, but this is not a common happening. Most poets are forced to double up on their outstanding talent, that is, a high skill with language. Academic jobs are a matter of controversy. Those who teach maintain that it is a decent complement to writing; those who do not tend to view the university as a carefully designed trap in which the artists are hamstrung if not prostituted. Poets affirm that it makes no great difference what one does for an income. If a person is a creative artist he or she will manage in some way to continue the work. Few contemporaries would approve of a system of outright subsidy for the artist; the objections are that subsidy is not only an unfair advantage in a democracy and a potential restriction to artistic freedom, but that the struggle for economic support is a necessary challenge to the writer's initiative. An unostentatious self-confidence generates the theme that the poet as interior person is superior to external conditions.

What of nonfinancial support from people? However dedicated and self-propelled, the poet needs a measure of human response to his efforts. The general public is not an important source of support, because the general public does not read poetry. Poets note that members of the public usually like poems for the wrong reasons—or are the wrong people. Liking for the wrong reasons is decried because the artist is not eager to be misunderstood; pride is not enhanced by having someone admire the lovely sentiment of a poem whose intent is ironic or satirical. The unintended consequences of poetic action need not be, but often are, harrowing to the conscientious professional. Liking by the wrong people indicates that the artist is not having the kind of effect desired, that the efforts may be at least temporarily wasted because ignored by those he or she respects. Auden gives a succinct analysis of this situation:

> The ideal audience the poet imagines consists of the beautiful who go to bed with him, the powerful who invite him to dinner and tell him secrets of state, and his fellow-poets. The actual audience he gets consists of myopic schoolteachers, pimply young men who eat in cafeterias, and his fellow-poets. This means that, in fact, he writes for his fellow-poets.[17]

If the general public is not prominent in shoring up poets' morale (and one must note that the public's disregard is often matched by a defensive rejection of popular taste by poets), they must gain their rewards from more selected, specialized publics. This they do, and the primary characteristic of the specialized audience is, of course, literary sophistication. Family and friends are important, in this context, only as they fill the role of literary expert; otherwise, spouse or boon companion is not to be trusted in matters of art. It is the in-group of critics and fellow professionals whose opinion weighs most in the scales of self-assessment. Again and again, poets speak of the vital place held by a few true perceivers, a handful of people who judge the artist's intent by strict but sympathetic criteria and rightly gauge the inevitable discrepancy between a vision conceived and a poem executed.

In many other fields we think it only sensible that specialists should receive their primary response from other specialists. Especially in scholarship and science, no one expects that the expert will speak to an extended popular audience. Perhaps modern technology and role differentiation have grown together, so that we anticipate specialization of function as a natural thing in science. The poet, however, is expected to create something widely enjoyable, or at last understandable. The image of the artist spans Western society in its prespecialized and postspecialized aspects; thus artists whose work does not emit the familiar ring of common evaluative and stylistic coin are thought of as deviants or cultists. Actually, the poet who has traditionally been the "whole man" seems now to be in one sense a technical specialist whose prospective audience has also become split and specialized. The width of his potential appeal is an unsolved question and probably rests as much on the extensity of common symbolic meanings in the total culture as on the poet's own attempt to elaborate the universal in the unique.

Group Membership

American poets, in contrast to poets of many other countries, do not today associate themselves with particular small groups or artistic coteries. While there may be an occasional banding together for launching a new journal or taking a specific public action (for example, awarding a prize or collecting funds for a distressed artist), contemporary poets tend to resist the attractions of the tightly knit artistic in-group. They feel that the comfort and intimacy afforded by such groups may be bought at too high a price of artistic conformity. They try to avoid labels and are fairly consistently truant from schools of thematic or stylistic dicta. It might be noted, too, that the poet's preference for catholicity rather than parochialism is abetted by geographical dispersion and the absence of congenial informal centers like the cafes of Paris.

If he or she seeks to avoid the limiting and labeling of coterie membership, however, it is not necessarily true that each artist is an isolated worker. There are various informal groups, loosely bound together by spatial or ideological propinquity. The Fugitive poets, a Southern group which flourished at Vanderbilt University in the 1920s, is an example of a small group sharing many characteristics yet generating very diverse types of writing and artistic careers. In Cambridge, Massachusetts, five or six established poets meet fairly regularly to read and discuss their work. Geographical proximity, which is seldom entirely accidental, tends to throw artists together, particularly in the case of summer homes.

In another sense the modern poet is a working member of an ill-defined group: contemporary professional poets. This craft membership is exceedingly important, although by ordinary sociological criteria we might hesitate to term poets a group. That is, they may exhibit a paucity of overt interaction, a refusal to agree on the identity of a leader, and a heterogeneity of sentiments. Yet they are bound together by some few group norms, such as the primacy of poetic activity and the integrity of critical judgment. Like an extended family, modern poets carry on an internecine war of attrition but rally to one another's defense if poetry itself seems threatened by outside forces. Interaction is actually vigorous, quite apart from interpersonal contact at parties, visits, or art colonies; the symbolic interplay of the printed word knits writers together through personal correspondence and, more importantly, through mutual cognizance of the created products. It is possible that poets have more profound knowledge of their fellow professionals from reading their work than do members of an organized group from daily superficial contacts with coworkers. We usually overlook this type of interpersonal network because the impulses which travel its channels cannot be measured, and the channels themselves are seldom visible. Yet the influences of second-level interaction, employing means other than face-to-face confrontation, are sociologically pervasive and are likely to become more so as modern society enhances its communicative virtuosity.

An artistic fellowship extending forward and back in time, sometimes grandly called "the republic of letters," constitutes the major reference group for the poet's behavior. The paradox of the role, the fact that it is a passionate devotion yet socially marginal, is partially resolved in the realization that the poet does not take business or professional elites as referential anchors. The poet does not, then, suffer from invidious comparison with individuals whose vocations entail unusual rewards of income and prestige. Growing as it does from the use of "relative deprivation" as an explanatory concept in *The American Soldier*,[18] the idea of the reference group leads us to ask, "Deprived relative to whom?" Modern poets are not deprived of reward or isolated from the dominant streams of action if they are seen (as they see themselves) in the context of a historically validated artistic community. Indeed, the essential behavioral genealogy is most distinguished and durable. When poets define their role as important, they are not isolated figures, brashly affirming a transitory place in the sun; rather, they envision themselves as links, however great or small, in a chain reaching back to Homer and the ancient Chinese lyricists. Since art as symbolic vehicle is a time-defying element of culture, poets can conceive their role as almost infinitely extensible. The vocational faith has been kept, and writers can find support for current behavior and exalted role ideal in the achievements of the past. They look also to the future, to the artists and audiences yet unborn. If the investment in posterity is intangible and hazardous, it is by the same token irrefutable; poets leave something behind, and considering the history of aesthetic taste, few would scorn them for banking on "a paper eternity."

The relation of poet to poet in the contemporary scene is ambiguous and complex. Fellow poets of today do comprise the primary reference group for each of their number; in a sense, they are "all in it together," and one's peers must be assumed to have the most precise basis for judging one's efforts. As in other groups of specialists, notably the scientific and scholarly fraternities, reputation and hence subjective prestige rest on the good opinion of peers. Again, the jealousy and bitterness which often characterize competitors in specialized fields, particularly those vocations demanding great personal devotion, are apparent in poets. The most skilled artist is of course not necessarily the most attractive personality; as one writer expressed it, "Most of the people one knows aren't poets, and most of the poets one knows aren't people." Yet the very zeal and discrimination which tend to make for unstable interpersonal ties among poets may also enrich those ties with a rare tenderness and significance. By reason of their common sensitivity, poets, of all people, can go "proudly friended."

The Self-Defined Role

> It is evident that a faith in their vocation,
> mystical in intensity, sustains poets.
>
> —Stephen Spender

> Does Madame recall our responsibilities? We are
> Whores Fraulein: poets Fraulein are persons of
> Known vocation following troops: they must sleep with
> Stragglers from either prince and of both views:
> The rules permit them to further the business of neither.
> ...The things of the poet are done to a man alone
> As the things of love are done—or of death when he hears the
> Step withdraw on the stair and the clock tick only
> Neither his class nor his kind nor his trade may come near him
> There where he lies on his left arm and will die:
> Nor his class nor his kind nor his trade when the blood is jeering
> And his knee's in the soft of the bed where his love lies:
> I remind you Barinya the life of a poet is hard—
> A hardy life with a boot as quick as a fiver.
> Is it just to demand of us also to bear arms?
>
> —Archibald MacLeish[19]

To paraphase Thomas and Znaniecki's trenchant aphorism, if poets define poetry as real, it is real in its consequences. It is significant that they do define poetry as real and that they view their role in terms of the intrinsic attributes of art rather than in terms of the writer's individual behavior. The social function of poetry as an art form merges with the function of the poet as person. There is in fact an ascetic tendency to think of the poet as important only in and through the poem; a writer remarked, "Let the language lead the dance—put the self behind."

Poetry is seen as a valuable thing in itself, primarily because it affects the hearts and minds of people by means of the distinctively human pattern of language. Poets see their role as a strenuous, concentrated effort to refine their own perceptions and trap them so exactly in words that others' perceptions may be sharpened. Conrad Aiken probably speaks for most modern poets in his philosophy that the artist's job is to increase awareness, to promote an ever more acute consciousness of the subtleties and riches, the "invariant doublets" of experience. Poets think of themselves as part of a vast company, the companionship of all who have tried to assess experience through art. Creative activity draws meaning and defintion from this context, but in daily behavior it is the battle with language, the endless struggle to wring from words an experiential exactitude, that gives the poet the keenest sense of role fulfillment. The faith of which Spender speaks previously is informed with love and challenged by the hazards of the creative process.

Modern poets do not seem concerned that they fall short of being "the unacknowledged legislators of mankind": they view their role as primarily judicial rather than legislative and are content if their judgments have an implicit relevance for society. They think of themselves as responsible citizens doing a responsible job, not as culture heroes or Commissars of Aesthetic Enlightenment. Their responsibility is essentially to themselves, to write the best verse of which they are capable.

Poets are tough and self-confident. Although they would welcome large sales of poems and increased stature in the total society, the belief in the intrinsic value of the work is strong enough to sustain them. Today they are not generally tempted to flee to some supposedly more congenial climate or to ally themselves with popular political or economic ideologies. Rather, poets intend to pursue their vocation and maintain their special integrity, relying on the pluralistic vigor of American society to accommodate them if it does not reward them.

Notes

1. David Riesman, *The Lonely Crowd* (New Haven: Yale University Press, 1961), pp. 14ff.
2. Stephen Spender, "The Making of a Poem," in *The Creative Process*, ed. Brewster Ghiselin (New York: Mentor, 1955), p. 124.
3. John Ciardi, *Mid-Century American Poets* (New York: Twayne 1950), p. xxvi.
4. Robert N. Wilson, "Poetic Creativity: Process and Personality," *Psychiatry* 17 (2) (May 1954), pp. 163-76.
5. Otto Rank, *Art and Artist* (New York: Knopf, 1932), pp. 235ff.
6. Arthur Quiller-Couch, *The Poet as Citizen* (New York: Macmillan, 1935), p.2.
7. Quoted in Martin Turnell, "The Writer and Social Strategy," *Partisan Review* 18 (March-April 1951.)
8. Matthew Josephson, *Portrait of the Artist as American* (New York: Harcourt, Brace & World, 1930).
9. Ibid., pp. xii–xiii.

10. Georg Simmel, "The Metropolis and Mental Life," in *The Sociology of Georg Simmel,* ed. K. Wolff (New York: Free Press, 1950), p. 409.
11. Edward Dahlberg, *Do These Bones Live?* (New York: Harcourt, Brace & World, 1941), p. 33.
12. Ezra Pound, *Patria Mia* (Chicago, Ill.: Ralph Fletcher Seymour, 1950), p. 41.
13. Ibid.
14. W.H. Auden, in Charles D. Abbott, *Poets at Work* (New York: Harcourt Brace & World, 1948), p. 175.
15. Gordon W. Allport, *Becoming* (New Haven: Yale University Press, 1955).
16. T.S. Eliot, *The Use of Poetry and the Use of Criticism* (Cambridge: Harvard University Press, 1933), pp. 147–48.
17. W.H. Auden, p. 176.
18. Samuel A. Stouffer, et al., *The American Soldier* (Princeton: Princeton University Press, 1949), p. 125.
19. Archibald MacLeish, "Invocation to the Social Muse," in *Collected Poems 1917–1952* (Boston: Houghton-Mifflin, 1952), p. 94.

5
Conrad Aiken: An Appreciation

A great deal of what went into these varied essays on creativity happened to me when I was a very young man. And a very lucky one too, I might add, honored to rub up against distinguished men and women and to learn from them. This memoir of Conrad Aiken, although it is of that time, is also a retrospective account, distanced by thirty years and hundreds of miles. I wrote it in mid life, partly as a matter of "mid life review," of trying to make sense of my recoverable past; but partly from less selfish motives, from a wish (if not an obligation) to share the privileged experience of knowing a great poet rather well. In a certain sense we are all witnesses at the trial of our times, required to testify as we are able.

Emerson tells us that, "the poet is representative. He stands among partial men for the complete man, and apprises us not of his wealth, but of the common wealth."[1] If Conrad Aiken was for me exemplary, we might well ask whether he was in vital ways representative of the genus *poet*. After admitting that a truly average or normative poet does not exist, the case for or against Conrad as a model for the creative life may be asserted convincingly either way. He enjoyed a long artistic career, wrote an astonishing range and quantity of poetry and prose, was esteemed by his fellow poets, was awarded the Pulitzer and Bollingen prizes, was Consultant in Poetry to the Library of Congress. Against this image of the committed poet as hero, we must counterpose the frankly antiheroic: the selfishness of the errant husband and absconding father, the once-suicidal and intermittently alcoholic personality, the poet for whom praise was always qualified, who was outshone at least in publicity by his contemporaries Eliot and Frost and who is very probably little read today. On balance, it is clear, I should opt for Conrad Aiken as heroic model. His old friend Malcolm Cowley perhaps says it best in recounting his last visit with the poet:

> He had done his work and knew it was good. He had proclaimed his religion of consciousness and had lived by its tenets. He had never compromised—as he was to say on his deathbed—and he could feel certain that, for all his hatred of intruders, the great world would some day come round to him.[2]

In any event, I spent much more time with Conrad than with any other creative figure, and the effort to generalize about the artist's work is inevitably heavily influenced by his remarkable presence. The richness of the encounter, the depth of insight and understanding I think I garnered, render this case history valuable in a manner that brief interviews or questionnaires involving hundreds of poets would not match. As I rather timidly ventured into the culture of modern poetry, Conrad proved to be very like the anthropologist's *key informant,* the individual who could be relied on for empathic explanation of the terrain and authenticating mediation in relation to fellow poets. As Casagrande shrewdly describes it:

> The relationship between the anthropologist and a key informant has many of the attributes of other kinds of primary relationships: between student and teacher, employee and employer, friends or relatives—as a matter of fact, it is often assimilated to the latter. In some respects it is more closely paralleled by the relationship between the psychiatrist and his patient. There is much of the same depth and intimacy, the same desire to gain insight, in the one case into the personality and in the other into the culture as it is reflected in the personality.[3]

The happy accident of history that made our lives intersect meant that I would learn much about poets and poetry as embodied in Conrad. He was not only teacher, guide, and friend, but a generous opener of doors to other writers. Knowing him in the several guises Casagrande suggests also underlined the fact that at some point in any truly absorbing social psychological research the professional and personal tend to merge. Here I could not be analyst of creativity were I not at once friend and apprentice, willing to give (or try to give) as much as I got in a blessed reciprocity.

On a summer afternoon in the year 1949, I met the Poet in the back room of the Grolier Book Shop in Cambridge. The meeting changed my life, because the poet was Conrad Aiken; I had never before been close to a practicing artist, and I was as ready for a whelming experience as I would ever be. At twenty-four, a graduate student at Harvard, I was toughened by army years in World War II, by early marriage, financial anxiety, a young child; but I was also curiously soft and innocent, my ideas of poetry bounded by Keats's pale visage and the roustabout Sandburg of the Chicago poems. Aiken put my feet to the fire of his uncompromising honesty, immense learning, exquisite taste, and avoidance of easy words. He always, now with gentle humor, now with savage wit, brought one up short in his naivete or pseudosentiment. Although he dressed like an itinerant handyman, there wasn't a sloppy bone in his body or an empty phrase in his vocabulary. Going to school to Conrad Aiken was one of the most important things that ever happened to happen to me. Knowing him closely forever altered my consciousness, and I should like to record the pace and tang of those days.

My mentor, the brilliantly innovative psychologist Henry A. Murray, one of the founding spirits of the Harvard Psychological Clinic, had arranged for me to interview Conrad in connection with research into the workings of the creative personality. Armed with an ancient Ford station wagon, a bulky tape recorder, and a psychological test, I had an appointment to drive Conrad to his house at Brewster, on Cape Cod, where we would begin our analysis and, as it turned out, our friendship. Perhaps the first thing that struck and surprised me was his lack of pretense, his robustly commonsensical and open way of encountering the world. Short, rotund, and ruddy, he fitted perfectly his wife, Mary's nickname: "Pinky." I felt straightaway at ease and was further relaxed by the three or four bar stops we made on the relatively short trip. Drinking was to prove one of the things we did best together, and my memories of Conrad are inseparable from the companionship of the bottle. Alcohol helped us both over a natural shyness and anxiety; with his absorptive body-build and long practice, Conrad was a more imperturbable consumer than I, but in any case the drinking pattern eased and burnished our intercourse. Among the other items I learned on that first journey were that he didn't drive a car, saying it made him too nervous, and that he had a most engaging rationale for putting away enormous amounts of gin or anything else going. It was, he explained, a matter of sensitivity to stimuli, and his nerves were so thinly sheathed against the incursions of the environment that they required a generous protective coating of alcohol.

When we arrived at Brewster, I met two of the prime sources of Conrad's remarkable stability, two supports of his dogged vocation. The most important was a person, his third wife, the painter Mary Hoover Aiken. Mary was yielding, hospitable, and wryly funny; she was also a very tough and practical woman who shielded Conrad's privacy, who nursed, badgered, shared, fed, and loved him with the alert protectiveness of one convinced she had a genius on her hands. Although herself an artist of considerable achievement, Mary put Conrad's poetry first. She had no doubt whatever that he was one of the foremost writers of his time, and she was at great pains to nurture his talent. The late A.J. Liebling once divided what he called writers' consorts into two kinds: those who were angry with their husbands for being writers, and those who were angry with the world for not sufficiently rewarding their husbands' work. Mary Aiken was thoroughly of the latter variety; it is hard to see how a poet could have enjoyed a more beneficent consort.

The other source of great security in his life, I think, was the Cape Cod house to which he ever and ever returned.The Aikens named the old, gray, weathered, rambling structure "Forty-One Doors," since this was indeed the number of doors identifiable on close count. It was as comfortable and secluded a house as a man could have. Every stick and surface was old and worn; the place exuded a rare contentment and calm, the necessary prosaic but inviting setting for a mind roaming free and far. I remember that first evening, perched on a stool in the big kitchen perfectly adapted to many-houred and many-layered sessions of drinking and cooking and talking, feeling somehow taken in and accepted as a peer among wonderous people. I was taken in warmly because that was the custom at Forty-One Doors, more especially so if the guest was young. One of the roles both Mary and

Conrad assumed superbly was that of teacher; they liked young people, and although both were quite capable of pithy obiter dicta, they had the true teacher's gift of listening to their students and taking seriously what they had to say. The house was often a harbor for students, whether those on a formal, paying basis, being tutored in poetry or painting, or simply young guests whose ideas the Aikens wished to entertain. In part, I think this was, somewhat deliberately, a strategy of Conrad's for staying in touch with the life of his times. But it was never artificial, never a pose, and the poet in his sixties had the essential creative individual's talent for seeming ever youthful, ever poised against the world with a naive curiosity.

After dinner, always an immovable and lengthy feast because of Mary's fine cooking, much wine, and much talk, Conrad often settled to the piano. He played well, including pieces of his own devising. In the half-light, buoyed by a boozy intimacy, he would meander over sad, lyrical songs that were a kind of thematic analogue of his distinctive voice in poetry. There were songs of mourning and love, and perhaps love of mourning; part blues, part jazz, in their haunting melancholy they were the authentic voice of the poet who, as in his *Brownstone Eclogues,* "preferred the black keys to the white."

Or, instead of the piano, Conrad might speak some of his own word-music reading from a work in progress. His voice was soft, beautifully modulated, not quite pure Harvard or the Savannah of his boyhood or the England he so loved, but something of all three. We would sit fixed, caught and transported; he said his poems with magic, and we were properly spellbound. I recall with special pleasure the night he read a draft of his elegiac "Vogage to Spring," with its alternations of vivid hope and quiet resignation, its blending of mature acceptance and unabashed longing. This most self-conscious of men was then so entirely absorbed in making poetry that one felt no separation between reader and page. In what Conrad celebrated as "the natural magic of natural things," here was poetry speaking itself.

When, on the next morning of our first encounter, I bearded the poet in his study with my psychological test, I discovered his acute gift for characterization, his wit, his taste for gnomic expressions. The test Murray had devised was a variation of his well-known Thematic Apperception Test, known in the trade as the TAT. It was composed of a series of picture cards that presented somewhat ambiguous situations and figures; the subject was supposed to respond to these stimuli with short narratives, plots telling what the figures shown were up to. The reasoning behind all this, of course, was that in the process of making up a story the respondent would project himself into the picture and reveal a good deal about his inner life. Aiken approached the task with good humor, and if he didn't reveal a great deal about his personality he did give glimpses of his poetic philosophy. I remember particularly his comment on the rather vacant face of a pretty young girl: "Susannah is just passing through. She has no tragic sense of life. And without a tragic sense, what have you got? You ain't got nothing." Conrad had a tragic sense, had it profoundly, and it informs his finest lyrics with a palpable sadness. Thus the second of the *Preludes for Memnon*, with its almost excruciating realization of all our brevity and old mortality:

> *Two coffees in the Español, the last*
> *Bright drops of golden Barsac in a goblet,*
> *Fig paste and candied nuts.... Hardy is dead.*
> *And James and Conrad dead, and Shakespeare*
>   *dead.*
> *And Old Moore ripens for an obscene grave.*
> *And Yeats for an arid one; and I, and You—*
> *What winding sheet for us, what boards and*
>   *bricks.*
> *What mummeries, candles, prayers, and*
>   *pious frauds?*
> *You shall be lapped in Syrian scarlet, woman.*
> *And wear your pearls, and your bright*
>   *bracelets, too.*
> *Your agate ring, and round your neck shall*
>   *hung*
> *Your dark blue lapis with its specks of gold.*
> *And I, beside you—ah! but will that be?*
> *For there are dark streams in this dark world,*
>   *lady,*
> *Gulf Streams and Arctic currents of the soul;*
> *And I may be, before our consummation*
> *Beds us together, cheek by jowl, in earth,*
> *Swept to another shore, where my white bones*
> *Will lie unhonored, or defiled by gulls.*
>
> *What dignity can death bestow on us,*
> *Who kiss beneath a streetlamp, or hold hands*
> *Half hidden in a taxi, or replete*
> *With coffee, figs and Barsac make our way*
> *To a dark bedroom in a wormworn house?*
> *The aspidistra guards the door; we enter,*
> *Per aspidistra—then—ad astra—is it?—*
> *And lock ourselves securely in our gloom*
> *And loose ourselves from terror.... Here's my hand,*
> *The white scar on my thumb, and here's my*
>   *mouth*
> *To stop your murmur; speechless let us lie,*
> *And think of Hardy, Shakespeare, Yeats and*
>   *James;*
> *Comfort our panic hearts with magic names;*
> *Stare at the ceiling; where taxi lamps*

> *Make ghosts of light; and see, beyond this*
> *bed,*
> *That other bed in which we will not move;*
> *And, whether joined or separate, will not*
> *love.*

Here, we have Aiken at his poetic pitch, characteristicaly alternating between an ancient wisdom and a fresh, innocent love of love. And we have, too, the musical quality so often remarked in his poetry; this is a quality so pronounced that a young scholar recently composed an entire dissertation on the relations between Aiken's poetry and the world of music.   Like any true artist, Conrad was an extraordinarily complex and many-faceted human being. F. Scott Fitzgerald says somewhere that there can never be a satisfactory biography of a novelist, because he is too many people if he is any good. So Aiken can't be pinned down as this or that sort of person. The best one can do is describe the many sides of the man, and accept (as he would readily have accepted it in others) the fact of conflict and complementariness, concentration and extension. Has philosophy of life and art could be best summed up, as he once did, in the exhortation to "be as conscious as possible." He thought that awareness was the highest poetic virtue, and he lived in the most aware fashion he knew. This meant that all aspects of experience had value and meaning for him; he would not willingly prejudge the worth of people or things, not knowingly cut himself off from a potentially enlightening encounter with the world. Hence, in matters of taste, he relished everything from Santayana and Li Po to the comic strips and grade-B movies—and in the latter case, if there had been a grade C he would have preferred to spend his afternoons with it. He loved the Boston Red Sox and the Harvard football team; although he could be perfectly at home in a Beacon Hill drawing room, Conrad was probably more comfortable in the lowest of working-class bars, such as the old Neptune on Capitol Hill in Washington, where we passed so many hours in beer and brouhaha.

Among the polarities of his nature, one of the most striking was his harsh, uncompromising *literary* judgment—often iconoclastic, rude, terse—poised alongside his *personal* kindliness and generosity. Conrad held classic, austere canons of artistic judgment; a scanning of his collected reviews of novels and poetry suggests in retrospect how prescient his evaluations were. But if he refused to suffer foolishness gladly in print, he was unfailingly polite and even courtly in manner toward all shapes of flawed and foolish human beings. He had an old-fashioned gentility and rectitude, politely answering all mail and retaining *Esq.* on a gentleman's address. Conrad showed a keen appetite for the bawdy, as witness his outrageous limericks, and his listener could be assured of a sexual pun every few sentences; yet he was never in what one would call poor taste. He was a lover of gossip, especially about his literary peers, and the more malicious and spiteful the better. (One of his best quips involved the search for just the right word to describe a very well known poet; according to Conrad, he and T.S. Eliot considered the matter overnight and triumphantly agreed on the word at breakfast, *superfluous.*) And still, and still, he was a gentle, supportive friend who warmed one by his attention.

I think we should have to call Aiken, paradoxically, a "tough romantic." That is, his essentially romantic view of life was something he had thought and felt through. He exhibited a schooled innocence, not an untutored ignorance. He had concluded that a romantic and tragic outlook was simply the truest vision of the way things were. If, as Goethe contended, "the eternal feminine draws us along," Conrad was steadily drawn; he recurrently fell in love with pretty girls, bedded many of them, and reported these episodes with a beguiling mixture of boyish delight and worldly matter-of-factness. One of his favorite heroines, I believe, was the English girl, Gloria, who is recalled in his autobiographical memoir, *Ushant.* A girl of liberal and widely bestowed affections, she characterized herself as a *pièce de non-résistance.*

This was a poet's poet, an artist who never wanted to be or do anything else. He said that as a small boy in Savannah he read in *Tom Brown's School Days* about "The Poet of White Horse Vale," decided that this was the role for him, and never after wavered. Conrad's lifelong employment was to be aware, to be supremely conscious, to serve as a delicate antenna for the most important signals of his time and place. He taught for one year at Harvard, but confessed that facing classes was too much of a strain for such a private, anxious man. He did a fair amount of reviewing and editing, and for several years wrote the *New Yorker's* "London Letter" under the pen name of Samuel Jeake, Jr. But Conrad could readily be said never to have been regularly employed, scraping along on a small unearned income and occasional grants or gifts from friends. Henry Murray was one of his generous patrons, as I discovered on my first visit to Forty-One Doors; a subvention from Harry had been used to remodel an old bathroom, which Conrad persisted in referring to in the English fashion as the W.C. And emblazoned on the wall was the legend HENRY A. MURRAY MEMORIAL BATHROOM, followed by the lines from which I later drew the title of my book about poets, *Man Made Plain:*

> *Was this the poet? It is man.*
> *The poet is but man made plain,*
> *A glass-cased watch, through which you scan*
> *The multitudinous beat-and-pain,*
> *The feverish fine small mechanism,*
> *And hear it ticking while it sings.*
> *Behold, this delicate paroxysm*
> *Obedient to rebellious springs!*

The poem is emphatically faithful to Aiken's conception of himself, as unswervingly and inevitably the poet and as representative of all men. Malcolm Cowley describes Thomas Wolfe as *homo scribens,* obsessed with getting every scrap of remembered experience on paper. Aiken might be called the Thomas Wolfe of our poetry, dedicated and disciplined to pouring out his consciousness of a long and full life.

For several years, at the Cape, in Boston, Washington, and New York, we were great pals, Conrad and Mary, my first wife and I. But time and geography drifted us apart, and at the time of Conrad's death, in August 1973, I had not seen him for a long while. I have never gotten out from under his impress, though; he taught me a great deal about what it means to be a poet, and what it means to be a man. Alfred North Whitehead said that education is impossible except in the constant vision of greatness. I feel immensely privileged to have been close, if only for a while, to a genius of the language. Conrad was exemplary, and he caught me at just the right time for shaping. If I am not better educated, not a better reader and writer, it is only that I did not pay close enough attention.

Notes

1. Ralph Waldo Emerson, "The Poet," in *The Best of Ralph Waldo Emerson* (New York: Walter J. Black, 1941), p. 227.
2. Malcolm Cowley, *And I Worked at the Writer's Trade* (New York: Viking, 1978), p. 248.
3. Joseph B. Casagrande, *In the Company of Man* (New York: Harper & Brothers, 1960), p. xi.

6

High Culture and Popular Culture
in a Business Society

Essentially, this essay may be seen as a more general companion to the analysis of the poet in America in chapter 4. Here the discussion ranges across a variety of arts and artists as they are situated in industrial (or postindustrial) societies of today. I was quite surprised when my former student, Ivar Berg, asked me to contribute a chapter on arts and entertainments to a volume he was editing about the distinctive place of business in American society. On the face of it, the assignment appeared quite remote from my central concerns with the sociology of art or Berg's absorption in the sociology of business enterprises. Yet as I tried to explore the connections I began to see that in certain fundamental ways the one made sense of the other.

In particular, two salient thematic conflicts suggested themselves as critical to understanding the persistent incompatibility, at times frank enmity, between high culture and business life. The first centers on the contrast so acutely and poignantly identified by Max Weber: man's virtuosity in means/ends problem solving, the pervasive "functional rationality" of high technology and double-entry bookkeeping, poised against that intimation of mystery and enchantment, that wonderful (full of wonder) characteristic of fine art. So we find the ordained rationalizaton of life colliding with the high culture that resists rationalizaton. (Not so incidentally, popular culture may be more comfortably attuned to rationalization, hence to business values, as seen for example in formula movie and television plotting). The second conflict is that of leisure versus nonleisure, whether the latter be construed as "work" or random "free time." We must ask, I think, whether a business society is *inherently* unleisurely, as Clement Greenberg avers, and in this sense intrinsically inhospitable to high culture. My extended analysis of leisure in relation to art and creativity (in chapter 8, "The Courage to Be Leisured") is in part a further development of these issues. It seems clear that high culture is inseparable from some ideal of leisureliness which may be difficult to achieve in a country dominated by a business ethos, and that popular culture, in the main, invites and is invited by a trivialization of leisure into quasi-empty free time.

In the sixteen years since this chapter was first published, several of the trends then perceived have become importantly accentuated. The volume of popular culture has increased enormously, but probably without a corresponding increase in variety. There is much more television programming, but unfortunately it also seems much more homogeneous. The publishing industry has become ever more concentrated on best-selling items such as diet books and romance novels. In these and other ways, there is evidence that popular culture and mediocre art are overwhelming. Yet there is evidence too that high culture flourishes in the United States as never before. Whether it be museums or symphonies, little magazines or modern dance companies, the fine arts show an encouraging vitality. Further, the support of the arts by business firms and government is increasingly generous: consider only the bank foyers lined with modern paintings, the rise of the arts council as local catalyst, the welter of people and activities subsidized by the National Endowment for the Arts and the National Endowment for the Humanities. The picture continues to be mixed and ambiguous, but on the whole promising for the healthy coexistence of high and popular culture.

Artists and intellectuals became acutely vulnerable to pressures from the commercial nexus in eighteenth-century England. Greatly heightened levels of literacy in the population, joined with cheaper techniques of printing and distribution, exposed the purveyors of high culture to a market situation.[1] England in the Industrial Revolution can perhaps be taken as a precursor of what we should today term a business society. Manufacturing, trade, and finance began to create an economic climate that affected all who worked in the arts—or in anything else. Of equal or larger significance, these activities were linked to political and religious themes to foster a climate of values sustaining the acquisitive thrust of a business society.

The shift from an economic base of aristocratic and other patronage to an increasingly open popular marketplace for art could be construed both as a favorable omen and as threatening exposure from the artist's point of view. It began to give him independence from the vagaries of whimsical patrons, making him more nearly his own man. Too, the expanded market offered a potential mass audience that could afford him a comfortable—and in rare cases a handsome—income from the sale of his creations. At the same time, the writer or artist became willy-nilly an entrepreneur, confronted by the iron dictates of popular taste; often an amateur, not to say naive, business-man, he was in many instances a ready victim of the manipulative printer or merchant. This was one meaning of London's Grub Street, the residence of poor writers so often mentioned in English literature; raw exploitation of the writer or would-be writer, whose literary skill often exceeded his talent for dealing with the exigencies of a developing business system.

The Discrepancy between Business and Aesthetic Values

Very early in the development of business societies in western Europe, artists and devotees of high culture began to enunciate a state of warfare between what they perceived to be the values of businessmen and the values of an aesthetic elite. Artists and intellectuals, being professionally articulate, were able to frame the terms of warfare and preempt the field of expression; businessmen and government officials, if they reacted at all,

waged the battle by obdurate inattention rather than by aggressive perse-
cution of the artist. Although the artist objected then, and objects now, to
many tangible features of a business system—the accumulation of material
goods, the focus on money as a measure of a person and his works, the
rigorous efficiency of factory discipline, the single-minded stress on a
narrow route to achievement—it is probably true that the fundamental
argument was and is with the abstract structure of values that underlies the
business society as the artist has experienced it. Thus Stendhal wrote, "Far
be it from me to conclude that industrialists are not honorable. All I mean is
that they are not heroic."

And César Graña, describing Baudelaire, poignantly expressed what the
artist asserts against the business system: "a retention of the uncontrollable
in human affairs and the philosophical anxiety and aesthetic intrigue of the
world." Surely a taste for philosophical anxiety and aesthetic intrigue is
quite far from the concerns of most members of a business society (or
perhaps any society). Baudelaire at one pole, and, say, Dickens' Gradgrind
or Defoe's Crusoe at the other seemingly have little to say to one another.
What, then, is the nature of the discrepancy in values between an aesthetic
dandy and a successful maufacturer?

A clue to one aspect of the discrepancy is in Stendhal's complaint that
industrialists are "not heroic." By this he means that they are calculating,
not that they are cowardly. Business activity rewards the individual who can
operate in a rational, foresighted, utilitarian manner, who puruses discrete
goals and husbands resources in a mode of disciplined efficiency. The
businessman dreams realizable dreams. To the Romantic artist, especially,
this apparently unexceptionable pattern of behavior is gross, demeaning,
grubbily undignified. The Romantic calls for a nonutilitarian orientation, a
gratuitous release of human resources, the quest for the unattainable.
Discipline derives from the exigencies of the tragic muse, not from the
factory clock or the margin of profit. The artist is inclined to prefer the
lifelong aesthetic gamble, the staking of the self against immense odds of
existence and creation, to the calculated risk of bringing off a commercial
venture.

Another facet of the separation between artist and industrial man concerns their conceptualization of experience. The difference in ways of
seeing and talking is at least partly rooted in the existence of two fundamental patterns of communication, which Suzanne Langer has described
as the *discursive* and *presentational* models. In discursive language—that of
prose—words and images point to discrete aspects of experience; they tell
someone about something in the fashion of logical pointing. In presentational language—that of poetry and the arts—the symbolic vehicles are
directed to recreating in the recipient an impression of a slice of life rather
than to making statements or propositions. Discursive language compart-
mentalizes life, deals with it in parcels that can be wrapped and labeled;

presentational language expresses and stimulates the rich whole of seamless experiencing at many levels of apprehension. High culture most nearly approaches the use of presentational language, while business must clearly be conducted in discursive terms.

At bottom, the differences in value are almost certainly matters of that indefinable property called style. When Sinclair Lewis jeers, in the opening sentences of *Main Street,* at the Ford cars and other small-town artifacts for which "Erasmus wrote in Oxford cloisters," he expresses a deep disappointment with plain American business style and a hunger for the grandeur of some alternative.

If the practitioners and audiences of high culture feel a disaffection, indeed a sharp enmity, for business society, what may be said of those dedicated to popular culture? Here, it seems, the polarization is a good deal less extreme. Popular culture is by definition closer to the dominant values and common tastes of the society in which it occurs; it is popular, in part, precisely because it is comfortable. The books, films, and drama of popular culture take advantage of business society in that they are supported by its affluence and its scheme of values. In turn, they tend to exalt those ideas, emotions, and customs that ensure a viable motivational base for the industrial-commerical enterprise. Popular culture is to a profound extent the creature of a business society, especially in its close connection to the ends and means of advertising. Indeed, we may find that one of the most important distinctions between high and popular culture is that popular culture accepts business values and exhorts its audience to do likewise, while high culture severely questions those values and easy assumptions.

What Is a Business Society?

A major hazard to sensible discussion about the roles of artists and art in society has been the lack of precision in defining just what kind of art and what kind of society are in question. The serious poet or painter or composer, for instance, is probably always in some sense at odds with society. Their activity is rare and singular; they work alone; they assess those perceptions and evaluations that most people around them take for granted (and perhaps *must* take for granted) in the conduct of their daily affairs. Similarly, popular artists are presumably always in tune with whatever version of social order surrounds them. They reaffirm its key tenets, do not interrogate its foibles too extensively, caress the surface of life as it is usually lived. They may probe the cracks in the facade of social consensus, but they are not likely to batter at its foundations.

Having generalized so boldly, I must try to specify what artists behave how in what sorts of societies. In the present context the burden is to characterize *business society, high culture,* and *popular culture* before much progress can be made in analyzing their relationships. By a business society, I mean the societies of western Europe, the United States, and Canada, those social structures marked by representative government, democratic polity, a more-or-less free economy in which entrepreneurial striving is prominent, and a developed industrial-commercial pattern. The business society is in this sense to be distinguished from industrial countries that do not have a strong entrepreneurial tradition or a relatively free marketplace (the USSR being the type-case) and from the so-called developing or underdeveloped societies. The primary referent of a business society is the contemporary United States.

Although a description of the United States in these terms could be a very elaborate essay, I shall confine my remarks to three major themes that are particularly relevant to the position of the artist and the processes of the arts. These are the primacy of the business calling, the organization of business enterprise, and the motivations and styles that accompany this calling and this form of organized effort.

We hear often today of Americans' disenchantment with business occupations and with the cluster of values centering on achievement of profit. Only a minority of college seniors frankly aspires to a business career. Public opinion polls show large percentages of the population to be skeptical about business ethics and the truth of advertisement and to question the contribution of business to the common good. Nevertheless, both the total distribution of vocations and the values demonstrated in everyday life leave slight doubt that Calvin Coolidge's words are as accurate now as when he spoke them in the twenties: the business of America *is* business. Our heralded affluence is as much the product of business values as of natural abundance, and that affluence in turn reinforces the rightness of energetic striving for gain. No matter that most people work for salary rather than for profit, in offices rather than stock exchanges, what is important is the way they work and the promises for which they work. The way they work is dutifully, in the veritable spirit of the Protestant Ethic; the promises for which they work are a combination of material plenty and that self-validation Max Weber traced from its religious origins.

With the exception of two professions—medicine and law—business occupations are perhaps the only ones in our society that usually require no explanation: no apology, rationalization, or explication is called for. In a country without an aristocratic tradition exalting leisure and amateurism, the businessman could become—as he has—the natural aristocrat. Linked to this ready acceptance of business callings as inherently right and appropriate to the masculine role, we find the most obvious measure of their primacy in the money economy. Business roles are rewarded in the marketplace on a scale that far exceeds the compensation for any other occupational category; it is a commonplace, for instance, that men at the very highest levels of government triple or quadruple their salaries if they move into the business sector.

If business occupations indeed constitute the primary model for occupational life, so the patterns of organized effort in business pursuits are models for understanding the organization of work throughout the society. Work relationships in a business organization are fundamentally bureaucratic in type, distinguished by specialization, interlocking functions, discrete formulation of goals and definition of means, hierarchy of authority, and rational accountability of effort. Accompanying and enforcing these themes is a conception of technical expertness—exemplified by the engineer, the accountant, the machinist—resting on trained capacity for specified work performances. The calculability of effort directed toward scheduled achievements is a pervasive characteristic of business enterprise; it is one very important mode of what Max Weber foresaw as the rationalization of life, the disenchantment of the world. Above all, contemporary business implies membership in a bureaucratic structure and adherence to bureaucratic norms. It enjoins a coordinated network of relationships to fellow members, the kind of intensive involvement and allegiance entailed in the vulgar designation "organization man."

Business callings and business institutions are underpinned by a distinctive American motivational complex that stresses the need for achievement, for the approval of one's peers, for the validation of self in tangible outcomes of striving. Although these motives are obviously not unique to the business society, they seem here to be peculiarly intense; what is crucial is not the desire for achievement itself but the zealous nature of the pursuit, the concentration on external criteria of individual worth, the calculated employment of human resources. Complementing these motivational springs of business effort is a style of life marked by activism, dutifulness, and the careful pacing of behavior toward a deferred reward. Considerations of functional efficacy are assumed to dominate the enterprise, so that we ordinarily ask, not "What kind of person is he?" but, "What can he *do?*"

What Are High Culture and Popular Culture?

It is patently impossible to attain perfect agreement about the boundaries of the two versions of cultural life with which we are concerned. We must at once note that our use of the term culture is narrower and more in keeping with common usage than with the anthropologists's concept. That is, we are confined to the intellectual-artistic sector of man's social heritage and patterned contemporary behavior and neglect the total range of styled choices that makes up the "culture" of a human group. Culture in our sense is connoted by those vehicles that are conserved, created, and transmitted to entertain and instruct through the imaginative representation of life. It embraces the arts, broadly construed to include novels, dramas, poems, paintings, sculpture, the dance, and music. It occurs in the traditional media—the book or performance—and the newer mass channels of television, movies, radio, magazines, and newspapers.

At their extremes, high and popular culture are relatively easy to distinguish. High or fine culture seriously aspires to comparison with the winnowed excellence of the past, with the few preserved exemplary works in the artistic and critical heritage. Popular culture, variously termed *mass* or *mediocre,* aspires only to contemporary acceptance by large audiences, is designed almost wholly for amusement, and is governed by no canons more rigorous than the producer's guess at what will stimulate an easy enjoyment. High culture is demanding and asks of its audience an imaginative participation, a deep and alert responsiveness along a spectrum of sensibility. Popular culture is undemanding, requires of its audience minimal attentiveness, and is satisfied with superficial responsiveness often limited to liking or disliking. But given these polar cases, we confront a fairly wide middle area of ambiguity. There would presumably be little dispute with the classification of, say, Picasso or T.S. Eliot as practitioners of high culture or the author of a television situation comedy as a promoter of popular culture. There is, however, that penumbra often designated as *middlebrow* or *kitsch* that seemingly aspires simultaneously to fastidious critical acceptance and mass response. Works and artists that do not fall clearly at either extreme inspire passionate debate among observers, who feel that a division is crucial and must be rigidly maintained.

Devotees of high culture are given to despair about the state of the arts. They are inclined to argue that a mass business society inevitably imposes a sort of aesthetic Gresham's Law, in which bad art drives out good. The good, at any rate, is taken to be the enemy of the best; a combination of business values and the proficiency of the mass media lends to this enemy an overwhelming advantage. Thus the great variety and bulk of popular culture are assumed to drown out the lonely but elegant voice of high culture.

There are other apostles of high culture, however, of whom Edward Shils[2] is an example, who maintain that a pluralistic society can fittingly sustain varied levels of culture. They contend that popular culture is not by definition "bad" in total and that a business society is not inherently inimical to the creation and appreciation of works of high culture. We might conclude that a pessimistic view is poised in fatiguing and apparently limitless debate against an optimistic one. As César Graña once observed in analyzing the pessimist: "The open industrial society can produce neither a social structure nor a set of cultural images to which a certain kind of intellectual can pay homage." Shils, and writers such as David White or Gilbert Seldes, adopt an optimistic stance. They do not exalt popular culture, nor do they proclaim the business society as a champion of high culture. Rather, they note that this society *allows* for high culture and that it is up to sensitive creators and critics to show an energetic persistence in their callings.

We have, then, a series of questions, often too sharply posed. Can high culture coexist with a business society? Are both high and popular culture so pervaded by the values and styles of a mass industrial social system that art has forever lost its noble autonomy? Such angular alternatives, and their issue in a vivid rhetoric of all-or-nothing, must probably give way to more intricate problems and tentative solutions under sober examination. We shall try to inquire into the complex of relationships among American business society, its arts, artists, and audiences.

Direct Articulation of Business with High and Popular Culture

The most obvious, if not really the simplest, relationship between business and the arts is strictly economic. In a money economy where business generates the money, both high and popular culture are dependent on business for essential support. Business is the patron of the fine arts and the acknowledged master of the popular arts. Surpluses from business activity, the basis of our affluence, pay the bills for the enterprises of high culture; these monies foster university and foundation—and now government—provisions for subsidies of artists and their works. Business fortunes and, increasingly, business salaries, go to buy paintings, to subscribe to symphonies, and to commission architecture and sculpture.

Popular culture is in great measure not so much the creature of business surplus as it is an integral part of expenditure in business institutions. Advertising is of course the primary route for this expenditure, and the products of popular culture are intimately attached to business because their media (television, radio, magazines) exist on business support. The historian David M. Potter describes advertising as the characteristic institution of an abundant society (the United States) and remarks on how little we know about this institution:

> But advertising as an institution has suffered almost total neglect. One might read fairly widely in the literature which treats of public opinion, popular culture, and the mass media in the United States without ever learning that advertising now compares with such long-standing institutions as the school and the church in the magnitude of its social influence. It dominates the media, it has vast power in the shaping of popular standards, and it is really one of the very limited group of institutions which exercise social control. Yet analysts of society have largely ignored it.[3]

And with reference to the context in which the popular artist functions:

> It is as impossible to understand a modern popular writer without under-
> standing advertising as it would be to understand a medieval troubadour
> without understanding the cult of chivalry,or a nineteenth-century revival-
> ist without understanding evangelical religion.[4]

Potter goes on to rehearse the basic argument advanced by many observers in recent years concerning the connection of media content to the desiderata of advertising. Popular culture, in this view, is constrained always by the businessman's understandable desire to reach the widest possible audience for his wares; the larger the audience, the more likely it is that a lowest common denominator of taste and subject matter will prevail. Thus popular art cannot shock, cannot be profound, cannot demand too much of its audience, and cannot treat matters that interest only a minority of readers, viewers, or listeners. In the words of an English critic quoted by Potter, American periodical writing "fixes the attention but does not engage the mind." And, contends Potter, this is exactly what the advertiser who supports the popular arts wants: to hold the audience without so stimulating or involving it that attention is seriously diverted from the accompanying commercial message.

Against this gloomy appraisal of the possibilities for popular culture there stand at least some significant examples of business support for works of popular excellence. Our business society has occasionally made fine drama available on televison, has widely distributed many good books (the paperback revolution in publishing), and has generated the techniques of reproduction and distribution that make prints of good paintings accessible to the meanest wall space. Two questions may be raised about the mass dissemination of excellence, involving respectively the identities of the creator and the audience. The first reservation notes the propensity of purveyors, in a commercial climate, to bet on sure things; certifiable works of high culture from the past are preferred to the ambitious efforts of contemporaries. Thus we may receive Shaw or Sophocles on television infrequently but Samuel Beckett almost never. Publishers are willing to risk bringing out a large cheap edition of Wordsworth (aided by the fact that his works are in the public domain), but the works of modern poets such as Ezra Pound or William Carlos Williams are much higher priced.

The second question really asks whether the nature of the aesthetic transaction, the interplay between the artist and audience, is transformed by number, distance, or the perceptual set of respondents. Is Shakespeare-in-the-Park still Shakespeare? Is Homer less than or different from Homer if his verse is on sale in thousands of drugstores? Those who yearn for an elite audience whose sophistication matches the quality of the work of art are perhaps at one with Kingsley Amis in his contention about expanding university enrollments: more is worse. Yet we cannot be very sure—was the tiny audience of the past in uniformly deep communion with the artist's highest intentions? Is the mass audience of the present so inattentive or obtuse as to destroy the aesthetic relationship? How can the value of many people enjoying a poem at a certain, perhaps superficial, level of receptivity be weighed against the value of a precious few responding with a full engagement of their perceptual resources?

Direct articulation of business society with high and popular culture clearly entails more than the content of the arts and the character of the audience. Conspicuously, it involves the economic position of those who create. Business values and organizational genius insure that the successful practitioner of popular culture will be handsomely rewarded. Never in history has the really popular writer, for instance, found the craft more lucrative. Dickens, or even Scott Fitzgerald, looks like a marginal literary sharecropper when compared with Harold Robbins or Irving Wallace or any regularly employed screenwriter. In Hollywood, on Broadway, and in publishing the economics of a mass business society offers an enormous jackpot to lucky winners. The support given artists tends, however, to be unevenly distributed and wildly oscillating in amount; a few are highly compensated, many are rewarded sporadically and modestly, many do not survive.

Creators of high culture stand in a peculiarly ambiguous position. Their art is not economically feasible in a business society; with very few exceptions painters, poets, or composers do not earn their way in the marketplace. It may well be argued that the fine arts have never been able to pay their own way and that the phenomenon specific to our society is not the fact of subsidy but merely a change in its sources. For church, state, or municipality, substitute universities, foundations, or business institutions themselves. An affluent business society probably offers more, and move varied, kinds of support for the serious artist than does any other social arrangement. Yet this economic flooring is not always granted to the artist as artist; it tends to come in the form of the second job, the paying employment of the artist as teacher, editor, professional, or businessman— or even producer of popular culture. If the second job is avowedly noncreative and substantially different from the task of art, its demands obviously divert the artist from investing anything like full time and energy in the artistic vocation. (However, some artists—notably the insuranceman-poet Wallace Stevens and the physician-poet William Carlos Williams—have asserted that the running of careers in tandem is psychologically satisfying.) In general, second jobs that are close to the artistic endeavor but not identical with it, such as teaching and editing, appear most congenial to the continued generation of products of high culture.

The serious artist as intermittent producer of popular culture presents a very interesting case. A poet and university don who writes mystery novels

(C. Day Lewis), a social historian who did the same (Bernard DeVoto), the many novelists who work on film scripts—each of these may handle his money-making chore with aplomb, indeed with relish. On the other hand, some critics maintain that the rewarding opportunities afforded by popular culture are likely to seduce artists, consuming their spirits with trivia. Ezra Pound, for instance, argued many years ago that the poet must be subsidized or else his art will suffer from the blandishments of the popular media:

> Villon is the stock example of those who advocate the starvation of artists, but the crux is here, to wit, that Villon had nothing whatsoever to gain by producing a bastard art. No harpies besought him for smooth optimism, for partriotic sentiment, and for poems "to suit the taste" of our readers. If he had nothing to lose by one sort of writing he had equally little to gain by any other.[5]

There is little evidence, however, that artists must inevitably be corrupted if they make excursions into the popular. We do not know that Fitzgerald or Faulkner was inferior as a novelist to what he might have been had he never served time in Hollywod; Richard Eberhart is not demonstrably a less able poet for the fact that his verse has appeared in a ladies' magazine of astronomical circulation. Perhaps the puristic critic underrates the artist's versatility as craftsman, his ability to work alternately at more then one level and for more than one audience.

Indirect Implications of Business for High and Popular Culture

It is tempting to suggest that the business society entirely determines the course of culture. Commercial-industrial-technological values are pervasive; the artist grows up in this climate, and is accordingly surrounded (some might say bombarded) at every turn by the sights and sounds, the assumptions and proclamations of business. Yet to regard this as the whole story would be to commit outselves to a species of vulgar Marxist determinism. For the creator does just that: creates. Artists envision possibilities and wrench perceptions in ways that neither their families nor their class can predict. The root meaning of creativity is that the artist will make, will invent something fresh. Who can say that the business society that influenced the authors of *Babbitt* and *Death of a Salesman* has not been equally influenced by those works, driven to examine its premises and its manners? The industrial climate that produced an Andrew Wyeth, a Martha Graham, a Richard Lippold, or an Alexander Calder, even a Gertrude Stein, has been in turn affected by those innovators.

Furthermore, the artist emphatically does not respond merely to contemporary circumstances. The autonomy of art is grounded in its having a tradition, a series of products and evaluations that transcends particular times and places. In the republic of art are many mansions, and it is to these, as well as to the everyday environment, that any given artist owes his or her stimulus and allegiance. We must then admit that although modern poets are undeniably influenced by business, they are shaped as much or more by, say, classic Chinese poetry or the rhythms of Gerard Manley Hopkins. The living presence of a tradition, of the forms and themes that are the vesssels for an artist's insight, points to a further aspect of independence in the universe of high culture: this is culture's capability of changing from within. As several social theorists, notably Sorokin and A.L. Kroeber, have maintained, the sophisticated patterns of high culture are distinguished by a potential for immanent change. What Kroeber termed "pattern fulfillment," the unfolding of art and science according to an internal logic of structural development, should make us wary of attributing the paths of artistic culture solely to the flux of its institutional environment.

There are, however, at least two ways in which a business society holds crucial indirect implications for high and popular culture. The first is the impact of business on the content of the arts themselves; the second is the influence of a business atmosphere on the people involved, on artistic career lines, aesthetic sensibility, and the audience's responsive capacity.

We have earlier remarked on the stock argument that advertising pushes the popular media toward the bland and the superficial. There seems little doubt that this is in general true. Advertisers are cautious about disturbing their public, and an art that does not disturb can scarcely be a vital experience. We may ask, however, how far the drive toward a comfortable and stereotyped popular culture is specific to business as such; it may always accompany a mass society, that is, a society marked by widespread literacy, interdependence, centralization, and shared awareness. Thus, although the United States is surely more nearly the prototype of a business society than is Britain, critics of recent shifts in popular culture in the two countries make quite similar analyses. For example, in the United States the critic S.I. Hayakawa has compared the leading themes of our blues and of popular music; he notes how much more closely the former hew to the facts of life, how much greater is their bite and pungency. But after indicting the lyrics of Tin Pan Alley as sugary unrealism, he notes a trend:

> The existence of the blues demonstrates that it is at least possible for songs to be both reasonably healthy in psychological content and widely sung and enjoyed. But the blues cannot, of course, take over the entire domain of popular song because, as widely known as some of them have been, their chief appeal, for cultural reasons, has been to Negro audiences—and even these audiences have been diminishing with the progressive advancement of Negroes and their assimilation of values and tastes in common with the white, middle-class majority.[6]

Paralleling this nostalgia for the integrity of a minority version of popular culture, Richard Hoggart writes of commercial dominance in British society as destructive of an older working-class culture:

> Inhibited now from ensuring the "degradation" of the masses economically, the logical processes of competitive commerce, favoured from without by the whole climate of the time and from within assisted by the lack of direction, the doubts and uncertainty before their freedom of working-people themselves (and maintained as much by ex-working-class writers as by others) are ensuring that working-people are culturally robbed. Since these processes can never rest, the holding down, the constant pressure not to look outwards and upwards, becomes a positive thing, becomes a new and stronger form of subjection; this subjection promises to be stronger than the old because the chains of cultural subordination are both easier to wear and harder to strike away than those of economic subordination.[7]

If the "chains of cultural subordination" are worn by the mass audience for popular culture, it must also be remembered that the business dollars forging the chains sometimes supply countervailing forces. Business has on occasion supported the dissemination of such contrary content, to use only the example of television, as *Death of a Salesman*, "This Was the Week That Was" (a satirical review of current affairs), and certain excellent presentations of "Playhouse 90."

Overt business themes tend to be almost entirely absent from high culture; serious artists have rarely dealt with business in any direct fashion. In the popular media, representations of businessmen and business life seem to be polarized. Business is portrayed either as a dramatic jungle, corrupt and corrupting (*Executive Suite*) or as a nonproblematic source of lifestyle (father's occupation in any situation comedy). Perhaps business is mainly a steady hum in the background, an unquestioned framework for the minutiae of domestic concerns. Certainly it does not engage the attention as a milieu for dramatic action, in the way statecraft and kingly plot did for Shakespeare or Sophocles, war for the Greek poets, knightly romance for the medieval singer.

Business Values and Artistic Careers

Artistic careers in high culture are almost diametrically opposed to the career lines favored by a business model. It might be said that the artist's fabled "deviance" in American society begins exactly in his not being a businessman. Why should his career be suspect and marginal? Perhaps in the first instance its difference inheres in its not being in the usual sense a career at all; training is haphazard, certification is virtually nonexistent, reward is capricious, the location and stated hours for work are not given but personally chosen, the criteria for evaluation of artistic competence are amorphous and notoriously unstable in the short run. Practitioners of high culture (and to a considerable extent the producers of popular culture as well) are far closer in spirit to the nineteenth-century business entrepreneur than they are to the bureaucratic business or professional man of today. Artists typically work in solitude and are therefore not heavily enmeshed in coordinated relations to others. Their roles are diffuse and wide-ranging, not narrowly contrived to fulfill a very specific function; everything human and natural *is* somehow a part of the frame of action. The life of the emotions is a integral part of their work, not an intrusion to be tightly disciplined during the performance of a task. Writers or painters must renew themselves daily in the battle to be creative, and this absorption may entail a conception of time different from that of most members of an industrial society. They are concerned with the immediacy of creative effort and the eternity of aesthetic judgment, not with the balance sheet of next week or the promotion of next month.

And indeed the study of artistic careers in the contemporary United States provides evidence that entry into the artistic role is difficult and that persistence in the role requires a hardy spirit. Neophytes are harassed both by the intrinsic difficulty of attaining competence and by the pressures interested parties exert to push them toward a business style. Mature artists probably suffer most from economic instability, an instability that is a direct consequence of nonmembership in the organizational nets within which most of their fellows work. But they are not immune from the knowledge that most people in their society regard their work as remote, possibly frivolous, and—in the case of men—in an important sense unmasculine. The roots of the suspicion that male artists are not wholly male are several: the traditional allocation of aesthetic interests to women in America; the seemingly high, and highly visible, numbers of homosexuals in certain arts (for instance, the dance); and the presence of a sensuous "feminine" component in art that is inhibited by the strictly male discipline of the business occupations.[8]

If business careers and artistic careers are so baldly discrepant, it is likewise no secret that the prevailing values of a business society offend the aesthetic sensibility. Science, technology, commerce, mass prosperity, the riotous profusion of things and services—all those seem to be inseparable from a style of rational and optimistic calculation. A well-ordered life, a planned life, an existence free from accident and marked by a cautious control over ends and means—the explicit goal of a middle-class business credo—appears as a living death to the majority voice in modern letters. Graña states the case succinctly:

> The prudence and prudery of the middle classes may look with horror upon lust, waste, irresponsibility, superstition, and violence, and middle-class

"reform" may seek to eradicate them from society as a whole. But for the literary imagination these traits are often the companions of amusement, charm, grace, courage, and the daily predicament of human triumph and failure and, within failure, survival, a spectacle always reassuring to those bored with the hygienic and relentless optimism of the present age.[9]

The Protestant Ethical spirit, the rationalization of life, and the organization of work according to bureaucratic modes all militate against any ready acceptance of business society by those who create works of high culture. Artists are at once more playful and more serious than the business style can countenance. They are more playful, not in the sense of unbridled hedonism or trivial pleasure seeking, but in their experimental and flexible posture toward the problems of life's meanings. They are more serious not in a tense sobriety, but rather more in a capacity to savor the bloody angles of existence and to accept the tragic mode as a real part of human affairs.

Business Values and the Audience

Opinions about the influence of a business society on the audience for the arts differ sharply. Some observers feel that the open industrial system, with its affluence and communicative élan, provides a varied opportunity for the wide consumption of both high and popular arts. Others are equally convinced that the milieu of business values is antithetical to true sensibility and alert responsiveness. To a considerable extent, these differing views revolve around the old question of whether "bad" culture drives out "good," whether the flood of popular products dulls the senses and steals the time of the cultural consumer.

A species of cultural double-play is postulated by many critics: business supports popular culture, which in turn diverts the potential audience from attending to high art. Indeed, there is rather convincing research evidence that audiences of all sorts do spend a great deal of time responding to the mass media of popular culture, notably television. What is especially interesting about this research is the general homogeneity of habits among people of widely differing educational and occupational levels. Steiner, for example, discovered that those of high educational attainment—those, presumably, who would be most likely to renounce the seductions of popular culture for the rarer delights of high culture—actually exhibited viewing patterns quite similar to their fellows in American society at large. He concluded that "the program mix of different educational groups is strikingly constant..."[10] Wilensky states:

> There is little doubt from my data as well as others' that educated strata—even products of graduate and professional schools—are becoming full participants in mass culture; they spend a reduced fraction of time in exposure to quality print and film. This trend extends to the professors,

> writers, artists, scientists—the keepers of high culture themselves—and the
> chief culprit, again, is TV.[11]

And again:

> Uniformity of behavior and taste is the main story. Nowhere else has a
> "class" audience been so swiftly transformed into a "mass" audience.[12]

Shils argues that the intellectuals have nobody to blame but themselves
for this state of affairs. That is, devotees of high culture allow that culture to
erode by their inattention and sloth; no one is forcing the arts to disappear
from the mass business society. Contrarily, Clement Greenberg believes that
the nature of an industrial system is such that consumers are compelled to
relax away from the job and are unable to muster the energy that response to
fine art demands. A business society, he contends, not only offers a diet of
popular culture but trains and strains its members away from the kind of
alertness required to apprehend products of high culture:

> To the exact end of greater productivity, capitalism, Protestantism, and
> industrialism have brought about a separation of work from all that is not
> work which is infinitely sharper and more exclusive than ever in the past.
> And as work has become more concentratedly and actively work—that is,
> more strictly controlled by its purposes, more efficient—it has pushed
> leisure out of the foreground of life and turned it into the negative instead of
> positive complement of itself. Work may be less arduous physically than it
> used to be, but its present standards of efficiency require one to key oneself
> to a higher pitch of nervous and mental effort, if only for the sake of the
> self-control and self-denial required by any kind of sustained activity
> directed solely toward an end outside itself. Leisure, in compensation, has
> become much more emphatically the occasion for flight from all purpose-
> fulness, for rest, respite, and recuperation. It is certainly no longer the
> sphere par excellence of realization, but a passive state, primarily, in which
> one's least passive need is for distraction and vicarious experience that will
> give those immediate satisfactions denied one during working hours by the
> constraint of efficiency. This in itself is a valid need, but when one's nerves
> insist that it be met with a minimum of mental exertion on one's own part
> only a base kind of culture can satisfy it, a kind of culture that has lost all
> efficacy as recreation (in the literal sense) and become entirely a matter of
> rudimentary entertainment and diversion—of the sort, exactly, that we see
> in lowbrow and much of middlebrow culture.[13]

What can we suggest to answer, or alleviate, Greenberg's persuasive
indictment? In a business society, after all, business and culture are indissolubly wedded. Must business, despite its overt financial support for high
and popular culture, inevitably debilitate the audience?

The United States as a business society has often been described as
pluralistic: it is marked by a great variety of values, lifestyles, occupations,
material goods, and cultural forms. Although empirical findings indicate

astonishing uniformity in television viewing, perhaps the total range of cultural response is more complex and diverse. Books, magazines, films, and other media afford immense opportunity for the satisfaction of more specialized tastes. As Wilbert E. Moore has averred:

> The very mass production that yields uniformity in some goods also yields the possibility of substantial variability in the combinations that particular consuming units may choose to put together.[14]

If cultural products are plural, we might ask whether the patterns of allegiance to the business style in occupational striving and discipline are not also plural. Is Greenberg's picture too sweeping, and can some considerable sectors of the audience retain or recapture the zest for high culture? There are at least some indications that a very rich business society may provide both the economic surplus for supporting artists and the leisure surplus for supporting audience receptivity. As the true revolution in production and information control that is commonly termed automation takes hold, it is conceivable that most members of the population will not only work fewer hours but will begin to cultivate a different attitude toward work and leisure. Enhanced leisure opportunities *may* lead people to reexamine life's meanings in a way that increases their potential interest in high culture. We cannot even dismiss the notion that our educational system may direct certain energies toward education for an informed and perceptive enjoyment of leisure.

Surely many of the relationships we have described between a business society and its various arts would apply to other types of society as well. Notably, much that pertains to the position of the mass media, the disciplines of industrial work, and the bureaucratic organization of effort would fit almost equally well the case of a nonbusiness but large-scale industrial system, such as the Soviet system has now become and the system China is striving to create. Yet the presence of advertising, of a democratic polity and pluralism, of venture capital for the arts, and of certain types of artistic freedom probably will continue for some time to distinguish the business society of the modern West from other mass industrial complexes.

Conclusion

We may conclude that the United States enhances the vitality of high and popular culture by providing economic abundance, widespread leisure, pluralistic values in which the arts can find a place, and an open forum for expressive variety. As a business society, America hampers the arts by its dedication to occupational efficiency and organization, its exaltation of the style of business callings, its insistence on profit as a measure of efficacy, and its assignment of recreation to the sphere of the trivial. On balance, it seems undeniable that the opportunities for the artist are as rich as they have ever been. The possibility of creating an audience of talented perceivers also appears great, given the foundation of very much expanded education and lesiure. And we must never forget the stubborn element of autonomy in aesthetic pattern and artistic creativity: art and artist are not utterly formed by a business, or any other, society. A fitting note of optimism is struck by the distinguished biologist, Theodosius Dobzhansky:

> The variety of human genotypes, and hence of inclinations and abilities, is increased, not decreased, by hybridization. I suppose the same is true on the cultural level also. A large and complex society should be better able to provide for specialized talent and to tolerate unconformity than a small homogeneous group. I, for one, do not lament the passing of social organizations that used the many as a manured soil in which to grow a few graceful flowers of refined culture.[15]

Notes

1. A particularly astute and well-documented account of this transformation appears in Leo Lowenthal, *Literature, Popular Culture and Society* (Englewood Cliffs, N.J.: Prentice-Hall, 1961).
2. See "The High Culture of the Age," in *The Arts in Society,* ed. Robert N. Wilson (Englewood Cliffs, N.J.: Prentice-Hall, 1964).
3. David M. Potter, *People of Plenty* (Chicago, Ill.: University of Chicago Press, 1954), p. 167.
4. Ibid., p. 168.
5. Ezra Pound, *Patria Mia* (Chicago, Ill.: Ralph Fletcher Seymour, 1950), p. 97.
6. S.I. Hayakawa, "Popular Songs vs. the Facts of Life," in *Mass Culture,* ed. Bernard Rosenberg and David Manning White (New York: Free Press, 1957), p. 401.
7. Richard Hoggart, *The Uses of Literacy* (Boston: Beacon Press, 1961), pp. 200–201.
8. Wilson, chapters 1–4.
9. César Graña, *Bohemian versus Bourgeois* (New York: Basic Books, 1964), p. 207.
10. Gary A. Steiner, *The People Look at Television* (New York: Knopf, 1963), p. 168.
11. Harold L. Wilensky, "Mass Society and Mass Culture: Interdependence or Independence," *American Sociological Review* 29 (April 1964): 190.
12. Ibid., p. 191.
13. Clement Greenberg, "Work and Leisure under Industrialism," *Commentary* 16 (July 1953): 57–58.
14. Wilbert E. Moore, *Social Change* (Englewood Cliffs, N.J.: Prentice-Hall, 1963), p. 109.
15. Theodosius Dobzhansky, *Mankind Evolving* (New Haven, Conn.: Yale University Press, 1962), p. 325.

7
The Sociology and Psychology of Art

In the early 1970s, when my good friend and colleague Harold Wilensky (an editorial consultant to the publisher) broached the idea of a brief monograph on the sociology of art I was rather reluctant to undertake it. The reasons for hesitation, perhaps nearly as cogent now as then, were several: the daunting complexity and scope of the topic; the weakness of conceptual grasp and relative scantiness of empirical evidence that characterized this field of interest; the marginal status of such an enterprise in relation to mainstream sociological concerns. In the event, I mustered up the needed audacity and tried to render these matters as shapely as I was then able.

Were one to embark on a similar effort today, I think he would enjoy a more favorable intellectual climate. As noted in the introduction to this volume, there have been notable advances in our understanding of the psychology of creativity, especially the synthetic achievement of Albert Rothenberg in *The Emerging Goddess*. Also, as remarked earlier, sociologists such as Howard Becker and John Manfredi have enhanced our knowledge of the social contexts of artistic production. Finally, there is encouraging fresh interest in the arts on the part of a number of younger social scientists, complemented by a rather more generous posture toward humanistic inclinations in the profession as a whole.

The Domain

Art is singular, individual, resolutely private and the creature of deep personal recesses. Its touchstone is concrete experience. Sociology is set in a collective framework, and is the study of patterned human groupings; its mode of discourse is often necessarily abstract. Yet the arts are protean, endemic in man's societies, and seemingly integral to the human condition. Thus what at first blush appears to be a contradiction in terms may be seen instead as an expression of the connection between the individual and the social, a bridge between private domains and public events. Yeats termed poetry "the social act of a solitary man," and his description is a clue to the curiously doubled nature of art, at once uniquely individual and profoundly social. Poetry, or any art, is a public act because it is a communication.

The chief problems of a sociology of aesthetics stem from questions about the precise nature of this communication: How does it originate in the artist's transactions with the world? How does the system of expressive symbols—the language of the arts—resemble and differ from other symbol systems, especially in its characteristic indirection, its intentional ambiguity? In what proportions do aesthetic symbols combine the cognitive and emotive modes of address? What are the properties of the aesthetic response, the reception by readers, lookers and listeners that completes the necessary artistic process, the interaction of creator, product, and perceiver? How is the shape and substance of what the creator produces, and the public's reaction to that product, related to other orders of events in society? This last broad question, of course, has been the traditional province of sociologists of art as they go about their inquiries: how is art influenced by wars and rumors of war, by systems of authority, by economic conditions, by the major themes embedded in adjoining systems of religious, political, and philosophic values? The reverse question is asked less often, and answered even less satisfactorily: to what extent are the arts themselves a causal force, helping to shape people's perceptions of reality and hence to influence their activities in nonaesthetic spheres of conduct? How much truth, in other words, inheres in Oscar Wilde's aphorism that "nature imitates art more than art imitates nature"?

The sociology and psychology of art, then, address themselves basically to a set of relationships whose center is the tangible piece of art. The art work itself links together the two critical parties to the transaction—the aesthetic experience—namely, artist and audience. To this core trinity of creator, work, and perceiver, are then added those satellite figures who influence the relationship in mediating roles: editors, critics, dealers, patrons, and the like. Finally, the entire cluster of relationships, which in modern industrial societies is increasingly dense and complex, must be viewed in the context of other human activities: politics, economics, science, work and lesiure, and the ways of valuing people and their environment.

The humanist and the sociologist, although ideally they are allied or even resident in the same person, have often been conventionally viewed as enemies. As many have observed, Sir Charles P. Snow's thesis that there are two cultures of science and letters, separated by a wide chasm of mutual ignorance, may be applicable as well to the relation between social science and the humanities. Because this misunderstanding exists, it may be well to define one thing the sociology of art is *not*, or need not be: it is not an effort to explain away artists and their work by a vulgar reductionism, either social or psychological. That is, a sophisticated student of the arts and human behavior does not subscribe to the "nothing but" fallacy, in which complicated patterns of talent and endeavor may be dismissed with a naive reference to the social class origins or neurotic personality of the artist. The autonomy and integrity of art are very real, and may not be undercut by attributing the characteristics of art solely to massive, blind social forces or to the personal compulsions of the artist as a singular human being.

The Broad Canvas: Art and Social Order

There have been several notable efforts to explore the relation between the artistic themes and forms characteristic of a given historical era and the general nature of the society that produces them. These efforts usually entail the assumption that at least a loose association exists between what artists do and the preoccupations of other members of the society. The social scientific axiom underlying the assumption is that a degree of social order exists, that human affairs are patterned—not random—in such a fashion that people's various endeavors cohere. Thus a certain element of society, such as the structure of the family, is so arrayed as to fit appropriately with the other important elements, such as the occupational system. At its root, this axiom of minimum orderliness in a society rests on the idea that no community, and no society, can long endure without a core of shared values; the reflection of these values in different guises affords coherence.

This is not, of course, to assume a unitary pattern of social values to which the arts conform. Indeed, most societies exhibit a pluralistic array of values, often internally contradictory ones, and the serious artist perhaps most often embraces the less popular of these. A function of art is to clarify alternatives in human values, to hold the most comfortable assumptions people make about themselves up to radical questioning. Nevertheless, the terms of the dialogue, the framework within which values are to be examined, are inevitably set by the shared culture embraced by a given human group.

The assumption that the arts are associated with other prominent features of a social group is also buttressed by an aesthetic axiom: that art may or must reflect its society of origin. One durable aesthetic theory holds that art has a truth value because of its correspondence to the real world of nature. And the theory may be extended readily to include art's correspondence to the social psychological universe, the real world of *human* nature.

Several formidable hazards assert themselves when a social scientist or a historian of art sets out to analyze the specific relation of an art work to a social environment. The causal networks under observation are dense and tangled; complex problems of definition and categorization abound. One often seems to be confronted with the discouraging options of making statements with perfect accuracy about a given work or time period, having little general applicability, or of essaying very sweeping statements that illuminate art or society and provoke thought, but have low evidential reliability. Further, the attempt to embrace huge historical eras and whole artistic traditions inevitably leads to a loss of concreteness, to a submerging of the individual artist, the tangible art object, and the veritable social psychological context that are really the crux of attention. Such unattractive alternatives are perhaps not essentially different from the inherent conundrums of sociological analysis: to speak confidently of trivia or hesitantly of significant things. Yet they bear a special poignancy for sociologists of art since they are dealing with such a richly elaborated and profoundly human range of phenomena.

Still another factor that bedevils students of human behavior as they approach the arts is what has been termed the autonomy of art. Like other complex symbolic activities in social life—science, law, philosophy—art may be seen as in important respects self-contained and self-sustaining. It has a tradition of its own and a capacity for immanent change. Hence a given expression of innovative form or content in painting or literature may as credibly be impelled by inherent unfoldings from earlier works in the tradition, as by, let us say, drastic shifts in the polity or economy in which the artist lives. In poetry, for example, the writer is influenced quite as much (perhaps more) by reading other poets as by mundane experience in the life of the times—whether that experience be grounded in an isolable interpersonal relationship or in response to economic depression or war.

Here it is possible to do no more than suggest the wealth of inquiry into the general propositions that art reflects society, or that society reflects the imaginative achievements of its artists. Hugh D. Duncan notes that, "the problem is no longer one of asserting that there is a reciprocal relation between art and society, but of showing *how* this relationship exists."[1] There are at least three chief directions investigators have followed in the attempt to specify how the reciprocal relation exists. Although these analytic modes are not mutually exclusive, they may be roughly categorized as: (1) valuative congruence, (2) social structural influence, and (3) specific interpersonal influences within the artistic vocation itself. In each instance, probably, one must also postulate a psychological mechanism through which the individual artist transmutes social themes into tangible artistic statements. Similarly, we require a theory of perception and symbolic process to account for art's effect on the disposition and behavior of its audience.

The most ambitious attempt to join the arts to social order is Sorokin's massive study of art styles and reigning social ideologies.[2] His essential position is that western European history may be divided into eras characterized by one of three overarching value systems, and that the arts of a given era embody the appropriate features of the dominant values or world view. Art, that is, reflects the primary cultural orientation of the society in which it is created; Sorokin deals less extensively with the reciprocal impact of art works upon social values, but clearly implies that artistic themes and styles reinforce the ideology that gave them birth. He distinguishes the three major value clusters as *sensate, ideational,* and *idealistic.* The properties of art are then shown to correspond to the guiding cluster of their age. Thus in the sensate, our own era, marked by a devotion to empirical reality and an enjoyment of the things of this world:

> Sensate art....moves entirely in the empirical world of the senses...Its aim is to afford a refined sensual enjoyment....For this reason it must be sensational, passionate, sensual, and incessantly new. It is marked by voluptuous nudity and concupiscence. It is divorced from religion, morals, and other values, and styles itself "art for art's sake."...*Its style is naturalistic, visual, even illusionistic, free from any supersensory symbolism.*[3]

This sensate art, notes Loomis, "is in strong contrast to the art of the ideational periods in which topics are mainly religious (God, His Kingdom, mysteries of salvation, redemption, saints, etc.). This art communicates the pious, ethereal, and ascetic. It does not admit any sensualism, eroticism, satire, comedy, caricature or farce."[4]

> It is a communion of the human soul with itself and with God....Its style is and must be symbolic....The signs of the dove, anchor, and olive branch in the early Christian catacombs [are examples].[5]

Loomis concludes that "No other sociologist has as effectively demonstrated how painting, sculpture, music, and literature function as vehicles for expressive communication."[6]

Yet the very abstract and general nature of Sorokin's categories at length renders his analysis questionable. His typology entails a forced orderliness that lumps too many disparate themes and styles together and tends to gloss over the concrete relationships between artists and their societies.

Other less sweeping illustrations of the approach to art through congruent values are Wilson's discussion of American cultural orientations in the novels of F. Scott Fitzgerald[7] and Kavolis's linkage of Puritanism to the style of abstract expressionism in painting.[8] Wilson, drawing on the scheme of value orientations devised by Florence Kluckhohn, demonstrates that certain core American postures towards time, nature, and human nature are vividly exemplified in Fitzgerald's life as well as in the lives of his fictional protagonists. For example, the bondage to future time is both a central theme of *The Great Gatsby* and a consistent thread in the novelist's own striving for literary achievement.

Kavolis contends that "abstract expressionism, the imageless, energetic style of painting represented by Jackson Pollock and Franz Kline, is one of the few modern styles completely without analogues in any of the civilizations of the past."[9] He suggests that this mode of painting is allied to Puritanism's abstract moral principle of independence from external things (human subject matter is excluded), to its tensions stemming from the uncertainty of salvation, and to its characteristic spirit of revolt against traditional authority.

The idea that art may not only express common values extant in a society but may itself help to shape that commonality, draws its firmest theoretical support from the tradition of symbolic interaction in social psychology.

George Herbert Mead and his followers contend that social cohesion is based on a cumulative symbolic sharing, such that the individual learns who he is and how to act as a consequence of observing others and incorporating their postures into himself. Art is, then, an obvious source of stimulation, of the learnings about one another that draw people together. Mead and one of his foremost interpreters, Hugh D. Duncan, would assert that art inspires agreement about values by rehearsing the problems and perceptions that people hold in common, but that they might not recognize so readily were the sharing not made articulate in the imaginative work. Art rehearses common meanings and allows us to enter the interior worlds of others:

> Our only hope is our curiosity, which may be called "the passion of self-consciousness." This teaches us that "we must be others if we are to be ourselves." Our best hope of becoming conscious of others is in art. The modern realistic novel has done more than technical education in fashioning the social object that spells social control. If we can bring people together so that they can enter each other's lives, they will inevitably have a common object which will control their common conduct.[10]

Perhaps the clearest example of a sociology of art premised on social structural influences is found in various Marxist interpretations. Prototypically, in this tradition, the substance of the work of art is viewed as an expression of the artist's position in the economic stratification of his or her society; or, if art does not express the artists' *de facto* economic status, then it embraces the economic interest of some group to whom they are obligated or allied. Although the effort to trace such a relationship may be revealing of influence overlooked in a purely aesthetic analysis, Marxist interpretations commonly founder on one of two major obstacles. The first of these is the protean nature of artists: their many-sidedness often leads to "betrayal" of presumed class interests, to an embracing humanism that leaps over the constraints of social categories. As Wellek and Warren have commented, "...the concept of humanism, of the universality of art, surrenders the central doctrine of Marxism, which is essentially relativistic."[11] Second, a direct, one-to-one correspondence between class and art product is very difficult to establish because of the congeries of other influences at work simultaneously, such as the thrust of artistic tradition and the psychological particularities of the artist. Thus Marx himself confesses that "certain periods of highest development of art stand in no direct relation with the general development of society, nor with the material basis and the skeleton structure of its organization."[12]

Vytautas Kavolis has offered the most recent review of the social structural approach to a sociology of art. His discussion is confined to visual art, primarily painting, but it is a comprehensive survey of prominent societal features and their associated art styles. Although Kavolis rehearses certain fairly well-substantiated links between economic or political conditions and stylistic tendencies (for example, the association of authoritarian polities with rigid, conforming styles), he is at pains to emphasize the futility of a search for simple correlations. He eschews a vulgar determinism, Marxist or other, in favor of a complex process of influence in which social conditions are mediated by what he terms the *fantasy dispositions* ("tendencies to impose a particular structure on experiences of the imagination") characteristic of various groups in the population. His summary of the relations between style and the economy illustrates this approach:

> The connecting link between economic variables and art styles is visualized as psychological congruity—a similarity in emotional quality—between attitudes toward economic action, or the tensions generated by economic conditions, and forms of artistic expression. An example of this kind of congruity is provided by the experimental evidence that achievement motivation (one of the main psychological stimuli of entrepreneurial activity) is reflected in such characteristics of style as restlessness, a preference for diagonal lines, and a tendency to fill up space.[13]

Hence, having begun with a quest for the stylistic consequences of social structure per se, Kavolis finds it necessary to invoke psychological dispositions and value choices as intervening variables in the art-society equation. A further illustration makes his posture clear. He attempts, rather successfully, to join the value orientation of a society (its fundamental stances toward time, activity, the nature of human nature, and so on) to its characteristic art styles. The key to this joining is his assertion that "one of the crucial social functions of art style may be the subconscious assertion of value orientations by filling the visible world with shapes emotionally suggestive of the value orientations held."[14] Kavolis then offers a brilliant discussion of abstract expressionism in painting as a style congruous with the continuing vitality of ascetic Puritanism in American culture.

Neither the attempt to establish valuative congruence nor to identify social structural influence has been markedly successful in dealing with the other side of the reciprocal relationship: how art may affect society. The reasons for this failure are not hard to find. It is extremely difficult to identify the susceptible audience(s) for the various arts, and still more difficult to assess the weight of artistic experience as a single factor in comparison with other kinds of impelling life events. Empirical investigations are few and rather unconvincing. We are left almost entirely with isolated individual reports, in which an elite perceiver testifies that a particular novel or painting has been moving or motivating. To move beyond the clinically subjective type of evidence, we need to answer questions about audience size and composition, about the differential salience of the arts in the life space of members of the audience, and about concrete attitudes or actions that have somehow been shaped by artistic experience. These are formidable tasks, and to date sociologists have not moved beyond fragmentary accounts of audience composition.

Theoretically, it may be assumed that the arts, like other components of the experiential mass, contribute some part to the formation of values and life styles. Most commonly, it is believed that art confirms a given definition of the nature of reality, and perhaps may have an impact in altering that definition. Thus Marxist theoreticians, notably Leon Trotsky, assign great significance to art as a molder of audience perceptions of a just social order, and the USSR has taken this proposition seriously, as seen in its fifty-odd years of censorship and prescription. Most crudely put, the portrayal of socialist realism in literature and painting is thought to promote widespread acceptance of approved postures toward the state and prescribed modes of individual conduct. There is really no substantial evidence that this is the case, however.

More subtle, but probably more profound, effects of art on society are hypothesized by philosophers and critics who concentrate on artistic style (as much as substance) in the shaping of perception. In literature, for example, it is often asserted that the artist helps to establish the language through which experience is categorized, and in so doing influences the fundamental meanings of social experience. We can only see what our perceptual classificatory scheme, embedded in language, directs us to see. The argument is compelling, combining considerable face validity with some substantial psychodynamic and anthropological evidence. Once again, however, we are hard put to demonstate the working of this sequence in any considerable audience for the arts, or its eventuation in specifically changed conduct that would constitute a social repatterning.

Art as experience, in John Dewey's phrase, has the special characteristic of existing as an end in itself. It is not necessarily or most importantly a means to any other purpose or function. Thus the anthropologist Jacques Maquet contends that "noninstrumental form seems to be a fair index of what specialists understand by aesthetic phenomena."[15] Maquet goes on to describe the mode of aesthetic experience as contemplative, and contends that contemplation is as valid and significant a behavioral posture as is, for example, cognition or action. To comprehend how the experience of perceiving art affects social behavior, we must perhaps inquire into how contemplation in turn influences choices among styles of cognition or feeling.

Because art exists only for itself, it focuses the attention and sharpens awareness in a way nonaesthetic experience rarely or never does. Leo Lowenthal speaks of art as that which is "more real than reality"; that is, the work of art has a coherence and pointedness that contrasts sharply with the relatively formless flux of everyday life,and hence seems to us more meaningful and tangible. The critic Roger Fry sums up the particular brand of attentiveness that is intrinsic to aesthetic involvement:

> The needs of our actual life are so imperative that the sense of vision becomes highly specialized in their service. With an admirable economy we learn to see only so much as is needful for our purposes; but this is in fact very little....In actual life the normal person really only reads the labels as it were, on the objects around him and troubles no further. Almost all the things which are useful in any way put on more or less this cap of invisibility. It is only when an object exists in our lives for no other purpose than to be seen that we really look at it, as for instance at a China ornament or a precious stone, and towards such even the most normal person adopts to some extent the artistic attitude of pure vision abstracted from necessity.[16]

Art, then, holds up life for our examination. But it is more than a mirror reflecting the social universe and teaching people how they do in fact behave. As source of models, organizer of experience, and refiner of perceptions, art also teaches them how *to* behave.

Clifford Geertz maintains that art forms not only reflect human subjectivity, but in fact shape that subjectivity. In a brilliant analysis of Balinese cockfights, Geertz notes:

> Enacted and reenacted, so far without end, the cockfight enables the Balinese, as, read and reread, *MacBeth* enables us, to see a dimension of his own subjectivity....Yet, because—in another of those paradoxes, along with painted feelings and unconsequenced acts, which haunt aesthetics—that subjectivity does not properly exist until it is thus organized, art forms generate and regenerate the very subjectivity they pretend only to display. Quartets, still lifes, and cockfights are not merely reflections of a preexisting sensibility anologically presented; they are positive agents in the creation and maintenance of such a sensibility. If we see ourselves as a pack of Micawbers it is from reading too much Dickens (if we see ourselves as unillusioned realists, it is from reading too little); and similarly for Balinese, cocks, and cockfights. It is in such a way, coloring experience with the light they cast it in, rather than through whatever material effects they may have, that the arts play their role, as arts, in social life.[17]

The third avenue of ferreting out the reciprocal relationship between art and society is the simplest, and undoubtedly the most congenial to the aesthetically responsive observer. Specific interpersonal influence within the artistic vocation is more tangible and easier to document than are the more unwieldly influences of values and social structure. Although values and social structure are still clearly involved, they are bounded by the institutions of the particular arts and hence are much more amenable to analytical grasp. At the same time, when we confine our attention to the internal functioning of an art as tradition or institution we are afforded only an indirect reading of those larger issues at the boundary interchange between the arts and society.

The Arts as Social Institutions

Art is engendered by a series of social relationships, similar to the ordered arrangements that engender science, law, scholarship—or even automobiles. That is, with the possible exception of an isolated and anonymous cave painter or lyric poet, artists do their work in a social universe marked by certain regularities of role recruitment and role performance, certain repetitive features of theme and technique, certain boundaries of audience demand, economic constraint, and the like. When we say that literature or painting is a social institution, we imply that an observable network of human relationships is organized around the production of specific kinds of communications, the objects of art.

It is probably only with the Renaissance in western Europe that we can begin to discern the contours of such human networks, because the idea of the arts as distinctive institutions seems inseparable from occupational specialization, from the division of labor in society. The definition of bounded institutions devoted to the arts in Europe and the United States was further stimulated by the development of a market economy in which art products could be bought and sold freely, and by specialization of audiences that complemented the specialization of types of artists. A competitive commercial arena for art, marked especially by the rise of a substantial middle-class consuming population, created new conditions of freedom for the artists. They could exploit their wares in any fashion the market would bear, freed from the constraints of aristocratic patronage. On the other hand, the tastes of large audiences could be quite as capricious as the whims of patrons, so that emerging mass audiences and open markets posed the possibility of economic ruin as well as of enrichment. For every Alexander Pope made wealthy by a single translation, dozens of writers starved on Grub Street or turned to other occupations.

Still another and very significant institutional consequence of specialization and the commercial nexus was the elaboration of social roles to facilitate the artistic transaction. The basic trinity of elements—artist, art work, and audience—expanded to include a variety of middlemen who intervened between the artist and the respondent. These middlemen ranged from dealers and publishers to critics and agents. They could be enormously helpful to artists in affording initial support and identifying potential clients; they could also, and perhaps with equal frequency, exploit them and drain off a great portion of their possible economic reward. Further, the holders of these ancillary roles were able to exert a very considerable force on the artist's prospects through their participation in molding audience taste and erecting critical judgments. This powerful, if often implicit and indirect influence, has become ever more important down to our own day because of audience fragmentation and the increasing numbers of relatively unsophisticated but affluent consumers.

A sociology of art directed to institutional analysis must ask the following kinds of questions: How are artists recruited and trained? How and by whom are critical canons established and popular tastes shaped? What predictable rewards, economic and other, are available to artists? How is art transmitted from its creators to its consumers? How are audiences cultivated and sustained? What is the relation of artistic institutions to other social institutions—economic, political, religious, familial? How does the artist-as-colleague influence—and how is he influenced by—fellow artists?

Clearly, the various arts differ in the degree to which they are formally structured and accompanied by a visible apparatus of organization. The performing arts, notably ballet, opera, and symphony, are characterized by rather firm patterns of recruitment, training, and internal operating structure. At the other extreme, the poet or novelist is seldom overtly recruited, may or may not undergo any formal training, and is typically only loosely linked either to a body of colleagues or to a specifiable audience. The painter or composer falls between these extremes of structure and organizational formality.

In recent years, several sociological studies of the arts have adopted an essentially institutional focus. They reveal much that is unique about art as a social activity, but also much that is comparable to other modes of vocational enterprise. Such analyses commonly begin by questioning how aspiring artists enter upon their vocation: since the artistic career is an unusual one, and most young people have very unclear visions of what its pursuit entails, what factors shape their choice? Three major types of influences seem to cut across the specific recruitment paths of the various arts today. These may be termed *exposure, initial experience,* and *exemplary encouragement.*

Exposure is clearly paramount; one must know that an art exists, must view it as valuable and enjoyable, if he or she is to aspire to creative activity. In a very real sense, it might be said that art products themselves are the tangible devices that lure youth into art. Relishing the act of appreciation, the neophyte begins to wonder how these marvels are brought about, how men and women actually fashion an original object. He may read about the lives of great artists, may begin in subtle ways to identify with them and model portions of his behavior upon theirs. The phenomenon was nicely summed up centuries ago by Dr. Samuel Johnson in *Lives of the Poets*:

> In the window of his [Abraham Cowley's] mother's apartment lay Spenser's *Fairy Queen*, in which he very early took delight to read, till, by feeling the charms of verse, he became, as he relates, irrecoverably a poet. Such are the

> accidents which, sometimes remembered, and perhaps sometimes forgotten, produce that particular designation of mind, and propensity for some certain science or employment, which is commonly called genius. The true genius is a mind of large general powers, accidentally determined to some particular direction. Sir Joshua Reynolds, the great painter of the present age, had the first fondness for his art excited by the perusal of Richardson's treatise.[18]

Contemporary accounts of how young people get into art are strikingly similar to Dr. Johnson's. One clue to the relative autonomy of expressive symbol systems, and their capacity for immanent change, is this fact that the artistic tradition breeds its own successors.

The nascent artist's first experience in doing the artistic job typically occurs early, probably earlier than is the case with most other vocations. Psychological theory suggests that the child's perceptual naivete and flexibility are more akin to the artist's bold questioning than are the more stereotyped perceptual frames of older people. Further, a first try at making art (except in the performing arts) does not require either the physical presence of a mentor or the supporting facilities of an organized workplace. In any event, artists report that the activity itself initially is pleasant and highly self-rewarding. It is a significant illustration of what Gordon Allport termed the functional autonomy of motives, or "function pleasure": the inherent rewards of process are sufficient to sustain repeated behavior, and this self-gratifying property continues to inform the mature artist's working life.

But in most instances the joys of appreciation and the absorption in one's early forays are joined by a third element. Someone in the aspirant's environment actively encourages the continued exercise of his or her talent. The teacher-pupil, or master-apprentice, relationship may be formally structured as part of a training sequence, as in music or art school, or it may be as haphazard as the exchange of letters between an older poet and a younger. Approval and counsel from a vocational exemplar is undoubtedly important in recruitment to most kinds of work; in the arts, however, it is lent special salience because formal criteria of certification are few and standards of evaluation of the work's quality are seldom explicit. A number of empirical studies have underlined the importance of this interpersonal transaction, which is perhaps the sociological crux of entrance to an artistic career. Griff documents the crucial part played by early encouragement in painting;[19] Forsyth and Kolenda trace the details of induction into ballet dancing;[20] Wilson describes the push established writers give to those on the way up.[21]

Training for the arts varies as widely in shape and substance as does recruitment. Once again, the performing arts are most likely to be characterized by formal and explicit educational processes; given a substrate of talent, the aspirant's achievement then rests heavily on skillful instruction and faithful rehearsal. Ballet and music are the prototypes of fields requiring arduous training and an almost religious discipline in which art comes first and last. The self is immersed in the search for perfection. Forsyth and Kolenda (1966) and Ryser[22] examine the extreme commitment of the dancer who must live for and in the dance, at the sacrifice of other interests, physical comfort, and economic well-being. Very rigid criteria of excellence are enforced with Prussian severity by a director whose authority is nearly absolute. Although preparation for the stage does not seem to demand quite the iron intensity that marks the serious dance, it exhibits many similar hazards: fierce competition for leading roles, in which by definition few can succeed; the aspirant's utter dependence on the mentor's judgment and favor; the demand for total dedication of the self to rigorous grooming, in a quasi-monastic situation where the world of art and the world at large are ideally coterminous.

Again literature falls at the other extreme. Here the training tends to be highly informal, although the number and quality of creative writing courses in universities is steadily increasng. It takes the form of editorial counsel, of a coaching relationship; the editor or friendly critic cannot usually show a writer explicitly how to do his or her work, but can suggest, shape, excise, and underline. Modern literature abounds in examples. Two of the best-known are the sage guidance given Thomas Wolfe by Maxwell Perkins, in which Perkins helped boil down masses of manuscript into still sprawling but recognizably formed novels; and the famous surgery undertaken by Ezra Pound on Eliot's "The Wasteland."

Relatively little is known about the audiences for the fine arts. In some sense they too must be cultivated, trained to respond with a measure of sophisticated discrimination. What one might term the socialization of perceivers is, again, covert, informal, and difficult to describe. On the one hand, an art dealer may be able to educate patrons to buy certain paintings through technical comments or simply by virtue of authority. Dealers may also appeal to purchasers on strictly economic grounds, since paintings have been overwhelmingly growth stocks in recent decades. Teachers of literature train readers by textual explication, comparative analysis, and perhaps most importatly, by showing infectious excitement in the face of art. But audiences are probably cultivated for the most part in more subtle, less than fully intentional ways: the chance remark of a friend, a newspaper review, the presence of art as an element of normal household atmosphere. As in the case of the artist, the audience is undoubtedly primarily educated through sheer exposure, through self-sought encounters with the worlds of art.

Although the composition of the audience and the roles of critics, agents, and other middlemen would apear to be inviting topics for sociological inquiry, there are few empirical studies of these phenomena. In literature there are recent French and Scandinavian examples. Robert Escarpit's *Sociologie de la Litterature* explores the social origins of French writers, their lifestyles, and the system of publicaton and distribution. He notes especially the sparse audience for serious literature and the economic difficulty of the contemporary writer's life.[23] In *Sociological Aspects of the Literary System*, Karl Erik Rosengren presents a meticulous statistical analysis of the structure of the Swedish literary world during two time periods, the 1880s and 1950s to 1960s. He studied literary reviewers of these periods, teasing out from their mentions of titles and authors the size and shape of the literary frame of reference. Rosengren discovered that the *size* of the literary system had greatly increased in the latter period, by some 30 to 40 percent; he further noted that this expansion may have had some unfortunate effects on Swedish literature of the 1950s to 1960s: "greater self-sufficiency, less internationalism and less international mobility."[24] Rosengren's method, adopted from statistical linguistics, appears promising for the comparative investigation of other eras and other countries.

In painting, two notable researches into the social structure of art are available. White and White's *Canvases and Careers*[25] traces the history of French painting in the nineteenth century by examining the structure of art institutions and the career patterns of artists. They show how the Academy and its system of exhibitions and prizes proved unequal to the demands of the thousands of aspiring painters for viable careers, and the changing composition of the consuming public. Dealers and journalist-critics moved into the gaps in the traditional system, and altered the opportunity structure for the artist, as well as the means of distributing art and shaping audience taste.

Rosenberg and Fliegal's *The Vanguard Artist*[26] is an absorbing account of the New York School of abstract expressionism, largely garnered from interviews with the artists themselves. It deals in striking detail with painters' self-perceptions, career lines, relationships to colleagues and to the booming market for art. Especially telling is the examination of how critics, dealers, and gallery owners intervene between artist and audience. These intermediaries are viewed with mixed feelings by painters—they are a convenient and economically enabling resource, but their influence on the consumer is seen as disproportionately heavy.

The identity of the audience for the serious arts is not well known, but most surveys indicate that it is very small, well-educated, affluent, and almost entirely upper-middle class. People who buy poetry or collect paintings tend to be the same people who prowl museums or attend symphonies or ballets. Although there are some indications that its size is increasing and its composition becoming more diverse, the audience is still a tiny fraction of the population. This has clearly been the situation in most societies throughout history, and the reasons for it are not obscure. Shils has argued persuasively that the audience for high culture has never been large.[27] Membership has nearly always required money, leisure, and educated taste—commodities in notoriously short supply in most times and places. Furthermore, attention to the arts is demanding, calling on more reserves of energy, discipline, and personal openness than people routinely possess. Great writers may not require great audiences, but they require good, alert, experienced ones. It is a mistake to think of the audience as a passive receptacle for aesthetic stimuli; the perceiver, whether reading or looking or listening, must make an active contribution to the total communicative process.

It is an open question whether the heralded American affluence and leisure of the near future will make an appreciable difference in this picture. The issue, of course, is how extra money and time are to be spent. The prospect of a greatly enlarged audience for high culture is deeply shadowed by the continuing vitality of the Protestant work ethic and its accompanying mistrust of sensual involvement. Indolence appears to be the reward and privilege of productive striving; when all that is not work is not serious, the mediocre and frivolous tend to drive out the best in a cultural version of Gresham's Law. It may be quite a long time before we can imagine a tired opera-goer falling asleep at his or her place of business.

As I have argued above, art is a self-propelling and intrinsically rewarding activity. Hence a discussion of the artist's gratifications must be grounded in the psychology of creativity. But beyond the psychic income derived from self expression, the artist seems to require at least two varieties of social support: economic gain and critical appreciation.

The economic rewards of art have been always and everywhere precarious in nature. Essentially, the absence of assured, substantial compensation for the artist's labors rests on the small size of the audience; we are willing to pay only for what we value, and high art is valued by few. Moreover, the dispositions of those who *do* support the arts, whether individual or institutional patrons, tend to fluctuate with changes in taste and in economic fortune. Historically, in the western European tradition, individual patrons have been overwhelmingly the aristocracy, and in more recent centuries the wealthy bourgeoisie. These patrons have often been capricious; Samuel Johnson's blistering complaint to Lord Chesterfield for supporting him in a tardy fashion is a conspicuous example. (Johnson compares Chesterfield's action to that of a reluctant rescuer who, having failed to throw a rope to a drowning man, embraces him eagerly as he staggers up the beach.) The individual patron, however, does insure a personal link between artist and audience, as contrasted to the faceless, anonymous public more characteristic of the arts today.

Institutional patronage of the fine arts has traditionally resided in the nation state or in the Church. In medieval and Renaissance Europe, of course, the Church was a primary support for certain of the arts, notably painting and architecture, and to a lesser extent music. The state has fluctuated in rewarding artists; it has often proved a generous patron, but often too it has demanded that the artist conform sedulously to prevailing ideological doctrine. Notorious in the latter respect have been the European totalitarian nations of the twentieth century, especially the Soviet Union. Taking art with deadly seriousness, the USSR has tried to enforce adherence to officially approved themes and styles, and continues to do so.

In the United States, government has offered little encouragement to the fine arts until the relatively recent past. In the 1930s, official subsidy took the form of artists' and writers' projects, under the Works Progress Administration. These supplied the artist a very modest but helpful income. How much they actually sustained the individual artist, and to what extent they enhanced the quality of artistic production, remain debatable issues. There was somewhat increased government recognition in the 1970s, particularly as represented by the National Endowment for the Humanities and the Kennedy Center for the Performing Arts.

There have also arisen two peculiarly American innovations in institutional patronage, the charitable foundation and the business corporation. Such foundations as Carnegie, Rockefeller, and Ford, together with many smaller ones, have been prominent in subsidizing art. In a sense, they represent a bureaucratic, durable form of the older patronage engendered by an aristocracy of wealth. The business firm has in the last thirty-five years enjoyed very broad legal rights as a donor to enterprises in the public interest, such as health, education, and art. (Before 1935, corporations were severely restricted from diverting funds to donees unless this could be demonstrated to be in stockholders' dollars-and-cents interest, narrowly construed.) Increasingly, businesses are indeed supporting the arts, although only at a very small fragment of the rate at which they might do so. Richard Eells has argued effectively that it is in the corporations' best long-run interests to support the arts more handsomely; the corporate patron can in this way foster a more sophisticated consumer public, can contribute to a richer community life, and can stimulate the creative skills on which its own health in the end is based.[28]

However economic reward accrues to the artist, from the free marketplace or a variety of patronage, that reward is rarely steady or high. Only a very small number of those who practice the fine arts in the United States can actually make a living from the artistic enterprise itself. Those who are at the very top of the performing arts or in painting reap high income; in serious literature, the poet or novelist can rarely exist on the returns from art alone. There is little chance, economically, for the merely competent craftsman, the journeyman of the arts. This situation results in a precarious and generally impoverished style of life for artists who choose to confine themselves to art as their sole job. Robert Frost's earlier career is exemplary: the unwilling schoolteacher, the farmer of northern New England's stony earth, the poet who enjoyed his first *succes d'estime* not in his own land but in Britain—Frost is a classic instance of neglect. He neglected his wife and children to follow the writer's angular and consuming calling; the public in turn neglected him, until the late years of *Life* magazine, the Kennedy inauguration, the Khrushchev conversations, the almost ritual obeisance paid by the young to the old, ripe poet whose own youthful talent went unremarked. Sir Arthur Quiller-Couch reminds us that all this has been a timeless characteristic of the poetic career:

> *Seven wealthy towns contend for Homer dead,*
> *Through which the living Homer begged his bread.*

Most practitioners survive only by taking up dual occupations: a remunerative job and the art job. The lucrative half (or more) of life may take several forms; most commonly, it is in a related field, such as teaching, criticism, or some commercial version of the craft. A minority of serious artists are successful in combining a seemingly unrelated professional or business vocation with art; Charles Ives, Wallace Stevens, and William Carlos Williams are prominent examples.

Less regular means of compensation are also available to support an occasional stint of artistic effort. Fellowships (for instance, the Guggenheim) and residencies at art colonies or universities may afford the individual an uninterrupted period of work. These opportunities, of course, are sporadic and time limited; they do not, in the usual case, represent a career-sustaining resource. And again, although such patrons attempt to seek out the talented young, the plums tend to fall to established "name" artists.

The other major type of reward on which artists depend is the approbation of a peculiarly qualified audience. This audience may perhaps be best characterized as a select jury of one's peers. With the fragmentation of the modern audience and the increased specialization of both artists and perceivers, the artist is unlikely to be in touch with a large, responsive audience of amateurs. Rather, he or she comes to rely on the judgment of fellow craftsmen and technically qualified critics; what is important is not their numbers but their quality. If one is taken seriously by an elite audience, a "saving remnant," one may feel slight need for a more popular acclaim. Hence the fine artist's moral support, the reward for excellence and devotion to craft, comes primarily from the university, the critical journals, and those respected as colleagues in art. In this sense, the structure of the artist's reward is strikingly similar to that of other professionals in science and scholarship.

As a radical perceiver, as one whose vocation leads him into severe questioning of values and styles prevalent in the environing society, the artist is almost by definition a deviant and isolated individual. Artists' angles of vision renders them exceptional. It is vital to distinguish this brand of deviance, however, from the typology of deviant behavior ordinarily embraced by sociological theory. Sociologists, in their concern for the nature of social order, have inclined to view deviance as an exclusively negative phenomenon. That is, the deviant person is the one who evades or contravenes the legitimate norms of the social group, through retreat, rebellion, or the adoption of illicit means of achievement; the addict, the thief, the political iconoclast are type-cases. Sociologists have not, unfortunately, been so adept at conceptualizing what we might term *transcendence* or *positive deviance.* Perhaps the single notable exception is the line of analysis embodied in the Weberian concept of *charisma,* the quasi-magical and magnetic style of the political or religious innovator. The creative person in science or philosophy or art has not been a prominent object of sociological interest, and is not well understood. Yet the artist's deviance, despite its occasionally partaking of elements of the negative deviant's style, is of a different sort altogether. Its aim is to refine old values and percepts, to suggest fresh ones, to rehearse alternative modes of valuing and of relating to one another and to the world.

If poets or painters must be in certain respects isolated, remote from the concerns of their fellows, and occupying the vantage point of a spectator in life, it would yet be mistaken to construe them as irrevocably lonely. Fiercely absorbed in a personal vision, sometimes a diabolical or despairing one, the artist remains a human among humans. A close study of artistic friendships would reveal much about the artist's talent for interpersonal relations (of all people, the artist is among the most likely to "go proudly friended," in Rupert Brooke's phrase) and also much about how artists support and influence one another in work itself. We noted earlier the manner in which art is self-perpetuating, in that the artistic tradition and presence attracts its own recruits. Similarly, colleagues reinforce one another, borrowing styles, offering criticism, offering the support of one who has been there and knows the territory. Artistic friendships are often passionate, shot through with jealousy and rivalry; at the same time, and consistently, they may, because of the devotion and intensity involved, be exceptionally deep and enduring. The mutual caring, about the creative job and about the person, can generate unusually close bonds.

We may then conclude that art is a social institution like any other, firmly anchored in those recurrent interpersonal behaviors that are the stuff of society. But with some few exceptions in the performing arts, this work is a private endeavor. Its content is no doubt the precipitate of social interaction, at least in large measure, and it may have consequences for patterned human relationships. Nevertheless, the artist creates alone and the audience perceives alone. The radically individual character of creation and of audience re-creation means that sociologists of art cannot sensibly restrict themselves to a conventional sociological frame of reference. They need to supplement the normal approach with psychological insight.

The Psychology of Art: Literature as a Case Illustration

A seemingly exhaustive classification of the manifold relations between literature and psychology is offered by Wellek and Warren:

> By "psychology of literature," we may mean the psychological study of the writer, as type and as individual, or the study of the creative process, or the study of the psychological types and laws present within works of literature, or, finally, the effects of literature upon its readers (audience psychology).[29]

Strictly speaking the second and fourth of these categories—analysis of the creative process and of aesthetic responsiveness in the reader—do not involve the psychological interpretation of literature itself; they are, rather, concerned with literature's antecedents and consequences. Yet all four avenues of approach are implicated in any attempt to explore imaginative literature as a characteristically human endeavor, to untangle the complex phenomena of people behaving as artists, as created figures within the work of art, and as appreciators who complete the artistic transaction through their engagement with the writer's voice.

Poems, novels, and plays have long fascinated the student of personality, both before and since the establishment of psychology as a distinctive academic discipline and scientific enterprise. And the reasons for this absorption are not hard to seek. Our own and others' behavior is the most compelling of all subjects, and our thirst for meaning impels the insistent search for understanding how and why people act as they do. Literature has always been for some observers a prime source of this understanding, since the writer is recognized as a peculiarly sensitive recorder of manners and motives. Further, the characters set forth in imagination exhibit a fullness, a coherence, that customarily eludes us in our mundane efforts to understand one another. Fictional protagonists are more accessible to us, we know more about them, and their image is concentrated for us in a way never achieved in the episodic patterning of real life. With L.A. Reid, one may contend that art has "more of essence, and less of accident"[30] in it than does the ordinary flux of existence. Even Freud (or perhaps especially Freud) confesses that imaginative writers revealed deep psychological truths before the advent of psychoanalysis.

On the other hand, the knowledge psychologists attain through examining literary work is always suspect: the data are by definition unique, uncontrolled, not replicable, and so on. Psychology is sometimes defined as the study of lives, and these men and women—the characters in a novel or play—never lived, or at least never lived in just the way represented by creative artifice. Moreover, the poet or storyteller is in turn commonly, although by no means always, suspicious of the psychologist's exertions; the psychologist is accused of a prying nature, a cumbersome if not inhuman repertoire of language and technique, a brutish insensitivity to nuances of aesthetic value. (See chapter 2 for quotes from Poe and Auden.)

Adopting Wellek and Warren's classification, I shall sketch certain leading issues in each of the four possible categories of psychological interpretation. My readily apparent bias is that psychology and imaginative literature have much to say to one another about their common subject: human beings in disguise and revelation, courage and fright, despair and obdurate hope. But this dialogue should not, and need not, be marred by a naive reductionism. Psychological interpretation can enrich our view of the work of art; it cannot be substituted for the art itself, which sustains its own integrity. A literary vehicle is never "nothing but" an expression of the author's neuroses—or of his health. Similarly, the artist's craft does not supersede the psychologist's theory or a slender but growing reliable knowledge. The novelist's insight and the poet's inspiration are different from and complementary to psychological analysis; they are not intrinsically superior or inferior to the psychologist's wisdom.

Psychological Study of the Writer

We may attempt to analyze writers as a type, to generalize about the personal characteristics and underlying motives of those people who devote themselves to the construction of imagined events. Here, the root assumption is usually that the nature of the task—the creative elaboration of verbal patterns—demands of its practitioners certain uniform dispositions, energies, and skills. Alternatively, we may probe the psychological composition of an individual author, trying to ferret out unique properties, strengths and weaknesses, recurrent life problems and modes of resolving them; this approach typically essays to establish convincing connections between the kind of person the author is and the kind of imagined worlds he or she makes. Study of the first sort, of the writer as type or class, probably promises more to the psychologist in the way of general propositions about the dynamics of personality. Yet it has been on the whole unconvincing, beset by conflicting and scattered evidence. Study of the second sort, of the peculiar qualities of a given writer in relation to his recorded art, tends to be at once more persuasive and perhaps less valuable to psychological science; it does more to enhance our understanding of literature than to advance generalizations about behavior.

The classical tradition in psychoanalytic theory affords only a murky picture of the writer as a type. Masters of literature appear now in the guise of heroes, if not readily understandable ones, now as refugees spinning fantastic tales in their retreat from some real world "out there." Thus Freud tells us that the artist is impenetrable, that psychoanalytic technique is not adequate to full comprehension of the poet. Jung avers that "the creative act, which is the antithesis of mere reaction, must forever elude our understanding."[31] And yet both men, as well as their followers for all the years since, find themselves unable to leave the problem alone. Jung believes that the artist's power derives from the ability to set forth archetypes, to draw on the most potent, but buried, themes that lie deep in the collective memory of the human race. Otto Rank, too, stresses the writer's role as the voice of others, as he who gives tongue to the dreams of the mass of inarticulate men. Nearly all psychoanalytic observers agree that the artist is in closer touch with the unconscious, is more vulnerable and sensitive to inner turbulence than is the nonartist.

Conflicting theories of the writer's personality revolve around the question of what is done with the inwardness, how healthy or ill is the writer as a consequence of wrestling with his demon. Freud, and more recently Daniel Schneider (himself both psychoanalyst and novelist), stress creative writers' essential healthiness in being able to master daydreams. They are able to bridle the wild horses of the id with the bit of ego-mastery, able to encounter despair and turmoil and terror within, and then to emerge with a message in the daylit world people are pleased to call reality. That is, writers return with hard-won treasures to our common universe of discourse where they are able to communicate something of their value to others. Here artists are seen not as mortally wounded outsiders, but as more capacious and more complexly healthy than other people.

Other interpreters, of whom Edmund Bergler is the most conspicuous example, profess to find the writer a sick person almost by definition. The inwardness, the obsessive involvement with the self, the recurrent absorption in fantasy—all these are construed as the stuff of insurmountable neurotic conflict. A healthy writer is to analysts of this persuasion a contradiction in terms. Well-balanced personalities work out their problems in daily living and have no need to strain for that exactitude of expression that marks the writer's craft. Fulfilling themselves in normal interpersonal relations, psychologically sound individuals are not compelled to stake out their wishes on paper, to invent other worlds or toy with a patterning of things other than they are.

Perhaps the most reasonable conclusion, based not only on psychological theory but on the wealth of writers' testimony about themselves, is that writers are on the whole as different from one another as they are from nonwriters. There appears to be no single or simple dynamic mechanism that drives people who create literature. It seems wise to suppose, with

Malcolm Cowley and others who boast intimate acquaintance with the tribe, that people who adopt the vocation of writer have a "doubled" nature; that, for whatever reasons, they are as adept at observing the behavior around them as they are at participating in it. Further, we may generalize that writers are more assiduous, if not always more successful, in the search for self-knowledge than are most people. Beyond this, the love of words—and the energy and caring to use the language with precision—may be the sole shared feature.

The more modest effort to interpret an author's personality in the light of his works, and vice versa, often yields genuine insight into each. It is of course confined in the main to writers of the fairly recent past, since they are the only ones about whose personal lives we have very much evidence. Instances of this approach are numerous, and some among them are very convincing. Characteristically, the analyst weaves back and forth between the events of the author's life and the imagined occurrences of his fiction. The picture of the person and the art that emerges depends on the writer's candor, on the analyst's skill, and on the artistic quality of the work; the more substance in the art, the more interesting the conclusions drawn. Writers with a penchant for self-revelation and a habit of using their experiences fairly directly in the act of compositon are most susceptible to this mode of interpretation. Thus F. Scott Fitzgerald, Ernest Hemingway, and George Bernard Shaw have each been the subject of illuminating inquiry. More reticent, private people, especially if they eschew an obvious exploitation of the autobiographical mass, yield less; T.S. Eliot and William Faulkner might be examples.

A close examination of Fitzgerald's life, joined to a thematic analysis of his novels and short stories, purports to show that Fitzgerald rehearses a consistent pattern of personal strivings. Dubbed the *Icarus Complex* by the psychologist Henry A. Murray, this pattern includes overwhelming ambition, the desire to be a cynosure, a craving for immortality, and dramatic fall from the heights of attainment, such as the mythic Icarus underwent when the sun melted his waxen wings. The novelist's life course, his observations about himself, and the life arcs of his fictional protagonists all hang together rather coherently in such a model.[32]

Hemingway has been a recent subject of psychiatric inquiry. The analyst discerns, again, a thematic consistency in his life experiences, in what he says about himself and his work, and in the central problems of his novels. Too simply and briefly put, Hemingway repeats a striving for robust masculinity, a constant need to reaffirm his manhood, combined with grave inner doubts about his durability and potency. His contempt for the weak and the womanly is a projection of these doubts. When, finally, physical illness and mental turmoil debilitate the writer and he can no longer sustain the self-image of adventurous invulnerability, he chooses suicide.[33]

In a somewhat different vein, the psychoanalyst Erik H. Erikson has employed Shaw's autobiographic writings for a dual purpose. He wishes at once to enrich our understanding of Shaw's personality and his posture toward a literary vocation, and to glean certain general principles of personality development.[34] And Erikson succeeds brilliantly in both: he shows us the playwright struggling and winning in a quest for maturity, for an identity suitable to his creative outreach; then he goes beyond to generate fresh psychological concepts about the problem of ego-identity, concepts applicable to nonwriters as well as to the lucid Shaw who has served as an exemplary fount.

Study of the Creative Process

Albert Camus made creative work the capstone of his ideas about individual morality and effort, viewing the process as the scene of courageous, intelligent self-mastery. Many psychologists would assent, on the grounds that the capacity to symbolize, to form and order the flux of existence, represents the uniquely human and most hard-won quality of man. Our understanding of creativity is very incomplete, either in terms of the personality of the creator, as sketched above, or in terms of the sequence of activities entailed in making something new. Some phases of creative work, in art as in science, are rather readily accessible to the observer; their credibility is also buttressed by consistencies in the testimony of acknowledgedly creative men and women. Thus we are persuaded that an initial immersion in the elements, the problems, the stuff to be worked on, is essential. Innovation does not take place in a vacuum. Again, the creative worker must be clearly adept in the craftsmanlike aspect of the metier, must know how to formulate and express the materials thrown up by the imagination. Artists must be dogged in the hard, hard labor of construction, revision, and polishing, the clothing of insight in meaningful garments. They need the child's playfulness in entertaining possible combinations and distortions, joined to adult energy and the power to stay the course.

So much we know—or so much artists roughly agree upon. What is concealed from forthright psychological analysis is the precise nature of the moment when the original pairing of elements occurs, when insight or inspiration present themselves in the mind's eye. As Paul Valéry said, "one line is given to the poet by God or by nature; the rest he must discover for himself." Something is known of how we prepare for insight, make ourselves ready to take advantage of it. A peculiar linking of intense absorption and playful relaxation appears crucial to creative readiness. Craft and vocational commitment are necessary if the *ligne donnée* is to be exploited. But the instant of the breakthrough remains shrouded, and there is sharp disagreement about how nearly it may be deliberately forced by the conscious will. Experience no doubt helps, and with it the confidence that what has happened once may be again coaxed forth. We are still very far, however, from being able to formulate a recipe for creativity or to instruct neophytes in its ways. The late Louis Armstrong once remarked that if you feel jazz you needn't be told about it, and if you do not feel it, no amount of telling will help very much.

Study of Psychological Types and Laws within Literature

The easiest and most obvious use of literature by the psychologist is an illustrative one. Imagined personalities may be regarded as exemplars of psychological dispositions which are already familiar from clinical experience. Here literature is employed to dramatize, to fill out, to render manifest and coherent the scattered observations that ordinarily underlie a diagnosis. Thus the Stones have gathered together excerpts from novels and short stories illuminating the chief features of various abnormalities.[35] Conrad Aiken's delicate story of a child drifting away from human contact, "Silent Snow, Secret Snow," is cited as a portrait of autism; a passage from Fitzgerald's Tender Is the Night, describing the heroine Nicole's condition, serves to exemplify schizophrenia. Presumably, the student of mental illness can gain from such a collection a sharper sensitivity to the nuances of personality deformation, perhaps especially in that the imaginative writer displays the interior world of the affected individual more richly than most "real" cases are able to.

Literature as illustration of either psychological types or principles of behavior is of course not limited to the aberrant. Dickens, Balzac, Tolstoy, all show us a wealth of character types, most of them well within the range of the normal. Since the novelist's aim is not to clarify our understanding of motivation or to classify textbook cases, he or she often presents a more many-sided and internally complex picture of human functioning than does the psychologist whose mission may be to simplify and generalize. The late Gordon Allport, a humanistic psychologist, pointed to the superficiality of some psychological descriptions: "Good literature never makes the mistake of confusing the personality of man with that of a waterskate. Psychology often does."[36]

Beyond the analysis of a given individual, literature is sometimes thought to express recurrent patterns in the behavior of specified groups. That is, the imaginative writer may characterize typical features of personality attached to an occupation (the merchant, the clergy, the military), a social class or status (the aristocrat, the burgher), or even members of a nation state (the "American character"). In this perilous undertaking, we move from psychological interpretation as such to a consideration of how social structures and social roles may impress their diverse inhabitants with certain uniformities of outlook or style. Buddenbrooks may be taken to represent the psychological style of the German bourgeoisie of the late nineteenth century, or The Great Gatsby to portray the striving behavior and bondage to an invented future typical of some devotees of the American dream.

All kinds of warning flags properly go up when the analyst shifts from the illustrative to the evidential use of literature. It is one thing to say that Mary Tyrone in O'Neill's *Long Day's Journey into Night* emerges as an addictive personality. It is quite another to say that Jay Gatsby instructs us in important aspects of American national character. For creative writers are selective: they devise a fictional personality to fit the story they want to tell, underlining here and omitting there. Moreover, in the absence of corroborating data of materials about a time and place and people drawn from extraliterary sources, one may slip into what Bernard DeVoto called "the literary fallacy." In this fallacy, the imaginative literature of an era is taken as wholly representative and self-validating. Still, in judicious and skillful hands, the effort to read off the temper of an age and its prominent models of individual conduct from literature may not only be intrinsically absorbing but may also inspire fresh ideas about the relation of personality to social milieu.

To the literary critic, the possibilities of interpreting imagined characters' behavior in psychological terms are inviting but pregnant with damage. They are inviting because psychological knowledge can deepen understanding of a protagonist's motivation, throwing light into dark corners of contradiction and obscurity. Dangers are of at least two kinds: by focusing on the intricacies of a single character, the interpreter may misgauge the significance of interaction *among* characters and thereby disfigure the total aesthetic force of a well-articulated plot; perhaps more serious, the effort to pin down idiosyncrasies often renders the fictional hero a clinical case, and in so doing misses or understates the hero's representativeness of universals in the human condition.

These arguments, particularly the latter, may be illustrated by the attempt to come to grips with Meursault, Camus' hero (or antihero) in *The Stranger.* To many readers, Meursault is an enigmatic figure because in his passivity and lack of caring he appears to be unmotivated, or at any rate motivated in a highly unusual fashion. It is then observed by the psychologist that Meursault is a type-case of neurasthenia. He does not know how to feel, or care that he does not; he has flat affect, an incapacity for emotional arousal; withdrawn from the interpersonal world, he is constantly fatigued; he cannot understand others' feelings, or how he affects them. So far so good, and the diagnosis is unquestionably correct. But as the psychiatrist R.D. Laing has pointed out, the plight of the existential hero is not only, and perhaps not most importantly, construed as an instance of individual pathology. Rather, Meursault's significance lies in his standing for everyman, for all who confront (as Camus did again and again) a witless, meaningless universe, for those who experience the full onslaught of absurdity. The situation of the absurd man may indeed be made plainer by psychological analysis. However, the psychology of absurdity speaks to large numbers of modern men. If what moves Meursault to his acts and refusals to act is a unique aberration of personality, then that aberration must be seen in a common framework the hero shares with all sentient creatures.

Effects of Literature upon Its Readers

Inquiries into the effects of imaginative literature upon the lives of its readers are remarkable for their scarcity. Neglect of such an apparently compelling topic has several roots. Behavioral scientists have not traditionally thought of aesthetic experience as a major species of life event. When exploring how personality is shaped, they have looked rather to apparently more direct, concrete, and immediate stimuli: the influence of parents and peers, the situational demands of household and classroom, the ambience of neighborhood and community. More recently, because of their physical intrusiveness, the mass media of communication—especially television—have gained some attention as possible factors in personal development. But reading has been consigned to a minor role, if any, in the formation of personality.

In addition to the psychologist's professional neglect of literary experience, there are other reasons for our ignorance. One is surely the tendency on the part of literary critics and other initiates of high culture to assume that aesthetic events are extremely important, but that their significance is so pervasive that no demonstration is needed. *Of course* literature molds our tastes and styles, our values and perceptions. *Of course* literature shapes our language, and hence our perceptual and cognitive possibilites; it teaches us about other people, other times, other private worlds we cannot yet—and may never—experience "on the nerve." Yet these manifold effects are assumed, not explicated, and in the taking for granted we close off a rich vein of investigation.

Finally, and perhaps most obviously, the psychology of readership is plagued by familiar problems of multi-causality and the sequence of cause and effect. Aesthetic experience is embedded in other happenings in the life space, so much so that it is hard to disentangle the impact of reading a particular book, or many books, from the impact of all else going on at the same time. Does the recommendation of a friend or a teacher that we read this novel or that play, that we make the acquaintance of a certain poet, forever color our view of the work in question? If an individual falls in love with the Romantic poets and with a real lover simultaneously, who is to say whether Keats or cuddling forever thereafter skews the angle of vision? And the direction of the causal chain is seldom clear. Many people have testified that reading a specific book was to them a vital experience, substantially altering their way of thinking and feeling. (For instance, Heywood Broun claimed that Bellamy's *Looking Backward* converted him to socialism.) Yet we can never be quite sure how far a predisposing taste led the person to take up a given author, prepared the ground for aesthetic reception, and how far the book itself acted as a fresh stimulus. Literary experience complements, supplements, sometimes contradicts other types of experience; it is one part, now large, now small, of the densely woven web of influences in the formation of literate personalities.

The obstacles in assessing literature's force upon the reader have led to the impasse described by several commentators:

> Indeed, it is not a great exaggeration to say that as a scholarly interest it [the response of the reader] is almost entirely neglected except as part of the analysis of literary influences on particular writers.[37]

> We have yet to find any comprehensive study of the effects of students' reading.[38]

A small-scale research into college students' literary experience provided tentative evidence that reading may contribute to individual development in a number of ways. One channel of influence concerns the psychological processes of identification and alienation; in this instance, students were asked to report on fictional characters who had seemed to them worthy of emulation, or the reverse—characters who repelled them. Interesting correspondences were found between the students' own personality configurations and the identity of ego-ideal and ego-alien figures in their remembered reading. Similarly, there appeared to be a congruence between fictional themes and important areas of concern in students' lives. Examples are the undergraduate who flees from reality, harboring unachievable aspirations and failing academically, and who joins these characteristics to an immersion in escapist science fiction; or the student who is marginally upper class, in some peril of falling from this status, who uses John Marquand's novels as a source of reinforcement, feeling they justify his status and that he can share a gentle in-group satire. Reading may be seen, too, in this group of individuals, as a gross category of experience, providing ammunition for domestic debate, affording an alternative to peer-group involvement, serving as a yardstick for making (or rationalizing) selected decisions about other people.[39]

> The subject may be asked to give a history of the fairy stories, fables, myths, adventure books, novels, plays, operas, pictures, paintings, sculpture and music that have most impressed him since he was a child....This procedure is based on the principle that a subject is most impressed by and remembers best the stories and creative productions which represent aspects of his own fantasies. A given presentation may light up hitherto latent tendencies or it may merely serve as a conduit for existent fantasies....Thus, a psychologist who simply notes a subject's artistic preferences may sometimes guess correctly the unconscious processes that are active within the subject.[40]

In addition to the effort to trace literary influence upon an individual's psychological make-up, there is a series of questions about the scope and uniformity of literary experience among population groups. Thus we may well ask about the pervasiveness of Shakespeare's imagination in molding English postures toward nationhood or interpersonal conduct. Or we may seek to uncover changing American interests and tastes by noting shifts in the content of bestseller lists, or fluctuations of literary critical reputation. In all these endeavors the problems of interpretation are compounded by issues of sampling, representativeness, and quality versus quantity. Is it more important to psychological dispositions, and to the fate of the language, that several million people read *Gone With the Wind* or that several thousand read *Four Quartets?* How much does one elite, fully absorbed reader weigh in comparison to a multitude of scanners? In any event, audience psychology remains relatively unexplored.

I think we might conclude that psychological interpretation *of* literature and *in* literature is a very risky but inherently absorbing enterprise. At its worst it may oversimplify or distort the writer's vision. At its bold but controlled best, a psychological approach to literary art may reveal unanticipated riches, may deepen and refine that enjoyment and comprehension of life itself that is literature's ultimate yield.

An Agenda for the Sociology of Art

This rather cursory overview of certain aspects of the sociology of art has perhaps raised more questions than it has answered. Part of the reason for our paucity of sure knowledge lies in the phenomena themselves: the arts are notoriously tricky and dense for any analyst, be it philosopher, critic, or social scientist. But a larger share of the reason lies in the lack of attention devoted to this realm of experience by sociologists. We have not thought long or hard, have not been conceptually or methodologically inventive, and have not made art a major focus of empirical research. In these concluding comments, I shall try to sketch in several items of a possible agenda for the sociologist of the arts.

Content Analysis

There is a great need for shrewd, fresh strategies in the analysis of the arts themselves. The art historian and the literary critic, the philosopher of aesthetics and the musicologist, each has developed elaborate vocabularies for handling artistic properties. Although social scientists can learn from these vocabularies, and perhaps use them as starting points, students of human behavior must create their own relevant classifications and conceptual tools. What, that is, are the significant categories of content and form in the various arts when our aim is to understand the social meaning of art?

Such a mode of analysis must clearly go beyond the obvious representation of social themes, ferreting out the messages and styles and symbols that appear initially remote from political or economic concerns. Leo Lowenthal sets the task for the sociologist of literature:

> The specific treatment which a creative writer gives to nature or to love, to gestures and moods, to situations of gregariousness or solitude, the weight given to reflections, descriptions or conversations, are all phenomena which on first sight may seem sterile from a sociological point of view but which are in fact genuinely primary sources for a study of the penetration of the most private and intimate spheres of individual life by the social climate, on which, in the last analysis, this life thrives. For times that have passed, literature often becomes the only available source of informations about private modes and more.[41]

And Lowenthal has in fact exemplified his own recommendations in a masterly fashion, tracing such facets in the changing image of man in western European literature.[42]

Similarly, Clifford Geertz advises the anthropologist to adopt this stance of sympathetic interpretation:

> The culture of a people is an ensemble of texts, themselves ensembles, which the anthropologist strains to read over the shoulders of those to whom they properly belong. There are enormous difficulties in such an enterprise, methodological pitfalls to make a Freudian quake, and some moral perplexities as well. Nor is it the only way the symbolic forms can be sociologically handled. Functionalism lives, and so does psychologism. But to regard such forms as "saying something," and saying it to somebody, is at least to open up the possibility of an analysis which attends to their substance rather than to reductive formulas professing to account for them.[43]

Only by close attention to the intrinsic qualities of novels and plays, paintings and dancing, can we arrive at the kernel of their social meanings. The arts are indeed products of something, about something, maybe the progenitors of something; but above all they *are* something.

Institutional Analysis

Although this is the aspect of the arts that has been best studied in sociology, we still require much more fully and precisely documented descriptions of the processes through which the arts are created and transmitted. Comparatively little is known, for example, about the relation of one artist to another and the effect their mode of interaction may have upon the art product. Nearly all of our clues about this type of intracraft relationship are drawn from the occasional and anecdotal observation. Artists, as the poet and critic John Ciardi has argued, are likely to be their own best guides to themselves; at the same time, the sociological observer may make somewhat different—and perhaps revealing—inferences about the significance of the interplay among colleagues.

In this era of specialization, with its elaborate and prolific repertoire of occupational roles, attention should be devoted to the network of people and organizations that mediate the aesthetic transaction. Illustrative role studies might be those of the literary critic, the art critic, the literary agent, the editor and publisher, the manager in the performing arts. Organizations that link art with publics are inviting subjects for investigation: the museum, the school, the voluntary agency such as the arts council.

Social institutions that impinge on the arts most directly, especially in the guise of support and/or regulation, should be examined for their postures toward varieties of art and artist. In the United States, such an examination might seek to chronicle the policies (and possibilities) of government, charitable foundation, and corporate subsidy. Cross-national comparison could be enlightening here, in that a very wide range of institutional sponsorship exists throughout the world.

Relations of High Art to Popular Art

For economy and clarity, my discussion has been confined to the sociological view of the arts as traditionally defined: "serious" literature and painting; "classical" music and dance. There is obviously a need, however, to juxtapose these traditional fine arts (or high culture) with the immense outpouring of popular art. Several key dimensions of such comparison are readily apparent, and have in fact formed the substance of a good deal of dialogue, often impassioned dialogue, in recent years.[44]

Probably the most vexed issue involves the competition among forms and levels of art for audience attention. It is often assumed by devotees of the fine arts that high culture must inevitably suffer from the increasing volume and availability of popular art. If we grant that time, money, and aesthetic receptivity are limited, conflicting claims for shares of these must seemingly ensue. Yet we should not be too quick to assume that levels of art are vying for a scarce pool of attention. It may be that the overlap in audience composition is not large, that various modes of art enjoy discrete publics. It may also be hypothesized that certain experiences with popular art stimulate the appetite for fine art.

Another problem of competition concerns the allegiances of creative talents, rather than audiences. To what extent do the economic and other rewards of popular art seduce the serious artist from his appointed rounds? Or, on the other hand, how far do such opportunities afford the poet or painter or composer a ready source of income which can then be used to sustain his or her activities as a maker of high culture? Serious artists may be radical critics of society's prevailing values; one of their tasks is to ask hard questions about common assumptions. If the fine artist often opposes the bland, the comfortable, and the conventional, what may we say about the stance of the popular artist? Values espoused in popular art deserve careful examination, since they may more accurately reflect the mood of a people at a given point in time than do the singular perceptions of the serious artist. This is especially likely to be case when we note the close links between popular art and advertising, which inevitably insure that the widely purveyed arts will not stray far from the presumed tastes of the consumer.

Finally, we must ask whether the mass media themselves, as a mode of communication, are working changes in the patterns of audience response. Does steady exposure to television actually shift the viewer's perceptual habits and possibilities, as McLuhan suggests? Does the torrent of print to which we are increasingly exposed mean that our ability to focus on a novel or play is altered?

Comparative Studies

The comparative method might be applied in two chief ways. First, cross-societal comparisons of the arts, in both their content and their institutional forms, would be very instructive. Several efforts have been made to develop thematic analyses in this vein, as exemplified, for instance, in McGranahan and Wayne's[45] contrast of German and American drama. Similarly, the content of the arts of the same society at different periods of time may be revealingly assessed in the search for the knowledge of social change. Cross-cultural investigation of the arts as social institutions might center on such aspects as differential patterns of recruitment, of governmental policy toward the arts, of audience preference.

A more challenging type of comparative analysis is found in the attempt to discern thematic and formal relationships among the various arts. Here, of course, the incompatabilities of media and form make the quest for intelligible categories of comparison very hazardous. Yet the fact that culture is patterned and society is systemic would argue for significant elements of congruence among the arts of a given period. Too, the practitioners of different fine arts often pay attention to one another's work, and are not seldom personally acquainted, so the tides of mutual influences can run pretty freely. An historically important instance of such influence is the Bloomsbury Group in early twentieth-century London, containing as it did painters, poets, novelists, and nonartist intellectuals.

Sociological Analysis of Creativity

Although I have maintained that the sociologist needs the psychologist for a deep understanding of the creative process, it is still true that there are little-explored sociological dimensions of creativity. These might be termed the antecedent, the associated, and the consequent conditions of creative work. The study of antecedent conditions would include such features in the life history of creative persons as familial origins, early experience, education in its several guises, and the influence of peers and exemplars on the growth of interest and talent. Investigations of this order would be relevant not only to the social scientific enterprise itself, but might have practical utility for a society whose problems demand a widespread cultivation of the capacity for original, bold thought of all kinds.

Conditions associated with creativity encompass the repertory of social roles enacted by artists in addition to the artist role itself: the modes of interaction with family members, friends, colleagues, middlemen, and representatives of the public. How does the artist's chosen life style, the habits of social engagement and withdrawal, mesh with the imperatives of creative effort? How is his economic level or the quality of recognition by appropriate audiences related to innovative elan and endurance?

Reciprocally, we may ask about the social consequences of creative success or failure. In what way does success as an artist shape the subsequent course of events in the individual life space? What are the implications of an artist's dedication to his or her vocation for other spheres of life and other favored roles?

Sociological Analysis of Audience Response

The questions to be posed in this part of the agenda are so obvious they need merely to be listed. How do people come to grips (if they do) with aesthetic experience? How are aesthetic responses learned? How are audience perceptions related to familiar sociological characteristics, such as social class, occupation, education? What are the consequences of aesthetic experience for future behavior?

The Arts and Social Change

Implicit in much of the earlier discussion is the fact that the arts in the modern West, perhaps especially in the United States, are caught up in the same very rapid processes of change as are all other parts of the society. Not only do styles and fashions within the arts themselves seem to shift ever more quickly, but changes in technology, values, living styles, community organization, education, and family composition all bear on the artist's universe of possibilities. Instantaneous transmission of words, images, and sounds, and instantaneous access to them through, for example, individualized television programming, appear to hold immense consequences for the arts. The vast range of options opening up to people, their freer choices of how to spend their time, how, where, and with whom to live—all these entail a correlative range of aesthetic choices. We not only need to consider how social change will foment change in ways of creating and appreciating; we also must attend to the role the arts may play in helping people to civilize their future.

Notes

1. Hugh D. Duncan, *Communication and Social Order* (New York: Oxford University Press, 1968), p.7.
2. Pitirim A. Sorokin, *Social and Cultural Dynamics: Vol. I, Fluctuations of Forms of Art: Painting, Sculpture, Architecture, Music, and Criticism* (New York: American Book Company, 1937).
3. Pitirim A. Sorokin, *Crisis of Our Age* (New York: E.P. Dutton, 1946), pp. 32-33.
4. Charles P. Loomis and Zona K. Loomis, *Modern Social Theories* (Princeton, N.J.: Van Nostrand, 1961), p. 460.
5. Sorokin, 1946, p. 31.
6. Loomis and Loomis, p. 460.
7. Robert N. Wilson, "F. Scott Fitzgerald: Personality and Culture," in *The Arts in Society*, ed. Robert N. Wilson (Englewood Cliffs, N.J.: Prentice-Hall, 1964).
8. Vytautas Kavolis, *Artisitc Expression: A Sociological Analysis* (Ithaca, N.Y.: Cornell University Press, 1968).
9. Kavolis, p. 165.
10. Duncan, p. 90.
11. Rene Wellek and Austin Warren, *Theory of Literature*. 3rd edition (New York: Harcourt, Brace, & World, 1956), p. 107.
12. Karl Marx and Friedrich Engels, *Uber Kunst und Literatur*. M. Lifschitz ed. (Berlin, 1948), pp. 21-22.
13. Kavolis, pp. 24-25.
14. Ibid., p. 160.
15. Jacques Maquet, *Introduction to Aesthetic Anthropology* (Boston: Addison-Wesley, 1971), p. 8.
16. Suzanne Langer, *Problems of Art* (New York: Charles Scribners Sons, 1957), p. 31.
17. Clifford Geertz, "Deep Play: Notes on the Balinese Cockfight," *Daedalus* 101 (1) (Winter 1972): 28.
18. Samuel Johnson, *The Lives of the Poets* (Garden City, N.Y.: Doubleday, n.d.), p. 12.
19. Mason Griff, "The Recruitment of the Artist," Wilson, ed., *The Arts in Society*.
20. Sondra Forsyth and Pauline M. Kolenda, "Competition, Cooperation, and Group Cohesion in the Ballet Company," *Psychiatry* 29 (2) (May 1966): 123-45.
21. Robert N. Wilson, *Man Made Plain* (Cleveland: Howard Allen, 1958).
22. Forsyth and Kolenda, pp. 123-45; Carol Pierson Ryser, "The Student Dancer," in Wilson, ed., *The Arts in Society*, pp. 97-121.
23. Robert Escarpit, *Sociologie de la Litterature* (Paris: Presses Universitaires de France, 1958).
24. Karl Erik Rosengren, *Sociological Aspects of the Literary System* (Stockholm: Natur Och Kultur, 1968).
25. Harrison C. White and Cynthia A. White, *Canvases and Careers* (New York: John Wiley & Sons, 1965).
26. Bernard Rosenberg and Norris Fliegel, *The Vanguard Artist* (Chicago: Quadrangle, 1965).
27. Edward A. Shils, "The High Culture of the Age, in Wilson, ed., *The Arts in Society*, pp. 317-62.
28. Richard Eells, "Business for Art's Sake: The Case for Corporate Support of the Arts," in *The Business of America*, ed. Ivar Berg (New York: Harcourt, Brace, & World, 1968).

29. Wellek and Warren, p. 81.
30. L.A. Reid, *A Study in Aesthetics* (New York: Macmillan, 1954), p. 275.
31. Carl Jung, "Psychology and Literature," in Brewster Ghiselin, *The Creative Process* (Berkeley: University of California Press, 1952), p. 209.
32. Wilson, "F. Scott Fitzgerald: Personality and Culture," in *The Arts in Society.*
33. I.D. Yalom and M. Yalom, "Ernest Hemingway—A Psychiatric View," *Archives of General Psychiatry* 24 (6) (June 1971): 485–94.
34. Erik H. Erikson, "The Problem of Ego-Identity," *Journal of the American Psychoanalytic Association* (January 1956).
35. Alan A. Stone and Sue Smart Stone, *The Abnormal Personality through Literature* (Englewood Cliffs, N.J.: Prentice-Hall, 1966).
36. Gordon W. Allport, "Personality: A Problem for Science or a Problem for Art?" *Revista de Psihologie*, 1938, 1: 1–15.
37. Thomas C. Pollock, *The Nature of Literature* (Princeton, N.J.: Princeton University Press, 1949), p. 205.
38. Douglas Waples, Bernard Berelson, and Franklyn R. Bradshaw, *What Reading Does to People* (Chicago, Ill.: University of Chicago Press, 1940), p. 12.
39. Robert N. Wilson, "Literary Experience and Personality," *Journal of Aesthetics and Art Criticism,* 15 (1) (September 1956): .
40. Henry A. Murray, "Techniques for a Systematic Investigation of Fantasy," *Journal of Psychology* 3 (1936): 115–43.
41. Leo Lowenthal, *Literature, Popular Culture, and Society,* (Englewood Cliffs, N.J.: Prentice-Hall, 1961), p. 143.
42. Leo Lowenthal, *Literature and the Image of Man* (Boston: Beacon Press, 1957).
43. Geertz, p.29.
44. Robert N. Wilson, "High Culture and Popular Culture in a Business Society," in Ivar Berg, ed., *The Business of America,* pp. 390–406.
45. D.V. McGranahan and I. Wayne, "German and American Traits Reflected in Popular Drama," *Human Relations* 1 (1947–48): 429–55.

8
The Courage to Be Leisured

In *Magister Ludi* the novelist Herman Hesse sets forth a vision of an ideal society, Castalia, in which the most honored pursuit is to master the playing of a game. The "glass bead game" that absorbs the Castalians is described as a rarefied mixture of music and mathematics, surely the purest of the arts and sciences. Hesse's fantasy exemplifies the intimate connection between play and art, leisure and creativity; indeed, it is perhaps not too much to say that the poet's vocation is a this-worldly analogue of the glass bead game.

It took me a long time to realize the centrality of leisure to human experience when at a pitch of intensity, when in the enraptured texture of close interpersonal encounters or in innovative symbolic forays. The integral relation of leisure to creative possibility eluded me because, as a creature of my culture, I held the world of work as the sole meaningful frame of reference for significant life activities. I grew up in a factory town, almost everyone I knew was involved in industrial production, and one of my major fields of graduate study was the specialty termed *industrial sociology*. As a faithful disciple of the Protestant Ethic, I looked upon leisure as most Americans do: trivial, orgiastic, compensatory, whatever, but in any event not wholly serious and inevitably tainted with some not-so-faint flavor of illegitimacy. Only when it fell my lot to teach an undergraduate course on the topic of "work and leisure," a course I had not designed but had inherited from a younger colleague leaving the faculty, did I have occasion to think hard about leisure. As time went on, I paid increasing attention to leisure, less to work, reversing the traditional proportions of the syllabus and the conventional assumptions of our society. I began to dare tantalize my students with the assertion that leisure was central and work peripheral, and gradually convinced myself that this turning of the accepted wisdom on its head was in fact a splendid idea. Wonderfully and surprisingly, my long-standing concerns with making and appreciating art, with the world of sport, with the nature of interpersonal closeness and psychological health, coalesced in a philosophy of leisureliness. It may be pertinent to reiterate that in considering leisure, as in considering creativity itself, a parochial outlook simply will not do: here psychology and sociology, to say nothing of philosophy, are indissolubly wedded.

I think artistic creativity is made more familiar and understandable by its comparison with a variety of other human activities under the rubric of leisure. To play, to experiment, to relish the events of daily living for their own sakes: such a posture does not render art mundane, but may lend it a quotidian homeliness, assimilating it more nearly to the common run of personal chronology.

In linking leisurely events to Suzanne Langer's *presentational* mode of discourse, I try to describe a generously receptive stance toward experience, including aesthetic apprehension. I speak of "spending the whole self" in a fashion more comprehensive, more demanding, but also more rewarding than a restrained logico-rational path of inquiry. In some ways all of the research assembled here partakes of a willingness to be immersed, to be vulnerable, to be importantly affected by undergoing a fresh experience. My work has changed me, made my life course different than it would have been had I pursued other topics. Had I not been shaped by the thrill of creative imaginings I could not shape these accounts.

Many of humanity's most significant activities, the processes of creativity, invention, discovery, are ultimately based on a certain detached, playful attitude toward experience. Many of the most vital achievements, the results of these processes, could not occur in the absence of civilized reflection and purposeful daydreaming. Yet the very behavior that is essential to these activities and achievements, the behavior of being leisured, is one of the least understood and seldom analyzed of human experiences. This is an attempt to define certain characteristics of leisure, to explore reasons why it is such a neglected topic, and to suggest that the avowed, conscious pursuit of leisure is, especially in the highly organized societies of the modern West, a genuine test of personal courage.

Introduction

The late psychiatrist Eric Berne, best known for his observations on the strategies people employ in playing the games of daily living with one another, once stated that the first problem faced by each individual is to get through twenty-four hours a day. That is, each of us must devise some terms of structure, some minimal order to instruct ourself on what to do next. Berne's assertion rings true, surely, for the majority of Americans, marching to clock time and accustomed from early years to emphasize the planned, scheduled piecing together of their days. Yet the idea that time is a problem, or a commodity to be rationally "used," is of fairly recent origin in history and appears to be largely confined to advanced industrialized countries. Our conception of time, and our exquisite sensitivity to its passage, militates against leisureliness. One might almost assert that leisure with a fixed clock duration is a contradiction in terms, that it cannot be fully free or true to itself.

Closely linked to an exaggerated time-sense as an enemy of cultivated leisure is the familiar work morality that Max Weber identified as the Protestant Ethic. Although at least some of its roots lie in Calvinist dogma, the obligation to busy oneself is today an entirely secularized condition of the mass-productive social order. Freud said that the mark of a healthy individual was a capacity to love and work; and indeed, work is central to the integrity of contemporary personality, a chief source of one's self-concept. The difficulty for leisure comes not from the importance attached to work as such, but rather from too-rigid definitions of work as a narrowly goal-directed enterprise, as an obligation to be performed instead of an activity to be savored. An individual who is not "working" in this limited sense of performing a specified routine for a stated time with a set product or result, is almost sure to suffer pervasive feelings of guilt. Bearing this guilt, confronting its sources, and at least partly curing ourselves of the compulsive habit of busy-working: here is the all too infrequently met challenge to our courage.

The pressure of time and the pressure of busy-ness are abetted and underlain by the language in which we speak of ourselves and our doings. Language to a very considerable extent shapes what we can perceive and how we think. Our language is beautifully adapted to the world of organized work, but ill-adapted to the world of unorganized leisure. We have many words, and many perceptual frames, to describe the production of goods or the rules of bureaucratic behavior. But our tongues twist or fall silent when we try to tell of contemplation or love, of writing a poem or pondering a philosophy. What Suzanne Langer calls *discursive* symbolism is exceedingly familiar and comfortable to us; this is the language of direct rational statement, of the textbook, the directive, the instructional manual. It is a superb vehicle for getting certain things done, or for pointing things out. However, our very mastery of discursive style tends to blind us from real appreciation of a significant alternative mode of discourse, one Langer terms *presentational* symbolism. Presentational discourse is geared to the reporting of whole experiences in all their richness, instead of pointing to items or aspects of experience. It is the language of art and religion. Most of us are less comfortable with this mode of seeing and speaking, and since this posture for dealing with the world is much closer to the spirit of leisure than to the ethic of work, it compounds our difficulty in either analyzing or enjoying leisured behavior.

Time pressure, the work ethic, and the dominance of discursive symbolism will be discussed in some depth; they are identified as three traps from which we must extricate ourselves if leisure is to be possible. I shall ask questions about the social and psychological conditions or concomitants of leisure, and assert that leisure is crucial not only to artistic and scientific creativity but to the creative interpersonal spheres of friendship and love.

The Leisure Process

Leisure is not static, is not a fixed posture. Even when, to the superficial outward observation, the person at leisure appears passive or immobile, he or she is engaged in a process of events. Tumultuous or calm, we are ever in motion. One of our great hazards in considering leisure is that it is so commonly thought of as a residue, an empty category of experience that is left over when other life-sustaining activities have been accomplished. We conventionally ask, "What is that person *doing*?" and lacking the language to describe creativity or contemplation we conclude, "Nothing." But leisure is precisely the most active way of doing nothing—that is, of doing nothing that is yet apparent, of nourishing an emergence.

The idea of leisure as an alert engagement with the world, rather than a quiescent onlooking, may be exemplified by the activity of responding to art. Aesthetic enjoyment is really at the opposite pole from the kind of sleepy—and sloppy—spectatorship we so often associate with watching television, say. Attending to a work of art requires that individuals mobilize their energies and adopt an attitude of vigilant perception. I remember the psychologist Christiana Morgan's shrewd remark that one cannot read Shakespeare when one is tired, that one must be somehow "up to" the level of intensity at which great art is wrought. To truly look at a painting, to listen to music with both ears (and perhaps with Theodore Reik's "third ear," the ear that catches the motive behind the sound), to read a poem in full following of the poet's voice: all these are in effect a reaching out for experience, the opposite of withdrawal or passivity. Suzanne Langer argues that attending to presentational symbols, the language of art, is more like having a new experience than it is like entertaining a proposition. Just so, and if it is possible to entertain a proposition with only a part of one's responsive repertory, it is impossible to have a genuinely new experience without spending the whole self.

The reasons why art demands our full involvement are clear. Art is many-layered, complex, often ambiguous, hence anything less than complete attentiveness will not do. Too, it may be asserted that the artistic transaction remains incomplete until an alert perceiver has done his or her part; the unlooked-at painting or the unread poem do not, in an important sense, actually exist as art. Only when the circuit of communication is closed by the perceiver's grasp, whether sure or hesitant, of the artist's intent, may we say that the process of art has in fact occurred. There are three parties to the process: the creating artist, the yield of his work, objectified in the art itself, and the aesthetically responsive individual confronting the art, attuning himself more or less successfully to the artist's voice, slipping with whatever degree of fit into the artist's skin.

Of course the perception of art is only one instance, although a particularly instructive one, of the leisure process. The aesthetic response is a useful example because it helps us begin to sort out the generic characteristics of leisure, to say what this behavioral mode is and is not. Leisure is identified as a process rather than a state; as a willing surrender of the whole self to experience rather than a parcelling out of some one or few of the individual's faculties. These features happen to be, not at all accidentally, also the distinctive marks of other leisured activities: of play; of creativity; of philosophic or religious or scientific contemplation; of the spirit of craftsmanship; and, crucially, of the most compelling interpersonal relationships, sexual love and committed friendship. What all these prized patterns of conduct have in common is a certain openness to the world, a relaxation of a tight, defensive hold on the boundaries of the self, a bold willingness to experiment and to let things happen without a brittle adherence to specified means and ends. And as they entail what we most value as the exquisitely conscious animals we are, so they entail great risks: the loss of the self, the fragmentation of a hard-won personal integrity, the frustrations and depressions that often accompany slow processes, the fear of failure attendant on the courageous quest for great riches. We shy away from this wholehearted giving of ourselves to the deep currents of emotion and intellection; this, surely, is one of the reasons why genuine lovingness and rich creativity are such rare happenings.

A further hallmark of leisure is its gratuitous quality. None of the activities that exemplify the leisured attitude has to be undertaken by a given individual at a given time. We might well argue that love and friendship, innovation and meditation, are required by society at large, certainly by what we are pleased to think of as a highly civilized society. Someone must be capable of leisure some of the time for the total health of the community. We might even argue that a talent for entering into leisure processes is an important feature of the best-integrated, most highly cultivated individual personalities. But for the individual the talent is not central to survival, or even to the modest enjoyment of life. Leisured behavior is by definition free, not forced.

True leisure is not, perhaps unfortunately, part of the common run of modern experience; it is rather more like what A.H. Maslow described as "peak experience," the apprehension of the world at full throttle, in utter involvement. The feeling of being at a peak when one is immersed in the most excellent leisure events is uniformly reported by people who try to describe their love, or religious experience, or creative activity. Its rare occurrence in most people's lives is probably one reason we are so inarticulate about the most intense, heightened sequences of leisure. Thus we fall back on words like *mysterious, ineffable,* and maybe most honest of all, *indescribable.*

If leisure is gratuitous and, at least in its superior manifestations, quite rare, it is also today a cultivated, learned, willed capacity. This property of leisureliness as an attainment is well expressed in Montaigne's observation that the test of a civilized person is the ability to sit alone in a room without being bored. The inwardness to which Montaigne refers, the idea of being comfortable with oneself, presumably demands a certain richness of personal resources, a cognitive and spiritual stock on which one may draw without fear of imminent depletion. But if the talent for being leisured must be learned and nourished, the learning can probably not take place in any very deliberate or mechanical fashion. Novices can no doubt be instructed to some extent in the arts of meditation, of spiritual concentration; but even here the teacher can offer only clues, and the patience and personal depth required of the learner insure that the mystical experience is not for everyone, or even for very many. Similarly, in art or science or love the apprentice is substantially self-taught. The would-be practitioner of creative work can only receive some cues and try to model himself on exemplary figures. And although the poet may claim that, "Nature's lay idiot, I taught thee to love," the teaching and learning of love occurs surely by indirection, implication, shared exploration. Love depends more on self-surrender (and self-knowledge) than on any explicit pedagogy, and this despite the solemn ministrations of our moden technicians of sex. The sex clinicians can instruct us, perhaps, in how to have sexual intercourse, but scarcely in how to fructify joy or delight in one another.

The leisured posture, then, is to be learned, at any rate by those of us caught in the traps of timeliness, busy-work, and prosaic language. But it consists in a learning by experience, by exposure to what might be termed, to turn a worn phrase on its head, the school of soft knocks. And some not so soft—which is why courage is needed. The will and ability to explore the self is of first importance, undergirding and complementing the ability to explore that world of other people and of symbols that is both "in here" and "out there."

For self-knowledge and for the sharpened perception that lets us really see our environment of nature and human nature, stretches of privacy are essential. Solitude in our age is hard to come by, real privacy the privilege of very few. We can be and are often lonely, but it is the loneliness of David Riesman's "lonely crowd." Beset with stimuli, we can be isolated but not calmly alone. No one has expressed the need for periodic withdrawal better than the then Archbishop of Canterbury, Michael Ramsey. His wise reflections bear directly on the nature of leisure and on important obstacles to its attainment:

Retreats and the World Today

When pleas are made about the desirability of retreat, many characteristics of our contemporary age are alluded to, as—for instance—that it is noisy and bustling and tiring. My diagnosis would be to use the word "over-crowded" —our age is over-crowded, and in particular the mind and heart of man are over-crowded. Each day a man or a woman does so many things, sees so many things, hears so many things, says so many things, and the mind has crowded into it a multitude of impressions, fleeting in and out. Some are important, others are unimportant. Some are good, some are bad. Some are worth preserving, some are merely of the moment. Some are worth pausing to consider, others are worth no consideration at all. Yet the mind and the heart are so over-crowded by this rapidity of sensations that for millions of people the power is lost to distinguish, to reflect, to reject or to approve thoughtfully, rationally, conscientiously. The power is lost to do what Saint Paul calls "to approve the things that are excellent."

It follows that purely from a humanist point of view, because man is so over-crowded in heart and mind, he is frustrated from being his own best self through a constant servitude to the haphazard. It is the reign of the haphazard that is so diabolical. From a theological point of view we can put the diagnosis a bit differently and say this: that man is the slave of the temporal flux of events, sensations, experiences, and therefore he misses the realisation of himself as a child of eternity. "There was silence in Heaven." "Be still, and know that I am God." So too man being enslaved to the temporal flux, fails to be able to "consider," in the biblical meaning of that word. Remember the very significant and telling way in which the word "consider" is used in the Bible. "Consider the lilies, how they grow." And they grow in a very leisurely way and if you are to consider how they grow you must have some affinity to their leisureliness. "When I consider the heavens, even the works of Thy hands, what is man that Thou are mindful of him?" "O, consider this, ye that forget God." The power to "consider" is undermined.[1]

Leisure cannot be enjoyed under "a constant servitude to the haphazard," since this bondage to a barrage of stimuli inhibits or even utterly forecloses the capacity to be reflective or introspective. If the individual lacks the time or the personal breathing space to "consider" in Canterbury's significant use of that term, then the days slip away unexamined and unsavored. Thoreau, surely one of the few American writers to have understood leisure, asserted that "most men lead lives of quiet desperation"; one might say that in the age of mass media and frantic overstimulation most men and women lead lives of noisy desperation.

It will be quite obvious, I think, that the various characteristics of the leisure process I have tried to rehearse run counter to the prevalent themes of contemporary American life. This thematic conflict is present not only in what we usually designate as the world of work, but also in those reaches of "free" or unfilled time that might be *potentially* the occasion of leisure. Our hours away from the constraints of occupations, of everyday jobs, are marked either by a fatigued withdrawal, a numbed respite from the harness of the work ethic, or else by an imitation of work life, a continuation of work attitudes now applied to the "uses" of discretionary time.

I believe it is futile to seek a strict definition of work or of leisure. Our felt experience of life does not fall into neat categories. That posture of leisureliness I have described may be adopted toward much of what we conventionally label as work; indeed, when it is the work that is likely to be more joyously and energetically done. Similarly, I should maintain, as above, that our dominant tendency is to carry over the stingy husbanding of the self, and the apprehension of being hemmed in by roles, rules, and short-term schedules that marks occupational life, into the realm of supposed freedom.

When I speak of "the courage to be leisured" I mean to imply that for us today a vulgar, foreshortened version of the Protestant work ethic is the natural and comfortable stance for dealing with our activities and relationships, and that to break with this pattern demands a stubborn boldness found in only a tiny minority of lovers and saints, poets and scientists. True leisure is premised on a willingness to wrench oneself away from the soothing ambience of busy motions and tidy calendars. And on a disposition, too, to let go, not to dole out the self in carefully measured portions, in grudging commitment and fragmented roles. As the poet Charles Olson once admonished, "Let the music lead the dance, leave the self behind."

The next section will focus on the three traps sketched in my Introduction, in an effort to determine why leisureliness should be such a hard-won and infrequent phenomenon.

Obstacles to Leisure: Three Traps

The young child at play, or the slightly older child dreaming the long daylight fantasies of a future in the great world, is by definition leisured. Free from the compulsion of inner appetite or of a schedule imposed from without, the child does what one does when one has nothing to do. Similarly, the poet has been described as an individual who, having nothing to do, finds something to do. This parallel, among many that indicate a kinship between the artist and the child, is a significant clue to the nature of playfulness and the nature of creative effort. The psychologist Robert W. White insists that children exhibit a propensity to reach out for satisfying experiences with their environment, to toy with the objects around them. He suggests the presence of what he terms *competence motivation*; this thrust toward manipulation and mastery, seen even in the crib-bound play of the infant, appears to operate in the absence of urgent biological needs. Thus White believes that we can identify a motive to be competent, to cope with the elements of experience, that drives the child toward play for its own sake. Undriven, freely chosen, gratuitous: this mode of behavior may be the child's analogue of adult leisureliness.

As individuals mature, particularly in contemporary American society, they appear to lose (or perhaps more accurately to have taken from them or smothered) the capacity for a playful approach to the world. They somehow can no longer indulge in guiltless fantasy, no longer pleasure themselves with an unpressured juggling of things and symbols. Why does this loss occur? Why does the adult shrink away from sheer playfulness? Can a childlike—*not* childish—posture of delight, curiosity, a sense of the world as wonderful (full of wonder) be sustained, or if once lost, regained?

St. Paul said that when he became a man he put away childish things. Must we also necessarily put away the best of childlike things, notably an openness to fresh experience and a talent for zestful wondering? It was said of Albert Einstein that the great mathematician and physicist was remarkable for the number of things he didn't understand. I think we may take this to mean that he refused the conventional scientific wisdom and dared to ask the fundamental, embarrassing questions. The genius is like the child in being bold enough to report that the emperor has no clothes.

In the modern West, at least three complex, interlocking sets of reasons may be adduced for the normal adult's loss of playfulness, and hence of true leisure and creative possibility. I shall call these the *rational linguistic trap*, the *Protestant Ethical trap*, and the *time trap*. The three hazards reinforce one another in obvious and subtle ways, so much so that we may seldom be aware of being trapped; or, if we occasionally struggle and squirm, we find the bonds of steel too strong to snap.

The Rational Linguistic Trap

> *When those who love God try to speak of Him, their words are like the tears of the blind lions searching in the desert for water.*
>
> —Léon Bloy

To speak of God, of love, of artistic creation and re-creation: all these partake of blinded tears and muted awe. Our stereotyped habits of language, overwhelmingly directed to one-dimensional labeling of phenomena and the connections among them, prevent us from leisurely perception and rounded contemplation. Ernest Schachtel has offered one of the clearest interpretations of our linguistic poverty, and of the way in which this narrowed repertory of expression forecloses our perceptual alternatives. In his extraordinarily provocative essay, "On Memory and Childhood Amnesia,"[2] he asserts that the habits of language impressed on the developing personality insure both that the concrete freshness of childhood experience will be forgotten by the adult, and that adults will also be hard put to attain such freshness in their present perception of the world. This is because the categories that language imposes on perception are confining and conventionally stereotypical. We can only make our experiences meaningful to ourselves by capturing them in language, and in our culture this is of course predominantly in verbal form: most of us do not have very rich resources of gesture or pitch, color or tone. Language sets limits on perception, in that we can see only that which we have been linguistically trained to see. Whether we fully accept the hypothesis advanced by Benjamin Whorf— that the categories of language wholly determine the span of possible experiences—it seems clear that our language importantly bounds what we can expect to perceive and how we record that perception for ourselves and others.

Schachtel notes that our language, and hence our experiential range, becomes schematized in a fashion that severely restricts our modes of seeing and diminishes the richness of the physical and interpersonal world "out there." He argues:

> Adult memory reflects life as a road with occasional signposts and milestones rather than as the landscape through which this road has led. . . . The signpost is remembered, not the place, the thing, the situation to which it points. . . . So the average traveler through life remembers chiefly what the road map or the guidebook says, what he is supposed to remember because it is exactly what everybody else remembers too. In the course of later childhood, adolescence, and adult life, perception and experience themselves develop increasingly into the rubber stamps of conventional clichés. The capacity to see and feel what is there gives way to the tendency to see and feel what one expects to see and feel which, in turn, is what one is expected to see and feel because everybody else does. Experience increasingly assumes the form of the cliché under which it will be recalled because this cliché is what conventionally is remembered by others. This is not the remembered situation itself, but the words which are customarily used to indicate this situation and the reactions which it is supposed to evoke. [3]

This line of reasoning is very like that advanced by Roger Fry in trying to analyze the difference between everyday perception and looking at a work of art; Fry says that the objects around us, in the interest of psychic economy, "put on a cap of invisibility," and that "it is only when an object exists in our lives for no other purpose than to be seen that we really look at it." [4] Presumably, too, this stereotyped packaging of experience, this snuffing out of wonder and freshness, is what Proust had in mind when, in *The Remembrance of Things Past,* he has Swann complain that "the flowers people bring me nowadays never seem to me real flowers." The repetition of the experience, and its storage in memory, have deadened his capacity really to see *these* flowers (rather than bouquets of long ago) in themselves—in their flowery essence, if you will.

Schachtel asserts that:

> The average adult "knows all the answers," which is exactly why he will never know even a single answer. He has ceased to wonder, to discover. He knows his way around, and it is indeed a way around and around the same conventional pattern, in which everything is familiar and nothing cause for wonder. It is this adult who answers the child's questions, and in answering, fails to answer them but instead acquaints the child with the conventional patterns of his civilization, which effectively close up the mouth and shut the wondering eye. Franz Kafka once formulated this aspect of education by saying that "probably all education is but two things, first, parrying of the ignorant childrens' impetuous assault on the truth and, second, gentle, imperceptible, step-by-step initiation of the humiliated children into the lie." [5]

Rather than initiating children into "the lie," we might say that adult society imposes on them a partial truth: that thin slice of the total perceptual range for which convenient stereotypes are at hand. And this fragment of possible expressions is severely weighted toward logical discourse, toward the process of cognitive pointing at isolated chunks of the environment. The intuitive faculties, the global awareness of the relaxed consciousness, are discouraged.

To Schachtel, the creative writer is that individual who acutely recognizes the discrepancy between actual experience and conventional words and in his work feeds on the tension. It is no accident that such a writer also may serve as a model of the leisured posture. Schachtel puts it this way:

> The lag, the discrepancy between experience and word is a productive force in man as long as he remains aware of it, as long as he knows and feels that his experience was in some way more than and different from what his concepts and words articulate. The awareness of this unexplored margin of experience, which may be its essential part, can turn into that productive energy which enables man to go one step closer to understanding and communicating his experience, and thus add to the scope of human insight. It is this awareness and the struggle and the ability to narrow the gap between experience and words that make the writer and the poet. [6]

Schachtel does not tell us, however, how some few people, those who move on to the intensity of leisured ferment, refuse fully to adopt the stereotypes and somehow sustain their awareness of the "gap." Perhaps we shall fail to understand true leisure until we can comprehend how the child survives in the artist or scientist.

Since our culture is premised on the efficiency of the linguistic trap, Schachtel and others see the poet and dreamer as a danger to conventional ordered society. The poet sees and knows too much. Recall James Joyce's dictum that the proper strategy for the artist is "exile, cunning, and silence." A French observer even advances the notion that certain of our definitions of insanity or madness are designed to "keep poetry out of the streets," to insure that official definitions of reality are not too widely questioned.

Our language, then, tends to inhibit the roaming imagination and the wholly savored experience by imposing a stereotyped reality on us. But there is something more: linguistic style in the modern West is heavily colored by a rationalistic bias. We suffer from what psychologists have termed, *left-hemisphere dominance,* in that the portion of the brain controlling the analytic, scientific, deliberative functions is exalted over the portion involved in synthetic, intuitive activities. This is one of the reasons why we find prose easier to read than poetry, why we distrust our emotional wisdom, why it is less demanding to pay attention to an advertising billboard than to a Jackson Pollock painting. To our great peril, because it impoverishes our life chances and life choices, we separate action from thought, feeling from analysis, subject from object in those persistent and tragic dualisms of the Western perceptual tradition. We seem experientially crippled, unable to reach the fusion described in Hans Speier's sage comment:

> We should learn from the poet. The notion that feeling and thought are hostile to one another is true only of perverted and exaggerated feeling or of barren thought. If uncorrupted, thought and feeling are at one. All great poets are wise. [7]

Another way of underlining the restrictive power of the linguistic trap is to adopt Suzanne Langer's concepts alluded to earlier. In her brilliant *Philosophy in a New Key*, [8] Langer sets forth two primary modes of discourse. She labels these as *discursive* language and *presentational* language. Discursive symbolism is by far the more familiar to us: it is the language of most prose writing, of science, the text, the instructional manual. It is instrumental, in the double sense that it assists in getting things done, shaping our mundane actions, and also that it is preeminently a means to an end, a pointer or reference to objects and events outside itself. The purpose of this kind of language is to inform in a deliberate, rational, analytic way. It carries a message or information, makes assertions that can be challenged. At its best, this is the speech of logical argument, appearing in its purest, most convincing form in a writer like Bertrand Russell. Langer notes that the discursive mode is so pervasive in modern industrial society that we are scarcely able to generate or respond to any other. This language is clearly the commanding discourse in our educational, occupational, and governmental structure.

Presentational language, in contrast, is noninstrumental. It does not set forth an argument, does not persuade or instruct us to do something. It is the vehicle of poetry and the other arts, and to a very great extent, of religion—especially of the mystical strain in contemplative devotion, as embodied in Léon Bloy's statement, or the poetry of Thomas Merton, or the novels of Par LagerKvist. I should argue that the capacity to create and respond to presentational symbolism, really to enter the domain of art or religion, is importantly akin to the ability to play. It demands a suspension of our ordinary, stereotyped frames of reference—perhaps Coleridge's "temporary suspension of disbelief." It entails a letting go of the self, a hospitality to the fullness of a new experience, a generous delight in something encountered for its own sweet sake without any necessary immediate points of application in conduct. All these are characteristics that the universe of presentational symbolism shares with the universe of play. Probably it would not be an overstatement to insist that an empathic talent for presentational discourse both requires and fulfills the best of civilized leisure.

It will be clear that I have begun with the rational linguistic trap because that undergirds and interpenetrates the other two great hazards to leisure and creative processes. The language in which we talk and think about work and about time largely determines how we perceive and enjoy them. The charged expressions we bring to the conceptualization of our experience betray how deeply ingrained, how value-laden are the injunctions to behave in certain ways and not in others. Consider only a few of the terms the linguistic trap offers to the Protestant-ethical and the time traps: duty; obligation; responsibility; punctuality; output; product; deadline; appointment; useful; useless; time is money; wasting time, frittering time away; loafing; not doing anything; lazy; hardworking; what's it good for?; only an intuition; hard facts; work-fare instead of welfare; the deserving poor; effort; achievement; success; failure; I want it done yesterday; tomorrow will be too late; schedule; program; break; rest.

The Protestant-Ethical Trap:

> The Puritan wanted to work in a calling; we are forced to do so. . . . In Baxter's view the care for external goods should lie only on the shoulders of the "saint like a light cloak, which can be thrown aside at any moment." But fate decreed that the cloak should become an iron cage. [9]

Max Weber, writing *The Protestant Ethic and the Spirit of Capitalism,* did not invent the work ethic, but he gave it a telling name and revealed its central significance in modern society. He traced the roots of the Western attitude toward work to their joint religious and economic sources, and offered a convincing description of the values clustered around the occupational sphere of life. It is not essential to subscribe wholeheartedly to Weber's causal thesis that a specifically Protestant posture was a precondition of capitalistic forms of economic organization; it is evident enough that an association exists, and that Weber brilliantly analyzed the accompanying values. Briefly, he traced the way in which Calvinistic ideas about virtue and predestination emerged, and how the individual's "election" to a state of grace gradually came to be signified by his or her works in *this* world. Although the religious background is important for understanding the emotional loading of job behavior, we now confront a secular ethic that is as powerful without God in his heaven as with Him enthroned.

The substance of the Protestant Ethic is that hard and successful work affords a tangible sign of grace and virtue, that the person who is economically dutiful and effortful in this life thereby gives evidence that he or she will be among God's elect in the next. So work, which historically had been a burden to be avoided if at all possible, which had been seen as humanity's harsh fate—"by the sweat of thy brow shalt thou get bread"—began to be transformed into a challenging task. In this task one might, indeed must, earn a hard-won salvation. Work became at once duty and opportunity, the individual's chief business in life, as life itself became chiefly business. The good person demonstrated goodness every day by unswerving devotion to production and accumulation. The caricatures embodying the most vulgar truth of the matter are perhaps the wonderfully named Thomas Gradgrind and Josiah Bounderby of Dickens's novel *Hard Times,* although Weber's exemplar was the Benjamin Franklin of *Poor Richard's Almanac.* At any rate, the proposition that immersion in work is virtuous in itself, that work is as much a matter of conscience as of exigency, had significant and largely negative implications for the spheres of play and leisureliness. If one's estimate of oneself, and one's presumed esteem in the eyes of others, rested preponderantly on an occupational activity, then all else in life was rendered somehow secondary—trivial or frivolous at best and sinful at worst. Non-work forms of behavior were seen to dissipate the energies of the economic athlete, to divert him from his appointed striving.

Two corollary features of the Protestant-ethical trap are its ascetic overtone and its power to foster guilt. The work ethic is ascetic in that work is not to be enjoyed, but to be endured. It is fundamentally grim and serious, sober and single-minded. Work that promises too much delight of the senses or too much pleasure of the mind is almost by definition not real work. Popular suspicion of the artist or scientist is partly rooted in the uneasy apprehension that they are in fact rewarded for doing things that are intrinsically satisfying, things they would be glad to do anyway without compensation. Another aspect of the ascetic strain is the notion that the individual at work should expend himself to the utmost, as in a crusade or pitched battle. Thus an executive of the National Aeronautics and Space Administration once boasted to me about the early age at which he had suffered his first coronary heart attack; he took this to mean he was really giving of himself, displaying professional zeal and valor.

If work has the characteristics I have described, then it is evident that failure to work, or failure to work hard enough, must generate substantial guilt and anxiety. And so it is that people caught in the Protestant-ethical trap will go to extraordinary lengths to pacify their conscience, to placate their super-ego, to demonstrate to themselves and to others that they are worthy-through-work. Work assumes a driven, overdetermined quality as the individual seeks thereby to validate himself. For men especially, the occupational role has been traditionally a source—often the primary source—of personal identity. When E. Wight Bakke sought to determine the effects of the Great Depression of the 1930s on unemployed men in New Haven, he found joblessness to be even more threatening to self-esteem than to economic survival itself. A man without work did not seem to be fully a man in his own or his family's eyes. On the other end of the scale, most rich Americans work very hard indeed. For instance, the numerous members of the Rockefeller clan, clearly affluent enough to sustain themselves for several lifetimes, all work long hours and sedulously ration their pleasures. Leisure is not the natural state of man, but rather something to be earned as a reward for, or surcease from, work. The man not working feels a deep compulsion to explain himself, to justify nonwork.

The abyss, the blackest doom, is failure at work. Willy Loman, in Arthur Miller's *Death of a Salesman,* is the prototype. There exists no more compelling case history of the pathology of the work ethic and the cult of success. Failing in his job, and lying to himself about the failure, dreaming of grandeur and finding the dream without substance, Willy ultimately sees his very identity dissolve and can no longer live.

A convincing illustration of the fact that the Protestant-ethical trap is peculiar to modern Western cultures, and not a universally shared human complex, may be found in one of the difficulties of the developing and underdeveloped nations. Here it is discovered that, although economic factors are enormously significant (especially problems of capital formation, and the shortage of technologically sophisticated manpower), motivational factors are also heavily involved. Docility and habituation to factory discipline and bureaucratic discipline is not innate, but must be learned. The need to achieve occupationally is not an invariant part of the individual's temperamental equipment. For instance, the psychologist David C. McClelland, who is noted for his research on the *achievement motive*—the personality disposition to strive, to accomplish—has been employed in India and other countries to try to stimulate or teach a need for achievement. He has succeeded in encouraging this motive through the use of competitive games and other educational techniques.

The power of the work ethic to ensnare us is reinforced by two distinctive cultural orientations which have been identified by Florence Kluckhohn. [10] These are not peculiar to America, but they have been pronounced in our society. She terms them the *doing* and *man-over-nature* orientations. *Doing* indicates the heavy value we place on activity as a mode of conduct, in contrast to cultures that emphasize *being* or *being-in-becoming*; that is, we stress performance (even if it may be often busy-work) rather than individual character or personal cultivation. Similarly, we conceive man to be vigorously engaged in the conquest of the natural world, to be a dominant force over nature. This penchant is sharply different from that observed in societies oriented to submission to natural forces or to the idea that man and nature should live together in harmony. There are, however, certain faint indications that the productive abundance of a very advanced industrial society, combined with worry over the spoliation and exhaustion of natural resources, is beginning to mute these value stances. If this occurs, it may enhance values more congenial to leisured processes.

I think I need not underline the way in which the patterns of rational language and the patterns of Protestant work values buttress one another.

They come together in what an English critic once called, "the American belief that all good things can be deliberately achieved." That is, we as a people have a touching faith that rational planning, ingenuity in solving problems, and intense organized effort can in some fashion enable us to dominate and encompass life. These attitudes leave little room for playfulness, receptive passivity, the slow accretion of wisdom, or generosity toward emergent inspiration. And they are further marked by an urgent, one might almost say hungry, posture toward time. Deliberate achievement must be dated; results are to be obtained by a specified year or month, hour or minute. The hound of time, and the conviction that the beast can and must be tamed, is well-expressed in a slogan of U.S. factories during the productive exertions of World War II: "The difficult we do immediately; the impossible may take a little longer."

The Time Trap

The late poet-psychiatrist Merrill Moore began one of his sonnets with this striking line: "The noise that time makes passing by..." Moore, a man voracious for experience and accomplishment, felt the passage of time as a tangible threat, a malevolent force stealing away his life chances. Perhaps most of us cannot hear the noise that time makes, but we are nevertheless exquisitely aware of its movement, watchful and alert as time slips past us. We are imprisoned, as Loren Eiseley remarked, in man-made time. The artificial demarcation, the splintering of life processes, is pointedly expressed in the phenomenon of jet lag, in the fatigue and dolour that typically accompany a sudden shift in the omnipresent clock. Here a second layer of chronological artificiality is imposed on the layer our bodies have learned to live with, and the result can range from minor discomfort to what is almost a wrenching of reality, a warping of one's private space-time coordinates. As a society of clock watchers, geared to the inexorable passage of the hours and days, the seconds and minutes, we stave off the possibility —or threat—of watching and knowing ourselves. Perhaps one reason for the familiar American complaint that "there is never enough time" is that we are exaggeratedly alert to its passage; we can seize the moment, but cannot relax our grasp and truly live in the moment. In the filling of our time to overflowing, we are in the situation De Grazia perceives: "The moment for being inwardly attentive is never allowed to come." Caught up in "that showy strife men call the world," we can absorb neither the rich fleeting moment nor the spaciousness of eternity. This hyperreaction to time's movement is akin to the habits of Thoreau's man who watched for the mail; Thoreau said that if we see a man constantly visiting the post office in search of letters, we can be sure that that man has not heard from himself in a long time.

Why is the time trap antithetical to play and creative processes? Primarily, I should say, because our bondage to a short-range future that is implicit in a heightened sense of time and an anxiety about its passage makes us basically unfree to be players. The dictates of the clock are obvious enough in factory discipline and in the patterning of bureaucratic and technologic organization. But time's tyranny is also present in subtler fashion throughout the space of life called nonwork. An individual's adjustment to the demands of time keeping constricts play by rendering it arbitrarily interruptible, by erecting cut-off points that intervene no matter in what valuable direction play might be leading him. Above all, an orientation to that moving hourhand in its thrust toward the next package of activity conspires with the linguistic stereotypes to make the past virtually inaccessible, to muffle it in the dead category of time that has vanished. We find it, then, very difficult to recapture and thereby reexperience the past that is the substrate of creativity. (This may be why Proust's devotion to the meaningful recovery of his personal history strikes us at once as so bizarre, so hazardous, so unusual.) We are also, in our vulnerability to what happens next, likely to dull and flatten the flavor of the immediate instant. We are seldom able to heed Blake's admonition to "kiss the joy as it flies," or to believe that, in the wisdom of another poet, "who can know, as the long days go, that to live is happy has found his heaven." The relaxed anticipation of unfolding events, internal or external, that is characteristic of leisurely experience, is replaced by an anxious longing for the imagined—and we think unimaginably better—future.

For all these reasons, then, I should argue that it is an act of moral courage and of psychological risk taking to dare to be leisured in contemporary American society. Civilized playfulness is far more demanding, requires more plenteous reserves of self-knowledge and of the capacity to mobilize mind and heart, than is most of our work life. It threatens our routine mechanisms for keeping our slice of the world under control, and our often-tenuous hold on a familiar and comfortable identity. Only the strong are equal to the challenge of that peculiar kind of loafing called *leisure*. The life of fantasy, contemplation, bold originality—in a word, of serious play and playful sobriety—is dangerous to seek and only intermittently possible to sustain.

The Spirit of Play

There is an undeniable propriety in calling all the liberal and imaginative activities of man play because they are spontaneous and not carried on under pressure of external necessity or danger. . . . By play we are designating no longer what is to be done fruitlessly but whatever is done spontaneously and for its own sake, whether it have or not an ulterior utility. Play in this sense may be our most useful occupation. So far would a gradual adaptation to the environment be from making play obsolete that it would tend to abolish work and to make play universal.

—George Santayana

I have speculated several times about the links between the world of leisure and the world of childhood. Nowhere are these links stronger or more evident than in the sphere of play. If most adults have forgotten or relinquished the child's aptitude for poetic perception, so too have they been persuaded to renounce the child's gift for playfulness. Our culture, although superficially pleasure loving and apparently exhibiting an almost frenzied dedication to play, is really quite uncompromising in its orientation toward this central human activity. Play is not honored for its own sake: it is either consigned to the domain of the frivolous and meaningless, or alternatively subsumed under instrumental goal striving as a species of work or preparation for work. Thus our often-remarked devotion to sport is unleisured in essence, being the grimly serious pursuit of victory or perfection. The child's play is construed solely as rehearsal for the solemn tasks of adulthood. (It is indeed this, but not only or most significantly.) The adult's play, when not viewed as a category of work (for example, the role of the professional athlete), is thought of as a kind of necessary evil, a timeout to refresh body and mind for the real world of work.

Play may be regarded as the essence of the leisured style. An essentially playful spirit underlies creative endeavor, as is seen in the case of the poet. And it also underlies, as we shall discover, that prototype of creative questing: sexual experience. The child's play, the artist's play, the lover's play—all are alike in being truly leisured, all alike in running perilously against the grain of contemporary American culture. Playfulness is the kernel of those behaviors that are distinctively human, that represent what men and women can be and do at their best. How then may it be identified?

Johan Huizinga is perhaps the subtlest historian and philosopher of play. In his classic *Homo Ludens* he argues convincingly that the most exalted activities, from poetry and philosophy to law and government, have their origins in play. Huizinga asserts that the first defining mark of play is freedom:

> For the adult and responsible human being play is a function which he could equally well leave alone. Play is superfluous. The need for it is only urgent to the extent that the enjoyment of it makes it a need. Play can be deferred or suspended at any time. It is never imposed by physical necessity or moral duty. It is never a task. It is done at leisure, during "free time." [11]

Play is chosen, not compelled; it is freely engaged in, in the best sense gratuitous. It might be construed as the voluntary construction of reality by humans at their most human, that is, when they are least subject to the urgencies of maintaining civil order or satisfying animal appetites. Play is thus very close to the classic ideal of elite leisure, the pursuit of those who need to pursue nothing except for its own sake.

I alluded earlier to Robert White's concept of *competence* and his speculation about children's play as an unpressured attempt to exercise themselves in the environment. White believes we must account for what seems to be "an intrinsic need to deal with the environment." Children exhibit a competence motivation which operates at times when other pressing internal demands and external challenges are absent. (Is this condition perhaps the child's equivalent of leisure?) White describes competence behavior as "constantly transactional," in which

> stimulation and contact with the environment seem to be sought and welcomed, in which raised tension and even mild excitement seem to be cherished and in which novelty and variety seem to be enjoyed for their own sake.[12]

He goes on to describe children's behavior in playful exploration:

> Typically, they involve continuous chains of events which include stimulation, cognition, action, effect on the environment, new stimulation, etc. They are carried on with considerable persistence and with selective emphasis on parts of the environment which provide changing and interesting feedback in connection with effort expended. . . . Effectance motivation must be conceived to involve satisfactions—a feeling of efficacy—in transactions in which behavior has an exploratory, varying experimental character and produces changes in the stimulus field. Having this character, the behavior leads the organism to find out how the environment can be changed and what consequences flow from these changes. [13]

Observed in these terms, the child's play would appear to be almost a precise analogue of the poet's adult play, a creative juggling of words and images in the service of nothing more (nor less) than full comprehension of the inner and outer worlds.

If *freedom* is the first mark of play, this untrammeledness, this loosening of the tight bonds of the familiar means-ends relationship, has several implications. One of the most important is that the meaning of play must be sought in the activity itself, not in the motivations that may inspire it or in the "ulterior utility" that Santayana rightly claims it may or may not possess. In the language of symbolism, play is *iconic;* its meaning is immediately embodied in itself. It does not refer to something else. The iconic property of play hints at the sense in which play, and leisure, may be called timeless. Play is freedom from both quotidian constraints and the stifling overlay of routinized experience. Play, like leisure, never has to occur, hence it eludes both the ticking metronome of clock time and the enchained wariness of instrumental striving. The player has, and must have, no answer to the persistent utilitarian question, "What's it good for?" Play's entrancing charm lies precisely in the fact that it is good for nothing, that is, nothing in our traditional vocabulary; it is good only for itself, and accordingly good for everything.

True playfulness, it may be argued, is the common element in lover and saint, friend and artist. This enduring core of leisure is marked by the freedom to be bold, self-yielding, and flexible. The leisured player, like the poet at his craft, enjoys the unrestrained capacity to toy with the stuff of existence, to juggle the modalities of perception and judgment, of cognition and feeling.

Clearly, the talent for acting in this fashion is quite rare. To let go of the clock, the schedule, the instrumental thrust of the means-end model, exposes the leisured person both to outer censure and inner fear. Thus when I speak of the courage to be leisured, I imply the courage to defy accepted ways of conducting ourselves and also the courage to rely on our inner composure. Leisureliness demands that the individual be strong enough to fight down the demons of work-shunning guilt, of comfortable routine, of the closely defended self. If you will, leisure calls for the strength to be weak and the self-control to be abandoned.

Our ineptitude as players is a key reason why our satisfaction in salient human interactions is so much less abundant than human beings have a right to expect. I refer to friendship and love, those central relationships that are so dear to us we find them nearly impossible to analyze, and of which we often dare not speak except in the language of mechanism or the argot of selfishness. Friends and lovers can be enjoyed only at leisure, and only fully savored when we approach them in the nonutilitarian, iconic posture of play. To befriend or to love is really impossible unless we are prepared to find the reward in the relationship itself, in the doing of it, to relinquish alike the selfish ego and the thought of a vulgar utility.

For the interplay of two personalities should be exactly that: a playing together that is dedicated to immediate mutual satisfaction. The satisfaction is immediate or it is nothing. If it is not discovered in the apprehension of rewarding play, then it is perverted and deferred in the interests of some ulterior goal. Our popular conception of the psychology of interpersonal relationships—and to a distressing extent our scientific conception as well —views the interplay as merely a means to the end of power or pride, in the service of a tawdry aggrandizement. Hence we speak of men and women as actors, intent on the applause of an audience or the attainment of status. Countless books and articles are written to instruct us in the strategies of relationships, to teach us the manuevers that are a logical consequence of seeing other people as objects to be manipulated. But love and friendship, like creativity, demand our full attention; they cannot be properly enjoyed if a part of ourselves is constantly looking outside and beyond, toward some end that is not embodied in the interaction itself. Yeats, in one of his wisest poems, tells us where to seek the rewards of friendship: "Think where man's glory most begins and ends, And say my glory was I had such friends."

The satisfaction is mutual or it is nothing. When our usual notions of relationship are not premised on the striving for external goals of money or power or pride of possession, they tend to be centered on a selfish indulgence of the needs of one party to the transaction. Unable to release ourselves to the fullness of play, we vigilantly guard the precious ego and implicitly reckon up the gains and losses of a brittle self-regard. Again this intent self-absorption is foreign to the spirit of leisured involvement. We speak of forgetting oneself as if this were some error, a sinful slipping out of control, when in fact self-forgetfulness is the essence of true relatedness. It is quite true that the individual has urgent personal needs for security, recognition, and sexual release, and that these goods are most readily obtained in the interpersonal context. But the meeting of each person's needs is more properly seen as a happy by-product of the relationship, as a corollary of free play and self-surrender, than as a goal of an interaction in which the other is merely a means to one's satisfactions. The situation is precisely that which long centuries of spiritual wisdom assert: only in the radical giving of the self can the self be found, only in generous yielding can meaningful gains be realized. And the present moment is all, the playing together for its own sweet sake. As Camus observed, "real generosity toward the future lies in giving all to the present."

Friendship, then, is based on the playfulness we have rehearsed. It is both freely chosen, and unbounded in its enactment. A friend is not a tool to be used but a presence to be cherished. Friendship and love, like creativity, retain always a kernel of mystery, of the inexplicable. We do not know what subtle movements of the affections, what wellings of sympathy and empathy, impel us toward one another. Yet, as in the case of art, we intuitively know that something important is happening. One might guess that a large share of that "something important" is an implicit compact to which both partners assent, and that the terms of the compact are the terms of an understood playfulness. No one *has* to become lover or friend; the relationships are in the best sense gratuitous, entered upon in entire freedom.

The second major aspect of play, its iconic property, is also a key to friendship. As we have noted, authentic relationships can only be based on intrinsic, self-contained rewards. These are arts, and akin to the poetry, painting, and music we ordinarily think of as art, they attain their full quality only when they exist for no other purpose than to be enjoyed.

If play and leisure are distinguished by the freedom to be bold and experimental, so too is friendship. A friend or lover is just that person with whom one can dare to be wholly oneself. The relationship is so special because here at last, and perhaps only here, can we drop the masks and posturings that mark so many of our ordinary human contacts. It is the freedom to have done with pretense, to speak or not to speak, to smile or not to smile, to be confident that one will be taken at more than face value;

these are the delicious bounty of leisured intercourse. They derive from the exquisite audacity of play. Again, however, the boldness of playful intercourse demands a plenitude of courage; the partners must have the self-confidence to take every risk, and the confidence in eachother to provide security, to cushion the potential terrors of self-forgetfulness and mutual exploration.

We should not draw too sharp a line between friendship and love, between comradeship and sexuality. It is is perhaps best to think of sexual love as a deepening and extension of playful friendliness. Making love partakes of all the characteristics of play and leisure that we have identified. Leisured sexuality might indeed be defined as the precipitate of a relaxed, free, mutually giving relationship. True sexuality, like play, can only occur in an utterly free, unforced manner; in it, one seeks nothing beyond the fact of being, the process of loving. The lack of a leisured capacity is fatal to the hope of a consummated sexual partnering. To conceive of the partner as merely instrumental, as a means to one's instinctual satisfaction solely or as a badge of possessive pride, is finally both irresponsible and self-defeating. If we recall the most fully realized lovers in literature, their gentleness and self-surrender, their playful merger, is surely what strikes us. Constance Chatterley and Oliver Mellors, Lara Antipova and Yurii Zhivago: how achingly they embody MacLeish's eloquent image—

> For love
> The leaning grasses and two lights above the sea—

The two faces of freedom—freedom *from* constraint and freedom *to* quest—are clearly integral to a ripened sexuality. And each rests on that leisured talent for leaving the self behind. A person gambles himself, courageously dares to anticipate that in yielding his individuality he will be returned a richened self. The too-closely defended and zealously guarded ego is unable to enter the realm of creative love. Robert Frost tells us that in writing a poem, "the figure is the same as for love." And so it is: creative acts of whatever order, in art as in love, call for a willingness to play, to follow the flight of hazardous processes, to surrender the self to forces beyond one's entire control. An experimental life, which is to say a vitally experienced life, is not led easily or safely.

Notes

1. From a speech delivered by Ramsey.
2. Ernest G. Schachtel, "On Memory and Childhood Amnesia," in *Metamorphosis* (New York: Basic Books, 1959), pp. 279–322.
3. Ibid., pp. 287–88.
4. Roger Fry,

5. Schachtel, pp. 292–93.
6. Ibid., p. 296.
7. Hans Speier, *Social Order and the Risks of War* (Cambridge, Mass.: MIT Press, 1952), p. 133.
8. Suzanne K. Langer, *Philosophy in a New Key* (Cambridge, Mass.: Harvard University Press, 1942).
9. Max Weber, *The Protestant Ethic and the Spirit of Capitalism,* translated and edited by Talcott Parsons (New York: Scribner's, 1930), p. 181.
10. F.R. Kluckhohn, "Dominant and Substitute Profiles of Cultural Orientations: Their Significance for the Analysis of Social Stratification," *Social Forces* 28 (May 1950): 276–93.
11. Johan Huizinga, *Homo Ludens* (London: Routledge & Kegan Paul, 1950), p. 8.
12. R.W. White, "Motivation Reconsidered: The Concept of Competence," *Psychological Review* 66 (September 1959): 328.
13. Ibid., p. 329.

Index